ANCIENT GREEK LOV

ANCIENT GREEK
LOVE MAGIC

~

Christopher A. Faraone

HARVARD UNIVERSITY PRESS
CAMBRIDGE, MASSACHUSETTS
LONDON, ENGLAND

First Harvard University Press paperback edition, 2001

LIBRARY OF CONGRESS CATALOGING-IN-PUBLICATION DATA

Faraone, Christopher A.
Ancient Greek love magic / Christopher A. Faraone.
p.   cm.
Includes bibliographical references and indexes.
ISBN 0-674-03320-5 (cloth)
ISBN 0-674-00696-8 (pbk.)
1. Magic, Greek.   2. Love—Miscellanea—History.   I. Title.
BF1591.F37   1999
133.4'42'0938—dc21   99-10676

For Susan

σὺ γὰρ ἐν σεαυτῇ τὰ φάρμακα ἔχεις

(Plutarch *Moralia* 141c)

CONTENTS

Preface   ix

1 INTRODUCTION   1

   1.1 The Ubiquity of Love Magic   5

   1.2 Definitions and a New Taxonomy   15

   1.3 The Advantages of a Synchronic and Comparative Approach   30

2 SPELLS FOR INDUCING UNCONTROLLABLE PASSION *(Erōs)*   41

   2.1 If *Erōs* Is a Disease, Then Erotic Magic Is a Curse   43

   2.2 Jason's *Iunx* and the Greek Tradition of *Agōgē* Spells   55

   2.3 Apples for Atalanta and Pomegranates for Persephone   69

   2.4 The Transitory Violence of Greek Weddings and
          Erotic Magic   78

3 SPELLS FOR INDUCING AFFECTION *(Philia)*   96

   3.1 Aphrodite's *Kestos Himas* and Other Amuletic Love Charms   97

   3.2 Deianeira's Mistake: The Confusion of Love Potions
          and Poisons   110

   3.3 Narcotics and Knotted Cords: The Subversive Cast
          of *Philia* Magic   119

4 SOME FINAL THOUGHTS ON HISTORY, GENDER, AND DESIRE   132

   4.1 From Aphrodite to the Restless Dead: A Brief History
          of the *Agōgē* Spell   133

   4.2 Courtesans, Freedmen, and the Social Construction
          of Gender   146

   4.3 Aelian's Tortoises and the Representation of the
          Desiring Subject   160

CONTENTS

~

viii

Glossary   175
Abbreviations   179
Bibliography   183
Subject Index   205
Index of Foreign Words   213
Index of Passages from Ancient Authors   217
Index of Magical Texts   221

PREFACE

Despite the well-documented separation and polarization of male and female spheres of action in ancient Greece, scholars traditionally treat love charms as one undifferentiated mass of data and assume that individuals of either gender could without discrimination use any type of charm they wished on any victim they so chose. I offer here a survey of ancient Greek love magic and a new bipolar taxonomy based mainly on the genders of the agents and their victims: those rituals used mainly by men to instill erotic passion *(erôs)* in women and those used primarily by women to maintain or increase affection *(philia)* in men. This taxonomy is not procrustean, however, and in the final chapter I discuss several important deviations from it, suggesting that most of the apparent anomalies in the gender of the person using a spell are not in fact anomalies at all, but rather give us some new and interesting insights into how ancient Greek ideas about gender were socially constructed. In the case of *philia*-producing magic, for instance, I show how freedmen and other socially subordinate males are constructed as female, according to widespread patriarchal notions of female inferiority. Conversely I argue that courtesans and prostitutes employ aggressive erotic magic—usually the purview of males—because, as autonomous operators free to indulge in their passions, these women are constructed as male in Greek culture. Finally, I discuss of how the Greeks constructed the victims of these spells as desiring subjects. My conclusions here may surprise some readers, as they did, indeed, surprise me, for they call into question the widespread orthodoxy of what we might call the "misogynist" model of Greek culture, which generally attributes men's mistreatment and control of women to their fears that women are "naturally" lascivious and are therefore a constant threat to male schemes for the orderly transference of property by means of betrothal and marriage. I argue to the contrary that the evidence assembled here suggests the existence of another, competing set of cultural assumptions, which I call the "misandrist" model, according to which men are the "naturally" lascivious and wild gender, who often need to be sedated and controlled by "naturally" moderate and chaste women.

It has been my goal to write a book for the generally educated person who has no familiarity with the ancient Greek language or the often equally arcane jargon of professional scholars. This approach has appreciably lengthened the gestation period of this study, during which I have published a series of more technical arguments in various professional journals, where I have laid out in considerably more detail the historical and philological evidence for some of the assertions in this volume. This does not mean, of course, that this book is without use to professional scholars or graduate students, but rather that they may from time to time want to consult these earlier studies for more detailed arguments.

Acknowledgments

This book is the fruit of some seven years' labor and as such requires a somewhat extended list of acknowledgments. My initial interest in the subject was sparked by one of the most stimulating teachers I have ever encountered: Jack Winkler, to whom I owe an entire Greek chorus of thanks for having challenged me to think for myself even when it meant that I ended up disagreeing with him, as I do from time to time in this volume. It saddens me greatly that he will not see the results of our many conversations about the nature and taxonomy of ancient Greek love magic and what such a taxonomy might tell us about Greek notions of desire and gender. Many thanks also to my friends and colleagues at the University of Chicago, especially to Bob Kaster, for first suggesting that I write a book on this subject and for supporting me in ways too numerous to mention; and to Jamie Redfield, for our many hours of team-teaching and conversation, which have taught me more about ancient Greek culture than most books on the subject.

I also owe many special thanks to Zeph and Diana Stewart, codirectors of the Center for Hellenic Studies, to the other junior fellows, and to the staff for making my stay during the academic year 1991–92 a particularly enjoyable and productive one; and I am deeply grateful to the Humanities Division of the University of Chicago for help in funding my stay there. For it was there and then that I laid out the foundations for this project and began to test many of my arguments. Timely grants from the

National Endowment for the Humanities in 1995–1996 and the Guggenheim Foundation in 1997 allowed me to finish the project, but none of this would have been possible in a department as busy as ours without the active support, flexibility, and encouragement from my chairmen, first Braxton Ross and then Bob Kaster, and especially from Philip Gossett, the Dean of the Division of the Humanities.

This book has benefited enormously from the time and energy of many other people as well. First, I should like to thank H. D. Betz, W. Brashear, R. Daniel, J. Gager, A. Henrichs, D. R. Jordan, R. Kotansky, F. Maltomini, D. Martinez, R. Merkelbach, E. Voutiras, and D. Wortmann, who in the last two and a half decades have spearheaded the renewed inquiry into ancient Greek magic with a steady stream of new editions, surveys, translations, and detailed studies of epigraphic and papyrological texts that have put the study of magical texts on an extraordinarily firm textual and historical basis. It is no exaggeration to say that without their primary research I could not have even conceived of this project, a point that all scholars should remember in this age when so much of the basic research in the arts and sciences is threatened. At its best, I think, scholarly research is a team effort, with each individual building on and contributing to the work of others; if we who study ancient societies allow such crucial colleagues as archaeologists, epigraphers, and papyrologists to go unsupported, the whole team suffers considerably and in time our endeavor will falter.

As it turns out, many of the individuals named above have also taken the time over the last seven years to answer queries and look over earlier drafts of lectures and essays that eventually made their way into this book. I am particularly grateful for the help and expertise of D. Bain, H. D. Betz, M. Blundell, M. Dickie, K. Dover, M. W. Edwards, H. Foley, D. Halperin, J. Henderson, A. Henrichs, R. Janko, D. Obbink, W. H. Race, E. Reiner, J. Scurlock, R. Seaford, L. Slatkin, H. S. Versnel, and F. Zeitlin. But the greatest thanks are owed to Danielle Allen, Maud Gleason, Fritz Graf, Sarah Johnston, Bob Kaster, Marilyn Arthur Katz, Ludwig Koenen, Roy Kotansky, Bruce Lincoln, and two anonymous readers at Harvard University Press, who read through various versions of the entire manuscript, offering me much important advice and saving me from numerous blunders. To those whose early comments and help I have inadvertently omitted, I offer my sincere apologies. Thanks, also, to Mr. Kenneth Wear for his help in assembling and typing the bibliography, and to Ms. Deva Kemmis Hicks for her assistance with the preliminary versions of the indexes.

I owe a very different and special kind of gratitude to my children, Alex and Amanda, and my wife, Susan, for their patience and their love.

Finally, I am grateful to the journals that have allowed me to use previously published material here. Parts of sections 2.3 and 3.1 appeared originally in *Phoenix* 44 (1990) 224–243, and a substantial part of section 2.2 was first published in *Classical Journal* 89 (1993) 1–19. Parts of sections 3.2 and 3.3 appeared in rudimentary form in *Helios* 19 (1992) 92–103 and 21 (1994) 115–135.

Note

A glossary of Greek and otherwise unfamiliar technical terms appears at the end of this volume, as does a list of abbreviations. In transliterating Greek names, it has seemed reasonable, if not entirely consistent, to use the familiar Latinized spelling of those names for which this has become "normal" English usage (e.g., Socrates or Pericles) and in other cases to use a direct transliteration from the Greek (e.g., Dike or Ladike). In my translations of Greek texts, I use a very simplified system of brackets: square brackets [] indicate a lacuna in an ancient text that has been filled in by modern scholars who extrapolate the missing word or words from the surrounding text, while parentheses () are used to supplement the Greek text by providing extra words or phrases or indicating the original Greek words, all with the goal of making a difficult original text less opaque to a modern reader.

Ancient Greek Love Magic

~

1

INTRODUCTION

In his *Memorabilia,* the fourth-century B.C.E. Athenian historian and essayist Xenophon reports how Socrates in the company of his students visits the home of a famous courtesan named Theodote and engages her in a spirited conversation about the contrivances she uses to attract her male friends. At the end of this conversation Socrates mentions in a very playful manner the use of love magic (3.11.16–17):[1]

> And Socrates, making light of his own laziness, said: "But it is not at all easy, Theodote, for me to get free, for much business, both private and public, keeps me busy. And I have also got my girlfriends *(philai),* who neither day nor night allow me to escape from them, since they are learning both love potions *(philtra)* and incantations *(epōidai)* from me."
>
> "Indeed, do you *also* know how to do these things, Socrates?" she said.
>
> "Why else," he said, "do you think that Apollodorus here and Antisthenes never leave me? And why do you think that Cebes and Simmias come from Thebes? Know well that these things do not happen without many love potions *(philtra),* incantations *(epōidai),* and *iunx* spells *(iugges)*."[2]

1. See Tupet (1976) 143, Henry (1995) 48–50, and Goldhill (1998) for discussion.
2. See the Glossary for the definition of frequently used technical terms.

As I discuss in greater detail below, Socrates humorously represents himself here as an aging courtesan who is busy teaching younger girls (his *philai*) the tricks of the trade, which include various types of magical charms.[3] At this point, however, I quote the passage simply to point out the utter banality of love magic in the episode. One gets the feeling that Xenophon and his audience were well acquainted with these somewhat technical terms for magical techniques and devices (*philtron, epōidē,* and *iunx*) and that they would not be at all surprised to learn that Theodote employs them or that Socrates would humorously pretend to do so. The passage also reveals quite nicely the potent explanatory value that such technologies provide, for the irony of the whole interchange hinges on Socrates' feigned surprise: "Why else do you think that Apollodorus here and Antisthenes never leave me? And why do you think that Cebes and Simmias come from Thebes?" The subtext here is, of course, Socrates' notorious physical ugliness:[4] how else can Socrates explain the fact that he, like the beautiful courtesan Theodote, is surrounded by attractive and well-born young men, who vie for his attention? As we shall see repeatedly in the chapters that follow, such accusations of love magic (both playful and serious) provide a rich source of information for the use of such rituals, since they reveal so much about the social relations of practitioners and victims. Finally I would note in passing the twofold purpose of Socratic love magic: to keep his current male companions from leaving and to force other men to come to him from afar, twin goals that mirror quite nicely the bipolar taxonomy of love magic that I offer below.

Love magic, then, seems to be part of the refined world of the wealthy courtesan, who could sometimes move, like the famous Aspasia, in the highest circles of Greek society. The ironic and lighthearted tone of the sophisticated essayist seems—to the modern ear, at least—to dismiss such practices outright as foolishness or (at best) to banish them to the boudoirs of disreputable women. But compare Xenophon's witty anecdote with these three different Greek magical incantations of later date, all of which are designed to force a person away from their homes, presumably

3. See section 4.2. Keuls (1985) 197 is probably right to suggest that this Theodote, like so many other characters in Plato's and Xenophon's dialogues, is based on a historical figure. See Goldhill (1998) for a different interpretation of Socrates' *philai*.

4. See Alcibiades' famous remarks in Plato *Symposium* 215b–c, with Dover's commentary ad loc.

like the charms that (Socrates claims) made Cebes and Simmias come from Thebes:[5]

> Bring to perfection the [content] of this binding love spell . . . in order that Theodotis, daughter of Eus, may never have experience of another man than me alone, Ammonion, she being enslaved, driven mad, flying through the air in search of me, Ammonion, son of Hermitaris, and so that she bring her thigh to my thigh and her "nature" to my "nature"[6] for intercourse always for the entire time of her life.

> Drag Heronous by her hair and by her guts to me, Poseidonios, every hour of time, by night and day, until Heronous comes to me, Poseidonios . . . Now, now. Quickly, quickly.

> Burn, torch the soul of Allous, her female body, her limbs, until she leaves the household of Apollonius. Lay Allous low with fever, unceasing sickness, incomprehensible sickness.

Gone now are the light humor and distanced view of the philosopher. Here we seem to see raw human motives and desires that appear—in comparison to the treatment of a literary author like Xenophon—perversely confessional in their violence and their hurried insistence: "now, now, quickly, quickly." Thus it would seem in the first example that we can look over Ammonion's shoulder as he orders a chthonic spirit to force Theodotis to come to him for sex. Indeed, we might even be tempted to psychoanalyze his deeper motives and to suggest that the sadism and violence of his requests reveal a vicious case of unrequited love.[7]

I juxtapose the passage from Xenophon with these later texts to illustrate two of the most dangerous pitfalls that await modern scholars who try to make sense of the social practice of Greek love magic from a disconcertingly wide array of sources. The distanced, ironic view that we find in Xenophon's anecdote is typical of most of the early modern scholarship on love magic, which often (wrongly) equates the minority voices of the

5. *SM* 38 (2d cent. C.E.); *PGM* O[strakon] 2 (2d cent. C.E.); *SM* 40 (3d cent. C.E.), all found in Egypt.
6. See Winkler (1990) 217–220 for use of the Greek word *phusis* to mean sexual organ.
7. Winkler (1990) 224–227; but see section 2.4.

philosophic and rationalist tradition with the typical Greek "man in the street" and infers that "most Greeks" would have dismissed such practices as the foolishness appropriate (in their hierarchical view of the world) to social inferiors like women, barbarians, and slaves.[8] On the other hand, we should not fall into the equally dangerous trap of romanticizing the Greeks as some perennially strange people, who reveal their truest and darkest souls in passionate outbursts on rooftops, late at night with a full moon beaming down.[9] Implicit in this second approach is, moreover, the mistaken assumption that actual incantations like those quoted above are a kind of ethnographer's windfall: cries of the heart that have fortuitously been recorded on scraps of metal or papyrus. Such an assumption is equally far from the truth, as the following text reveals:

> . . . take away the sleep of that woman until she comes to me and pleases my soul . . . lead [BLANK SPACE] loving, burning on account of her love and desire for me . . . force her to have sex with me [BLANK SPACE] . . . impel, force her to come to me loving, burning with love and desire for me [BLANK SPACE] . . . drive [BLANK SPACE] from her parents, from her bedroom . . . and force her to love me and give me what I want.[10]

8. For the inadequacies of this approach, see Dover (1974), Winkler (1990) 17–44, and Faraone (1992c) 11.

9. E.g., Bonner (1942) 467 thinks an inscribed gemstone designed both to attract and to paralyze the victim "tells a story of despair and love changed to hate," but this is a pattern common to several other spells and seems generic; see Faraone (1992a) 94–95. Similarly Moke (1975) 275, who suggests that a handbook formula (*PGM* LXI. 39–59) "surges with the irate hostility of a man whose bed has been robbed"; and Bernand (1991) 287–288, who assumes that errors in spelling and syntax in some erotic spells result from the "haste and heat" of the agent (e.g., the woman who wrote or commissioned *PGM* LXVIII "semble aussi ardente et impatiente que la Simaïtha de Théocrite") and who suggests (p. 298) that the formulaic threat to Osiris in *DT* 270, which shows up on nearly identical Greek spells of fourth and fifth century C.E.—see Brashear (1992) 85–87 lines 15–21 and *SM* 45.11–15—displays the author's personal brutality. Winkler (1991) 216 warns that his approach to love magic "runs the risk of romanticizing Mediterranean passion (as did Stendahl and Browning for Italy)," but then on pp. 222–230 he makes precisely this error. This is not to say that generic spells can never be the vehicle for creative and idiosyncratic expression; see Versnel (1996).

10. *DT* 230 (1st cent. C.E.) is inscribed in Latin but has most probably been translated from a Greek model; see below, note 64.

The person in Carthage who commissioned or wrote this text on a lead tablet a full century before the earliest of the three spells quoted above, made a crucial error: he forgot to add the female victim's name in the blanks left on the tablet and thus made it impossible for the four invoked demons to find their target. For modern scholars, however, such a text is a great boon, revealing as it does that as early as the first century C.E., such spells were to some degree generic and could be copied by a scribe ahead of time and set on shelf with blank spaces that could be filled in later by or for a specific customer. Indeed, as more and more magical texts are deciphered and published, we have begun to realize how stereotyped such expressions are, and we are able to see that many have been copied from handbooks, often with very few changes over the centuries—except, of course, the names of the victim and the practitioner. Thus even when dealing with actual magical texts we need always remember that these spells, no less than lyric poems and tragic choruses, are to a large degree shaped by generic conventions and expectations; they tell us as much or as little about the psychic state of the scribes, practitioners, and clients who used them as ancient literary texts tell us about the individual neuroses of their authors.

1.1 The Ubiquity of Love Magic

Love magic appears or is alluded to in the literature of every epoch of ancient Greek history, beginning with Homer and ending with early Christian hagiography.[11] In the fourteenth book of the *Iliad* Aphrodite lends Hera her magical belt *(kestos himas)* to repair her parents' estrangement, but Hera uses it instead to seduce her husband, Zeus.[12] A similarly seductive power probably lies behind the gifts she gives Pandora, Hypsipyle, and Amphitrite on the eve of their weddings.[13] Two famous episodes in the embedded tales of the *Odyssey* also seem to reflect indirectly themes and beliefs about love magic: Greeks in the later periods, for example, interpret

11. For surveys of Greek literary allusions and references to magic generally see Riess (1896b), (1897), and (1903); Eitrem (1941); and Tupet (1976), all of whom I have used extensively for what follows.

12. Petropoulos (1988) 218 and Faraone (1990) 220–229; see section 3.1.

13. For Pandora, see section 3.1; for the presumed power of the other gifts of Aphrodite, see Scodel (1984) 141 and Brown (1991) 332–333.

Circe's potion as a perverse form of love charm,[14] and the Sirens' song is
similarly equated with erotic incantations that attract their victims against
their wills.[15] In book 3 of the same poem, Nestor seems to allude to a
tradition that Aegisthus used a love charm to seduce Clytemnestra;[16] and
Demodocus' embedded tale of the binding of Ares and Aphrodite in book
8 can perhaps be linked with the later use in love spells of images of these
two deities bound in an erotic embrace.[17] A fragment of the Hesiodic
Catalogue of Women preserves parts of the well-known story of Atalanta,
seduced by the apples of Hippomenes. The fragment does not describe the
effect of these apples on the young woman, but Hellenistic sources state
explicitly that they kindled erotic desire in the girl, an assumption that
apparently underlies the use of specially charmed apples, quinces, pomegranates, and other fruit to strengthen marital affections of brides-to-be,
both in early Greek myth and in actual wedding ceremonies.[18] There are
also a number of allusions to or imitations of erotic magic in early lyric
poetry. Sappho's *Hymn to Aphrodite* most clearly reflects the form, content,
and intent of later erotic spells;[19] and Alcman probably alludes to similar
arts in his *Parthenion,* where he mentions in passing a woman named
Aenesimbrota, who apparently was skilled in making others fall in love.[20] It
is Pindar, however, who gives us the earliest detailed account of an erotic
charm, when he describes how Aphrodite taught Jason to use a magic *iunx*

14. Dedo (1904) 32, Page (1973) 51–69 and Parry (1992) 226. Plutarch (*Moralia* 139a)
implicitly makes this assumption when he cites the Circe episode as a cautionary example for
why brides should not use love potions on their husbands; see section 3.2.

15. In a discussion of love magic (Xenophon *Memorabilia* 2.6.11), Socrates calls the Sirens'
song an incantation (*epōidē*) that they used to attract and bind men, precisely like a love
charm. Parry (1992) 270 notes the same equation in a Hellenistic epigram.

16. Page (1972) and Faraone (1996b) 91–92 n. 50.

17. Picard (1942–43) publishes a fifth-century vase painting from the Hephaestus sanctuary on Lemnos (= *LIMC* s.v. "Ares" no. 60) which shows an armed man and a naked female;
both he and Burkert (1983a) 8–9 n. 7 connect it with Demodocus' song. In Chapter 3 I discuss
later scenes on a small terracotta relief and gemstones that may have been used in some form
of love magic.

18. Hesiod frag. 76.17–23 (West). See Faraone (1990) 230–238 and section 3.2 below for full
discussion.

19. Sappho frag. 1. See Archibald Cameron (1939) and (1964), Segal (1974) 148–150, Burnett
(1983) 254–255, Petropoulos (1993), Faraone (1992b) 323–324, and section 4.1 below for a
detailed discussion.

20. Alcman frag. 1.73–77. See West (1965) 199–200 for discussion.

charm and to recite "prayerful incantations" designed to set Medea aflame with desire for him.[21]

Attic drama occasionally reflects the use of love spells or accusations about them. In Sophocles' *Women of Trachis*, Deianeira mistakenly kills her husband, Heracles, with poison, thinking that she is giving him an aphrodisiac;[22] and a tiny fragment from another of his plays suggests that the melting of a wax effigy as part of an erotic spell may have played a role in the plot.[23] Euripides twice uses erotic magic to heighten the drama or ambiguity of his tragedies. In the *Andromache*, Hermione ambiguously accuses Andromache of using *pharmaka*—"drugs" or "incantations," the word can mean either[24]—to seduce her husband Neoptolemus, to inhibit Hermione's sexual performance with him, or to render her infertile.[25] The Nurse in the *Hippolytus*, on the other hand, gives us more precise details about such contemporary practices and beliefs (509–515):

> It just dawned on me, in the house I've got enchanting charms for passion *(philtra thelktēria erōtos)* which will put an end to this disease of yours without any shame or damage to your mind—if *you* do not become cowardly. We've got to get some token *(sēmeion)* of

21. *Pythian* 4.213–219. See Faraone (1993a) and section 2.2 below for detailed discussion.

22. Faraone (1994a) and section 3.2 below.

23. Sophocles *The Root-cutters* frag. 536 (Radt): "having melted a doll with fire." There is, however, no agreement as to the context or meaning of the fragment, and other readings have been proposed; for discussion see Radt ad loc.

24. Since the word *pharmakon* has a vexing spectrum of meanings ranging between "poison," "drug," and "incantation," I shall, throughout this volume, leave it untranslated unless the context makes its precise translation clear. The meaning "incantation," though cited by LSJ s.v. i 3 as "enchanted potion, philtre: hence charm, spell," is often ignored by modern scholars. See Pharr (1932) 272–274 and Graf (1992) 276–277 for discussion.

25. *Andromache* 155–158. Burnett (1971) 134 and Kovacs (1980) 13–28, esp. 19–20. The dramatic situation here—two "wives" in the same house—would not have been tolerated in ancient Athens (see Chapter 3 for discussion of a similar dramatic situation in Sophocles' *Women of Trachis*), but the rules were apparently different in other places. Dionysius I of Syracuse married two women on the same day, a Locrian named Doris and a Syracusan named Aristomache, both of whom came to live in his palace. This arrangement, however, apparently produced the same rivalry we see in the *Andromache*, for later on—when Aristomache was unable to produce a child—Dionysius had the mother of Doris put to death on the grounds that she had bewitched or drugged *(katapharmakeuein)* her daughter's rival. See Plutarch *Dion* 3.3 and Caven (1990) 175.

that man you desire, either a lock of hair or a thread from his cloak,[26] and then fit together one benefit from the two.

The wording here is purposely ambiguous and can be taken to mean either a spell for dissolving Phaedra's love or a spell for captivating Hippolytus and subsequently curing the queen's pains by fulfilling her desire.[27] Phaedra's reply to the Nurse's offer—"Is this *pharmakon* an ointment or a potion?"—is equally ambiguous, for it can refer either to an aphrodisiac given to Hippolytus or to an antaphrodisiac given to Phaedra.[28] Either way, Euripides is clearly referring to the contemporary use of *ousia*, a later technical word for the magical "material" or "stuff" (almost always the victims' hair or bits from their clothes) that is used to target the spell most precisely.[29]

Comic writers make many passing allusions to erotic stimulants in the form of love potions, special foods (especially bulbs and shellfish),[30] and specialized magical gear like the *iunx* or the *rhombos*.[31] Aristophanes refers to the rite of apple-tossing (*Clouds* 996–997), and in a fragment from his lost *Amphiaraus* he parodies the form and content of a popular hexametri-

26. Reading with Barrett (1964) and most editors Reiske's conjecture *plokon* ("lock of hair") for the MSS *logon*. Commentators have, however, generally missed the practice alluded to in the exceedingly opaque last line, which probably refers to a magical ritual in which the hairs or threads of two people are magically intertwined with the hope of similarly joining the two individuals in love. The symbolic joining of two individuals is common in later magic: a third-century C.E. charm (*DT* 271.42–43) names a couple and then prays to a demon: "Yoke them in marriage and desire, sharing their lives"; and both Wortmann (1968) 85–102 and Brashear (1992) publish pairs of wax *sumplegmata* (male and female effigies in an erotic embrace) found with Greek erotic charms. See Rosenqvist (1986) 60 for a similar Byzantine love charm used by a rejected suitor to get his fiancée back.

27. Goff (1991) 48–50.

28. Barrett (1964) insists (in his comments on lines 516–521) that this can *only* be interpreted to mean a self-applied medicine designed to cure Phaedra's love; but see section 3.1 for examples of self-applied ointments used as love charms to beautify the woman and to increase the man's affection.

29. For *ousia* used elsewhere in literary love spells, see Apuleius *Metamorphoses* 2.32 and 3.15–18 (hairs) and Lucian *Dialogues of the Courtesans* 4 (clothing, shoes, hair); Jordan (1985b) 25 collects many examples of actual Greek spells found with hair attached.

30. Athenaeus (62e–64b and 356e–f) has a wide-ranging discussion, peppered with quotations from Attic comedy. Menander frag. 397 (Sandbach) mentions *hupobinētiōnta brōmata* ("foods that encourage screwing").

31. For the use of the *rhombos*, see Eupolis *Baptai* frag. 83 (K-A) and Aristophanes *Heros* frag. 315 (K-A). For the *iunx* see his *Lysistrata* 1110, discussed in section 4.2.

cal incantation that turns up repeatedly in Hellenistic and Roman-era charms for erotic purposes.[32] Although most of Attic comedy is lost, it seems clear that Lucian writing in the second century C.E. owes much inspiration to Menander and New Comedy for his satirical sketches of the magical spells performed by courtesans in Athens.[33] Later poets remain deeply interested in such themes. An anonymous Hellenistic epigram, for example, purports to be the dedicatory poem for a bejeweled *iunx* wheel—originally a gift from a Thessalian sorcerer—that has the power "to draw a man from across the sea and youngsters from the women's quarters"; and another by the poet Asclepiades refers to a magic girdle with powers similar to those of the Homeric *kestos himas*.[34] Horace, on the other hand, describes the macabre rituals of the sorceress Canidia, some of which clearly reflect contemporary love spells;[35] and even Dido's elaborate ritual at the end of book 4 of the *Aeneid* has been interpreted as a form of love magic aimed at keeping Aeneas in Carthage.[36] But by far the most detailed and best-loved literary descriptions of love spells are those found in Theocritus' *Idyll* 2 and its Virgilian rendition, *Eclogue* 8. In each poem a lovesick women enacts an elaborate incantation designed to force her wayward lover to return to her.

The prose authors of antiquity offer less evidence for the use of love magic, but they are not silent about it. Oratory provides us with occasional but important glimpses of such activities. In Antiphon's speech *Against the Stepmother* the unnamed speaker accuses two women of poisoning their lovers, one knowingly and the other under the illusion that the *pharmakon* was an aphrodisiac.[37] Another Athenian woman charged with homicide in similar circumstances was apparently acquitted by the Areopagus when she

---

32. *Amphiaraus* frag. 29 (K-A) and Faraone (1992b).

33. Herzig (1940) 12–19 and Kofler (1949) 86–98 exhaustively discuss Lucian's most detailed descriptions of erotic magic: *Dialogues of the Courtesans* 4.4 and *Philopseudes* 14–15. For the general influence of Attic New Comedy on Lucian, see Fantham (1986) 55–56 and Rosivach (1998) 144–145.

34. *Iunx: AP* 5.205 = Gow and Page (1965) 207 no. XXXV. Magic girdle *(zonion): AP* 5.158 = Gow and Page (1965) 45 no. IV.

35. E.g., Riess (1893), Kuhnert (1894) 44–53, Dedo (1904) 42–44, and Freudenburg (1995). Dedo (1904) 38–39 discusses a lost poem of Catullus that apparently also imitated a love charm.

36. Eitrem (1933) is the classic discussion; see also Tavenner (1916) 33–35 and Tupet (1976) 247–248.

37. Antiphon 1.9.2; see Faraone (1994a) 118–119 and section 3.2 below.

argued that her intent was to get the man to love her more, not to kill him.[38] Demosthenes, on the other hand, mentions the prosecution of a woman who, if we can trust the scholiast, was condemned to death for "making love potions *(philtra)* for young men."[39] We find occasional references to such activities in the philosophers as well. In addition to the anecdote about the courtesan Theodote, Xenophon's Socrates makes several playful references to love magic in the *Memorabilia,* as one might expect in a dialogue devoted to the causes of friendship and affection.[40] The historical tradition, given its concern for public events, is understandably silent about such activities, but love magic or accusations about it do turn up occasionally in discussions of the private lives of kings and other important leaders. Herodotus, for example, describes Queen Ladike's prayer to Aphrodite to make her impotent husband virile (2.181); and later, more sensational biographers like Cornelius Nepos, Plutarch, and Suetonius mention the use of aphrodisiacs by Romans and Greeks alike.[41]

But by far the best prose sources for ancient love magic are the numerous discussions of the magical powers of plants, minerals, and animals that can be gleaned from naturalist, medical, or encyclopedic writers. Aristotle, for example, gives us a detailed discussion of the famous aphrodisiac *hippomanes;*[42] and his student Theophrastus, despite his own obvious skepticism about their efficacy, dutifully records in his *History of Plants* the claims of local drug-sellers and root-cutters about the effectiveness of various herbs in stimulating desire.[43] Pliny the Elder, Dioscorides, Aelian, Galen, and other authors pursue this scientific tradition in Roman times;

38. [Arist.] *Magna Moralia* 16. 1188b30–38; see MacDowell (1978) 114–115, Faraone (1994a) 118–119, and section 3.2 below.

39. Demosthenes (19.281) claims enigmatically that Aeschines' mother Glaukothea "used to convene meetings, for which another priestess has been put to death." The scholia explain that he is referring to a woman called Ninos, who had been executed either for making *philtra* for young men or for mocking the Mysteries. Derenne (1930) 224–227 and 233 argued that both charges may have been true, an argument revived by Versnel (1990) 116.

40. See the index of individual passages.

41. Cornelius Nepos frag. 52 (Marshall) (= Plutarch *Lucullus* 43.1–2); Plutarch *Antony* 37; and Suetonius *Caligula* 50 and *De poetis* 16.

42. Either a black, fleshy substance on the forehead of a newborn foal or a secretion from a mare; both were believed to have aphrodisiac properties; see Aristotle *HA* 572a30–b4 and 577a10–15, Theophrastus frag. 175, Aelian *NA* 3.17 and 14.18.

43. Lloyd (1983) 129–130, Preus (1987), and Scarborough (1991) 146–151.

and—beginning as early as the Hellenistic period—there is another important and perhaps competing "theosophical" tradition of pseudo-Orphic, pseudo-Democritean, and pseudo-Pythagorean writers who often discuss the magical properties of plants and stones and even pass on recipes for amulets and rituals.[44] The most illustrious of the latter was Bolus of Mendes, a Hellenized Egyptian active in the second century B.C.E., who under the name of Democritus wrote and compiled many (now lost) works on a wide range of subjects, including demonology, astrology, and necromancy, as well as a treatise on sympathetic and antipathetic magic. His sources seem to have included native Egyptian and Mesopotamian writings, and his works were widely excerpted by Pliny and others.[45] The late second-century C.E. Christian philosopher Sextus Julius Africanus wrote in a similar vein an eclectic work called *Kestoi* in twenty-four books, a miscellany of magical and medical recipes and observations.[46] The "Orphic" *Lithica* and more elaborate compilations such as the *Cyranides* date back even earlier, to the first century C.E., and seem to draw on all these various traditions as they discuss the magical properties and practical uses of various gemstones, plants, and animals.[47] And since the ancients often used herbs and amulets on their livestock to encourage breeding, important information also turns up in various Byzantine handbooks on the care and breeding of animals, such as books 16–17 of the eclectic compilation known the *Geoponica*.[48]

As we saw in the discussion of Socrates' conversation with Theodote, the consistent problem with many literary materials is the offhand manner in which they mention or allude to love spells. In publicly performed genres like epic recitation, oratory, or drama such references must have been easily recognizable to most of the audience, but they can be quite cryptic to the modern reader, who must supplement them with archae-

44. See Brashear (1995) 3412–13 for summary and bibliography.

45. Brashear (1995) 3412 and Dickie (forthcoming).

46. Thee (1984). The title *Kestoi* seems to refer to the *Kestos himas* of Aphrodite (note 12 above) and probably should be translated as *Magic Bands* or *Magic Girdles* (see Chapter 3 note 4).

47. See Abel (1881) and Halleux and Schamp (1985) for the *Lithica* and (for the present) Kaimakis (1976) and Waegeman (1987) for the *Cyranides*. For dating and authorship see most recently Fowden (1986) 87–88 n. 57. David Bain is launched on a new and superior edition of the *Cyranides*, which takes into account many more manuscripts.

48. Beckh (1895).

ological, epigraphical, and papyrological evidence in order to appreciate them fully. Fortunately, there is an abundance of such nonliterary data, beginning with the late eighth-century B.C.E. "Nestor's Cup Inscription"— among the earliest attested examples of written Greek—which seems to be an incantation designed to charm a cup of wine with amorous power: "Whoever drinks from this cup, desire for beautifully crowned Aphrodite will seize him instantly."[49] Another inscribed cup calling itself a *philtron* ("love spell") was dedicated in the sixth century B.C.E. to Aphrodite in her temple at Naucratis.[50] The bulk of our nonliterary evidence for Greek magic comes, however, from the two large corpora of extant spells: the "binding spells," which survive mainly on inscribed lead tablets;[51] and the so-called magical papyri.[52]

The former date as early as the classical period in Sicily, Attica, and the Black Sea area; and by the late Hellenistic period we find them scattered throughout the Greek-speaking Mediterranean. The usual practice was quite simple: a person inscribed the victim's name on a metal or wax tablet, rolled it, pierced it with a nail, and then deposited it in some underground place, such as a grave or a well. Since the focus of these binding spells is on the restraint of the victim,[53] they are occasionally used in agonistic situations that involve love—for example, when people try to bind or restrain their rivals in love.[54] This is not, of course, love magic per se, as it does not attempt to make another person fall in love. Rather it is designed to reduce the competition, by inhibiting the words, the actions, and even the sexual performance of a rival. Thus, for example, three fourth-century B.C.E. Greek binding spells appear to be written by women who wish to

49. S. West (1994) and Faraone (1996b).

50. Gardiner (1888) 66 no. 798 and Faraone (1996b) 106.

51. They are called *katadesmoi* in Greek and *defixiones* in Latin. The most important corpora and surveys of Greek spells are *DT, DTA,* Preisendanz (1928) and (1933), and SGD. Latin spells are included in *DT* and have been surveyed further by Besnier (1920), Garcia-Ruiz (1967), and in the appendix to Solin (1968).

52. *PGM* and *SM* are the most important corpora.

53. Kagarow (1929), Preisendanz (1972), and Faraone (1991a) provide general discussions. With increasing frequency in the Hellenistic period, the same media are used to preserve a different genre of malediction that Versnel (1991a) has aptly labeled "judicial prayer": usually a prayer to an Olympian (i.e., not chthonic) deity in which an aggrieved party claims to have been wronged and seeks redress; see below, section 2.1.

54. Petropoulos (1988) 217–219 and Faraone (1991a) 13–14.

prevent their husbands or lovers from "marrying" other people, a term that can mean either formal marriage or in slang merely sexual intercourse.[55] A tablet from Athens, for example, employs a simple wish-formula: "Let him not 'marry' another woman or boy";[56] and in a recently published Macedonian tablet a woman attempts to inhibit a relationship between her husband(?) and another woman, presumably his girlfriend:

> I consign (i.e., for purposes of binding) the sexual fulfillment *(telos)* and marriage *(gamos)* of [Theti]ma and Dionysophon and also (the marriage) of all other women, both widows and maidens, but especially Thetima . . . May he (Dionysophon) indeed not take another woman other than myself, but let me alone grow old by the side of Dionysophon and no other woman.[57]

Yet another late-classical spell from Athens binds "Glycera, Dion's wife . . . in order that she be punished and not consummate her marriage."[58] All three texts provide us with some important background for understanding Hermione's accusations that Andromache was using magic "to make her hateful to her own husband."[59]

Although this tradition of binding rivals in love triangles continues unabated into later antiquity,[60] by the late classical period we see signs that it is being adapted to another popular form of love magic, the so-called *agōgē* spells, which—as we shall see in great detail in section 2.2—seek to bind a female victim and force her to come and make love to the practitio-

55. This slang usage is found in Hellenistic epigrams and persists in modern Greek; see Robert (1967), Shipp (1979) 187–188, Cameron (1982) 163–164, and Petropoulos (1988) 218.

56. *DTA* 78. See Voutiras (1998) for this translation, which corrects Faraone (1991a) 14.

57. For Greek text and this translation, see Voutiras (1998). I thank Professor Voutiras for kindly giving me access to his ongoing work on this text.

58. Willemson (1990) 145–147. The final words in Greek are *atelēs gamou,* literally "unfulfilled in her marriage." But given the slang usage of the word *gamos* and the fact that Glycera is a typical name for a courtesan, we might also translate: "Glycera, Dion's woman . . . in order that she . . . have a rotten sex life." For courtesans' use of magic, see section 4.2.

59. See note 25 above.

60. See, e.g., *DT* 271.46 (3d cent. C.E.): "make him obey like a slave . . . desiring no other woman or maiden"; and *PGM* V. 304–369, a recipe for an elaborate binding spell inscribed on a lead tablet, which adds: "If (you are binding a) woman, (write:) 'in order that Ms. So-and-so may not "marry" Mr. So-and-so.'"

ner. Thus, in a recently published lead tablet from late fourth-century B.C.E. Acanthus, a man named Pausanias puts a binding spell *(katadesmos)* on a woman named Sime "until she embraces him."[61] Because of long-standing and intensive archaeological excavations, Roman Carthage provides us with our most extensive evidence for this important sea change, yielding numerous love spells inscribed in the Latin language, but often written either with the Greek alphabet or with selected parts in the Greek language,[62] a language not widely known or used in this area of the Mediterranean at this time.[63] The fact that several of these spells were copied by scribes from handbooks only increases the suspicion that they reflect an evolving Greek tradition of *katadesmoi*.[64] In Roman-era Egypt and Hadrumentum (a city near Carthage) this same early Greek tradition of binding spells yields yet another composite: the so-called binding love spells *(philtrokatadesmoi)*, which aim to prevent the victim from having sex with others and (at the same time) to encourage him or her to have sex with the person performing the spell.[65]

Miraculously, another even larger corpus of Greek magical texts has survived,[66] and it contains an enormous amount of information about love magic: seven sizable papyrus rolls filled with magical charms, which appear to be the personal library of a professional magician working in Upper

61. Jordan (1999) no. 3; see section 4.1 for full discussion.

62. *DT* 227 (Latin spell written in the Roman alphabet with a border of nonsensical Greek letters around it), 230 (Latin spell written in the Roman alphabet with the names of the demons written in Greek), 231 (Latin spell written entirely in the Greek alphabet), and 304 (same).

63. Rives (1995) 193–120, esp. 197–199.

64. For example, *DT* 230 (quoted earlier), seems to have been copied out ahead of time with the appropriate blanks left for personal names. For further evidence for scribes in third-century Carthage working from Greek handbooks, see Jordan (1988d) 120–126 (three Greek curses against charioteers follow same formulary) and (1994b) 325–333 (the same Greek formula being used in Beirut and Carthage; in the latter case, the scribe apparently knew no Greek). See section 4.1 for a tentative sketch of the history of these types of spells.

65. See, e.g., *SM* 38 (= SGD 161 = *CTBS* 34) and *PGM* IV. 296–466.

66. I say miraculously, because many of the longer handbooks—*PGM* IV, V, X, XII–XIV, and perhaps I–III, VII, and LXI—seem to come from the library of a practicing magician in Upper Egypt in the fifth century; had this one cache remained hidden, *PGM* would only be one-fifth of its present size. See Betz *GMPT* p. xlii, Petropoulos (1988) 216, and Brashear (1995) 3402–05.

Egypt in the late fourth or early fifth century c.e.[67] About one-quarter of these texts are concerned with love and sex.[68] Finally, there are scores of magical gemstones that date roughly to the Roman imperial period and are particularly popular in the eastern Mediterranean basin; at least one specifically magical design can be traced back to the second century b.c.e., a fact suggesting that here, too, we have evidence for a much earlier tradition.[69] Many of these gemstones have short Greek inscriptions and stereotypical scenes involving Aphrodite and Eros that clearly indicate their use for amorous purposes.[70]

1.2 Definitions and a New Taxonomy

There is, then, rich and plentiful evidence for the ancient Greek tradition of love charms, aphrodisiacs, philters, and the like in myth, historical anecdote, and actual practice. The manifold nature of these sources and the many varieties of this form of enchantment have, however, dissuaded modern scholars from attempting any precise definition or taxonomy of the phenomenon, and therefore it is extremely important that I begin by saying precisely what I understand to be the scope of a book titled *Ancient Greek Love Magic*. The chronological and ethnic boundaries are, perhaps, easiest to define: for present purposes "ancient Greek" refers to a variety of peoples living in and around the Mediterranean basin from the eighth to the first centuries b.c.e., who spoke the Greek language, lived in small city-states, and shared in a very loose manner a shifting body of religious practices and beliefs that can be said to characterize traditional Greek religion.[71] This is not to say, of course, that I am uninterested in the later Roman and late-antique periods, for we have already seen that some of our best evidence for actual magical spells—those inscribed on gemstones,

67. Fowden (1986) 168–174 and Brashear (1995) 3402–05.
68. Petropoulos (1988) 215.
69. Galen (12.207 Kühn) quoting Pseudo-Nachepso; see M. Smith (1979) 132 for discussion.
70. Bonner *SMA* and Delatte and Derchain (1964) are the classic collections. On the importance of the gemstones, see Eitrem (1939), M. Smith (1979), and Schwartz (1981).
71. Burkert (1985) 7–9. This level of generalization is not, of course, unproblematic. See Finley (1971) 62 and 120–133, and my discussion of the synchronic approach in section 1.3.

papyri, or lead—date to the first four centuries C.E. Nonetheless, the beginnings of the first century B.C.E. provides the best terminus for this study, because it is an important watershed in the history of ancient Mediterranean magic—a point at which the local, oral, "amateur" traditions of magical knowledge and *praxis* begin to yield to an international and conglomerate tradition that is heavily dependent on professional magicians using handbooks (written in Greek, Demotic, Hebrew, and Aramaic), in which we find a fascinating mélange of Greek, Roman, Jewish, Syrian, and Egyptian forms of invocation and ritual mixed with or assimilated to one another.[72] Although these later and somewhat complicated "Graeco-Roman" or "Graeco-Egyptian" forms of magic are themselves quite beyond the scope of this study, I will at times argue that the originally Greek contributions to them—often signaled by traditional poetic forms and meters or technical terms—can be readily identified and used to reconstruct and understand the much earlier native Greek tradition of love magic.

So much for the first half of my title. "Love magic" itself, however, is not so easy to define, since in many societies both "love" and "magic" are more culture-bound than most ideas and therefore can be extremely difficult for outsiders to grasp. To begin negatively, by "magic" I mean neither the illusions and parlor tricks of a Houdini[73] nor "magic" in the more diffuse literary sense of "fantastical" such as one finds in the so-called magical realism of recent Latin American writers. Rather, I mean a set of practical devices and rituals used by the Greeks in their day-to-day lives to control or otherwise influence supernaturally the forces of nature, animals, or other human beings.[74] This type of magic was traditionally mundane and unremarkable to the ancient Greeks. Thus when Hera dons a magical cord to help her seduce Zeus, or when Deianeira smears her husband's shirt with a magic potion to make him more affectionate, such activities

72. Faraone (1991a) 14–15, Graf (1991), Brashear (1995) 3413–14 and 3445–46, and Faraone (1996b) 96–97.

73. The Greeks were not, of course, without a sense of humor. Indeed, there is evidence in the magical papyri of a Greek tradition of *paignia* ("playful tricks") that were apparently used at drinking parties, e.g., *SM* 76, 83, or *PGM* VII. 167–185, which is labeled "The *Paignia* of Democritus." Bain (1998) provides an overview.

74. This definition is similar to that of Versnel *OCD* 909, who describes the" family resemblance" of magic as "a manipulative strategy to influence the course of nature by supernatural ('occult') means."

per se would not have been any more remarkable to a Greek audience than Socrates' conversation with Theodote about *iugges* and *philtra*. I would argue that in both cases the poets are simply putting practical tools (magical amulets and ointments) into the hands of literary characters (usually gods or heroes), much the same as they dress them in clothes typical of the period or arm them with familiar human weapons. I might contrast the use in a modern literary text of an unremarkable device of practical technology (for example, a fax machine or a telephone) with a fantastical conceit, such as a large invisible rabbit named Harvey or an elixir that brings eternal youth. Just as we believe in the mundane power of a fax machine and find it unremarkable, by the end of this book it will be clear that many Greeks believed in or at least feared the practical efficacy of magic spells.

A more precise theoretical definition of "magic" as a category distinct from "religion" or "science" lies at the center of a long-standing controversy among anthropologists and historians of religion and need not detain us here.[75] Suffice it to say that these traditional modern divisions are for the most part inappropriate for ancient Greece because (1) until very late the Greeks had no developed system of empirical science to test the efficacy of magical spells and thereby distinguish between magic and science; and (2) as extremely tolerant polytheists the Greeks had a very flexible sense of religious orthodoxy, one that allowed them to worship a wide diversity of divinities and to perform an enormous variety of ritual acts, many of which we might call "magical" today. The ancient lack of interest in distinguishing magic and science is perhaps best illustrated in Pindar's description of early fifth-century medical practice, which included incantations, surgery, drugs, and amulets.[76] In this environment, at least, modern notions of magic as "bad science" or "quackery" are at best unhelpful in

75. The bibliography is staggering and still growing; see Brashear (1995) 3446–48 n. 353. For some helpful recent studies pertaining specifically to magic in classical antiquity, see Versnel (1991b) and Graf (1995), who cite and discuss some of the contemporary debates. Versnel argues rightly that any modern definition of ancient "magic" other than an "outsider's" (etic) one is impossible. Thus in this volume I follow the recent trend in ignoring the distinction altogether for Mediterranean cultures before the advent of the Christian Roman empire; compare, e.g., Fox (1986) 36–37, Phillips (1986) 2711–32 and (1991), Rives (1995) 15, J. Z. Smith (1995) 13–20, and Brooten (1996) 109–111. Graf (1995), however, tentatively tries to recapture an "insider's" (emic) definition in fifth-century Athens (mainly in philosophic circles) and republican Rome.

76. Pindar *Pythian* 3.47–54 and Kotansky (1991a) 108–109.

understanding ancient Greek beliefs and the social milieu of their magical rites. Nor would most Greeks dismiss magical practices as a form of "bad (i.e., unorthodox) religion." Indeed the ancient Greek tendency toward extreme diversity in religious belief and ritual practice was ensured by the peculiar decentralization of political, economic, and religious authority in the Greek city-states well into the Christian period.[77]

Defining the narrower topic of Greek *love* magic is even more difficult. Again, I start negatively, by excluding any detailed investigation of antaphrodisiacs[78] or other spells that are used to bind or impede love,[79] as both fall more easily into the category of inhibitory magic. For our purposes, "love magic" will refer almost exclusively to a large body of traditional ritual techniques used by the Greeks to instill or maintain various forms of desire and affection. The most common and best-known forms of love magic are, of course, those that one person uses to make another person desire or love him or her. Greek males did, however, apparently use magical substances or techniques on themselves from time to time as a form of self-help or medication, presumably in cases of impotence, a practice with a long prehistory in the eastern Mediterranean basin, beginning with early Mesopotamian "potency spells."[80] In the Greek world, the earli-

77. Each city-state had its own pantheon of deities and its unique repertoire of rituals, and there were rarely any professional or hereditary priesthoods (as in Egypt or the Near East) that rigorously enforced religious principles or jealously guarded their own prerogatives by resisting innovation; see Burkert (1985) 8 and 216–217. Parker (1996) 152–153 notes that it is a delicious paradox (at least to modern scholars) that traditional polytheisms are subject to constant change; this is one of their most important traditions.

78. The Greeks and Romans were well aware of the ability of certain herbs to suppress sexual desire and even sexual dreams. Thus, e.g., the herb *numphaea* was thought to "relax" the phallus for a few days (Dioscorides *Materia Medica* 3.132), make someone incapable of intercourse for twelve days (Pliny *NH* 25.75), and take away sexual desire and sexual dreams for forty days (ibid. 26.94). Pliny claims similar power for lettuce seed (20.68); condrille (22.91); *agnus castus* (24.59, where he notes its use in the Athenian Thesmophoria; and 61–64); *brya* (24.72); rue (20.143); purslane (20.214); and willow (24.58).

79. For "separation spells" *(diakopai)* see Jordan (1985b) 222–223; for "hate spells" *(misēthra)* see Lucian *Dialogues of the Courtesans* 4.5 and Bevilacqua (1997).

80. Biggs (1967) is the standard commentary on this series of cuneiform "potency incantations," which were copied faithfully well into the seventh century B.C.E. and which were designed "to get and maintain an erection sufficient for sexual intercourse" (p. 3). See Leick (1994) 204–210 for a Mesopotamian ointment of magnetite and oil designed for a similar purpose.

est example may be the "Nestor's Cup Inscription," which tells us that if a man drinks from this particular cup, he will immediately be struck with desire for making love.[81] The late sixth-century B.C.E. poet Hipponax, on the other hand, seems to describe a ritual designed (like the Mesopotamian spells) to increase a man's potency by rubbing or striking his testicles;[82] and we have a number of other references, beginning in the classical period, to penis creams that were believed to encourage erections or to increase their duration: Aristophanes, for example, has a joke about a bride and groom who are told to use a special wine in this way;[83] and Aristotle's junior colleague Theophrastus, drawing on the oral traditions of fourth-century B.C.E. drug-sellers (pharmakopolai), discusses one herb that when rubbed on a man's penis is said to produce twelve erections in succession.[84] This same Greek tradition of sexual self-help shows up repeatedly in later magical recipes, which recommend rubbing the penis with various herbs, oils, and liquids to encourage a prolonged erection[85] and in a few cases to increase women's desire as well.[86]

Aristophanes and Theophrastus also mention special foods that have an aphrodisiac effect on males, especially bulbs and the herb *eruca sativa*,

81. Faraone (1996b).

82. Hipponax frag. 78 (West); West (1974) 142–143 compares a similar rite in Petronius 127.9 and 131.8. Hipponax may also allude to a love potion to be drunk when one sees the first swallow in the spring; see Degani (1962).

83. Aristophanes *Acharnians* 1048–68.

84. Theophrastus *HP* 9.18.9 (also cited by Pliny *NH* 26.99); Lloyd (1983) 120–126 and Preus (1988) 78–80 discuss the *pharmakopolai*.

85. *SM* 76.5–6 (anoint the penis with the juice of the "deadly carrot" in order "to play with a woman"); *SM* 83.11–5–6 (rub "yourself" with swallow dung and honey "to have fun with a concubine[?]"); *PGM* VII. 185–186 (anoint your "thing" [*pragma*] with honey and pepper); and PDM lxi. 58–62 (rubric: "For an erection"). See Riess (1896a) 83 n. 1 for parallels in the medical writers.

86. Theophrastus, in his discussion of the herb used for multiple erections (see above), mentions in passing that women "are considerably more eager when they (i.e., their men) use this *pharmakon*." Demotic Egyptian handbooks preserve several recipes for penis creams (PDM xiv.1046–55, 1155–62, 1190–95; and lxi.58–62) where the aim is "to cause a woman to love her husband" or "to make a woman love copulating," a feature known in two Greek recipes—*PGM* VII.191–192 ("A binding love spell that lasts forever") and XXXVI.283–294 (to ensure faithfulness in a woman)—and attested in the Middle Ages and Renaissance; see Kieckhefer (1991) 32–33 (if the wife is indifferent) and Brucker (1963) 10 (to ensure her faithfulness).

more commonly known as rocket or arugula.[87] This tradition continues unabated down through the Roman period, where we also find repeated mention of a plant called *saturion*, apparently a general name for aphrodisiac plants in the orchid family.[88] Pliny the Elder, in particular, provides abundant evidence, much of it culled from earlier Greek sources, that men believed they could increase their sexual potency or stamina by eating or wearing parts of a number of special plants[89] or strange animals such as the crane and the skink;[90] and quite similar beliefs also show up from time to time in the much later magical handbooks.[91] Although encyclopedic sources like Pliny may often tell us vaguely that such materials stimulate sexual desire or activity without designating the gender of the desiring subject,[92]

87. E.g., bulbs (Aristophanes *Eccl.* 1092 and several other Attic comedians cited by Athenaeus 63e–64b, 64e–f, 356e); arugula (Theophrastus *HP* 1.6.6); and cyclamen (Theophrastus *HP* 9.9.3).

88. For *saturion*, see Dioscorides *MM* 3.134 and Pliny *NH* 26.96–99; for arugula, see Hor. *Satires* 2.8.51; Dioscorides *MM* 2.140 and 169; Pliny *NH* 10.182 and 19.154; and Ovid *Ars Amatoria* 421–424). See Freudenburg (1995) 211–212 and Maltomini's note on *SM* 76.12 for discussion of arugula.

89. Pliny offers many other examples: *terebinth* (24.28); *donax* (24.87); *clematis* (24.140); *xiphium* and *ormenos agrios* (26.94); *orchis* (27.65); *phyteuma* (27.65); radish (20.28); *staphylinus* (20.32); leeks (20.47–49); garlic with fresh coriander in wine (20.56–57); Megarian onions (20.105); wild asparagus mixed with dill (20.110); *hebrotonum* placed under the pillow (21.162); sea holly (22.20); asphodel (22.71); *buprestis* (22.78); chervil (22.80); and the pith of a *tithymallus* branch (22.99).

90. Pliny *NH* 28.261–262 provides a long list of animal materials used to stimulate coitus, including wearing the right testicle of an ass in a bracelet. Other examples: eggs (Ovid *Ars Amatoria* 421–424; Athenaeus 63e); the brain of a crane (Aelian *NA* 1.44); the tail of a deer (*Geoponica* 17.5.3 and 19.5.4); a reptile called the skink (Pliny *NH* 38.91 and—when mixed with *saturion*, rocket, and pepper—30.119–200); the flesh of lascivious birds (Athenaeus 9.384e–f) and the *salpe*-fish (*Cyranides* 1.18.50; see Bain [1998] 268). For the magical use of materials from sexually excited animals, see Leick (1994) 207–208 (in Mesopotamia) and Kieckhefer (1991) 34 and 36 (in medieval Europe).

91. *SM* 83.5–9: "To copulate a lot: bruise the seed of arugula and small pine cones and drink on an empty stomach"; and *SM* 76.11–12: "To screw a lot: drink, in advance, celery and arugula seed." See also *PGM* VII.183–185 (small pine cones with wine and pepper).

92. In his discussion of the materials listed above in notes 88–90, Pliny says that nearly all of them are useful for exciting sexual desire (e.g., *concitatrix veneris; veneris causa; venerem excitat* or *concitat* or *stimulant; libidinem excitat; libidinis causa; ad stimulandos coitus*), without specifying the gender of the person. He does specify, however, that both arugula and *saturion* increase desire in the male (10.182 and 26.96). As far as I can tell he makes no specific mention of the arousal of female desire.

the general focus on male potency is often made clear by references to a desired erection[93] or evident in more subtle ways, for example, in the derivation of the name *saturion* from the often ithyphallic satyr, in allusions to the sympathetic relationship between plant bulbs and testicles,[94] and in the frequent crossover between these human aphrodisiacs and those used to encourage stud animals to mate.[95] Perhaps related is the scantier evidence that images of a couple in an erotic embrace *(sumplegmata)* may have been placed in the home to promote a man's erection or to encourage in a more general fashion a couple's lovemaking, but here, since some of these images were apparently displayed openly in the house, any alleged "magical" effect merges quickly into the more mundane power of erotic images to create sexual desire.[96]

93. Pliny *NH* 26.96, on the benefit of eating arugula. Martial 3.75.3 suggests eating *saturia,* eggs, and arugula for an erection. The *Cyranides* suggests the use of arugula mixed with spices and honey for a large and pleasurable erection (1.5.10–18) or carrying the tail of a lizard (2.14.10–13) or the right molar of a skink (2.29). Medical writers claimed that the condition of satyriasis (continual and painful erection) occurred in places like Crete where men had too much *saturion* in their diet; see Gourevitch (1995) 153–154.

94. This is explicit in Pliny's discussions of *orchis* (*NH* 26.95 and 27.65), *saturion* (26.99), and sea holly (22.20). See Scarborough (1991) 148–149 for the logic of this "doctrine of signatures" in the herbals.

95. Pliny *NH* 26.99 (discussing *saturion*): "They tell us that sexual desire is aroused if the root is merely held in the hand; a stronger passion, however, if it is taken in dry wine; that rams and he-goats are given it to drink, when they are too sluggish; and that it is given to stallions from Sarmatia, when they are too fatigued for copulation." He also discusses at 8.165 and 26.181 the similar effect of *hippomanes* on humans and stallions. Julius Africanus *Kestoi* 3.5 and the authors of Greek horse-breeding manuals suggest the flesh of the skink given with wine as an aphrodisiac for stud horses; see Thee (1984) 230 n. 1. *Geoponica* 17.5.3 and 19.5.4 prescribes a similar use of the tail of a deer.

96. For Mesopotamia, see Leick (1994) 294 n. 12, who discusses a tablet with a couple embracing on one side and the sign "ZI" ("rise" or "have an erection") inscribed over and over again on the reverse. Ovid mentions small painted tablets depicting "the various unions and forms of sexual love" traditionally on display in Roman homes (*Tristia* 2.523–524), and Clement of Alexandria (*Protrepticus* 4.57–61) rails at similar images in Greek homes, which show Aphrodite naked and bound in a sexual embrace; Montserrat (1996) 213–215 discusses these passages and publishes some examples from Egypt (plates 21, 23, and 24). See, too, Delatte and Derchain (1964) 238–239 no. *329 (a magical gemstone from Tarsus depicting Eros and Psyche in two different scenes of sexual intercourse). These are, of course, quite different from the *sumplegmata* that are buried in graves and under thresholds; see section 2.1.

It would appear, then, that the Greeks—especially the men—used magic and herbal techniques on themselves to enable or to enhance their own sexual performance. There is also occasional evidence that Greeks might use magic to cause someone to fall in love with a third person. In a few cases, in which the object of this love is particularly inappropriate, these spells are simply a curse hurled against an enemy, for example, in the apocryphal story of how the poet Homer, when rebuffed by a priestess, cursed her with a lust for old men.[97] In his lost poem *Arae* (Curses) the Hellenistic poet Moero apparently told a similar story about a Corinthian housewife named Alcinoe, who mistreats her servant and dismisses her unjustly. The angry servant prays to Athena for revenge, and the goddess responds by forcing Alcinoe "to fall madly in love with a Samian stranger . . . and to abandon her home and children and sail away with him."[98] Here Athena's action—striking a woman with *erōs* and forcing her to flee her home—has precisely the same goals as the three Greek erotic spells quoted earlier, but here they are the result of an enemy's curse, not of an incantation performed by the Samian stranger with whom she elopes. Broadly speaking, both of these stories are not unlike like the plot of Euripides' *Hippolytus,* in which the vengeful goddess Aphrodite causes Phaedra to conceive an inappropriate passion for her stepson. As all of these instances involve pleas or plots for revenge, one might argue that these are curses pure and simple, but even this approach raises some interesting questions, for, as we shall see in section 2.1, crossovers between the technologies of cursing and erotic magic were extremely common in ancient Greece.

On the other hand, sometimes a friendly third party is at work. Simichidas, in his prayer to Pan in Theocritus' *Idyll* 7, asks the god to bring the boy Philinos into the arms of his lovesick friend Aratus, a request that is, in fact, a clever parody of an erotic spell.[99] Two other cases involve the

---

97. [Herodotus] *Life of Homer* 30 = [Homer] *Epigram* 11. He prays: "Hear me as I pray, O Kourotrophos. Grant that this woman may refuse the affection and bed of young men, but let her find joy in old men with wizened temples, whose strength is blunted but whose desire remains keen." In the past scholars have debated the identity of the goddess Kourotrophos, some preferring Aphrodite, while others (noting the place of the sacrifice at the crossroads) have identified her—correctly, in my view—as Hecate. See Markwald (1986) 199–200 and 204–206 and Watson (1991) 139–140. Gigante (1991) 33–36 suggests that she is Hera of Samos, but I am unconvinced.

98. Parthenius *Tales of Unhappy Love* 27. See Watson (1991) 227–228 for discussion.

99. Fantuzzi and Maltomini (1996).

well-intentioned attempts of parents to manipulate the affections of their own child or someone else on behalf of their child, a credible use of magic in a culture that depended upon arranged marriages. Thus in Heliodorus' novel *Aethiopica* the father of the heroine—who lacks a male heir—hires a professional magician to cause his daughter to fall in love with his nephew,[100] and one of Lucian's courtesans—in an effort to explain why a soldier suddenly became passionate for an aging and ugly rival—claims that the woman's mother, a sorceress *(pharmakis)* knowledgeable in "Thessalian charms," put *pharmaka* in the man's drink which drove him mad with desire for the daughter.[101] An oddly formulated third-century C.E. Greek spell may in fact have been written by a parent on behalf of a daughter who was having marital problems: "Yoke them (i.e., both) in marriage and in passion, as they live together for the whole time of their lives. Grant that he, like a slave, be subordinated *(hypotetachthēnai)* to her as he lusts *(erōnta)* for her, desiring to hold as his life-mate no other woman or maiden but Domitiana alone for all their lives. Now, now, quickly, quickly."[102]

In this study, however, I shall focus mainly on the interpersonal use of love magic, that is, spells used by persons to force others to lust after, fall in love with, or be more affectionate toward themselves. I do so because such spells are by far the most frequently attested in our extant sources and because the Greeks themselves so frequently call attention to them in their myths and stories, a noteworthy fact when one searches in vain for any mention of the practice in ancient Mesopotamian or Egyptian myth or

100. Heliodorus *Aethiopica* 2.33. At 3.9 the same father wishes aloud that his daughter might "feel a lover's longing" for the nephew.

101. Lucian *Dialogues of the Courtesans* 1.2. This accusation helps explain the otherwise inexplicable: a soldier in love with an ugly woman. Note that the role of the "mother"—here probably an aging courtesan who has "adopted" and trained the younger woman, just as Socrates pretends to do. This pattern of adoptive families of courtesans is apparently a well-known Mediterranean phenomenon; see Chapter 4, note 80.

102. *DT* 271.39–46. The use of "her" instead of the usual "me" in this spell is striking, and cannot be explained by the intermediary of a professional magician working on behalf of Domitiana, for the handbooks always give first-person formulae, e.g., "force X to come to me." David Jordan informs me by letter of a similar third-century C.E. spell from Cyprus (unpublished) that seems to take the husband's side: ". . . lay hold of the name Strategis and restore her and their former marriage to Sosibios and bind her to the (former) marriage with indissoluble bonds."

literature. This apparent Greek fascination with such spells and their effects arises, as I will show, from the danger perceived in them, for in a culture devoted so radically to personal autonomy (be it a man's body or its extension, his home and wife) the very existence of this kind of technology creates some very unsettling problems. It is one thing for a man voluntarily to use an aphrodisiac on himself—this was apparently quite unproblematic for the Greeks, with the exception of those philosophers who are generally suspicious of the carnality of the body. But it is another story entirely if a woman, for example, uses a similar ritual or herb against a man without his knowledge or permission. Popular Greek erotic spells aimed at the removal and seduction of the daughters and wives of other men similarly threaten the autonomy of a Greek man's household, but, as we shall see in section 2.4, the discourse on these types of spells is frequently connected in a positive light with stories about courtship and marriage. Thus it is not at all surprising that love spells directed against another, unwilling person are the most-discussed forms of erotic magic in ancient Greece and form the central topic of my book.

With our preliminary definitions in place, some complicated questions arise concerning native taxonomy. Did the ancient Greeks have a word for our modern category of "love magic"? The answer is "no, not exactly." Our word "aphrodisiacs" probably comes from the rarely used Greek adjective *aphrodisiakos* ("lecherous" or "salacious"), which occasionally designates gemstones or foods that have this effect on people.[103] The Greeks of the classical and Hellenistic periods, however, preferred a variety of overlapping (and sometimes interchangeable) words. General terms such as *thelktērion* (from the verb *thelgein*, "to charm or enchant"), *pharmakon*, and *epōidē*, which simply denote a magical incantation, can also be understood by context to mean specifically a "love charm."[104] Conversely, the two other terms used above by Xenophon (*philtron* and *iunx*) in their original and primary meaning apparently denoted a specialized form of erotic spell,

---

103. Pliny *HN* 37.148 mentions "stones that make one lecherous" *(aphrodisiaca)*, while [Aristotle] *Problems* 954a3 and Galen 14.241 (Kühn) refer to foods with similar qualities *(edesmata aphrodisiatika)*.

104. For *thektērion*, see LSJ s.v. For *pharmakon*, see note 24 above. The word *epōidē* (poetic form is *epaoidē*) means either "a song sung over or to (i.e., a sick person or a damaged limb)" or "a song sung against (i.e., an enemy or a demon)," and it is usually translated (like the similarly formed Latin *incantamentum*) as "charm, spell." See Lain Entralgo (1970), Kotansky (1991a), and Furley (1993).

but as early as the fifth century B.C.E. come to be used generically for any kind of magic spell. Thus, for example, the word *philtron*, formed from the verb *philein* ("to love"),[105] means a "love potion" or "love incantation" and more generally a "magical potion" or "drug" of nonamorous power.[106] The development of the term *iunx* follows a similar trajectory: Pindar describes it as a bizarre magical device—a bird tied to a wheel—that is employed with prayers and incantations to seduce Medea, but other fifth-century writers occasionally use it less precisely to mean any "magic spell" that draws people unwillingly.[107] The definitions of other special terms, however, remain fairly stable. The poetic words *stergēma* and *stergēthron* (from the verb *stergein*, "to love") consistently mean "love charms," while *charitēsion* (from *charis*, "beauty" or "grace") designates spells or devices that make the user more beautiful or charismatic.[108] The word *saturion* is derived from the word "satyr" (the hybrid goat-man famous for its randiness) and is commonly used throughout the Roman period to denote plants in the orchid family thought to produce erections and male lust.[109]

The rubrics of the papyrus magical handbooks provide a good overview of the Greek terminology employed by the professional magicians of the Roman and late-antique periods, but there is surprisingly little crossover with the popular terms discussed above.[110] The most popular rubric by far is *agōgē* or *agōgimon*, which means "a spell that leads" and designates a variety of techniques used to force young women from their homes,[111]

105. Smyth *Grammar* 232, in a discussion of words with the suffix –*tron* (an indication of instrumentality or means of action), defines a *philtron* as "that which brings *philia*." A scholiast to Theoc. 2.1 defines *philtra* as "*pharmaka* used to encourage *philia*."

106. LSJ s.v. The Latin word *venenum*, apparently derived from the name of the goddess Venus, undergoes a similar transformation from the specific ("aphrodisiac") to the general ("drug, poison, charm")—a range almost identical with that of Greek *pharmakon*.

107. *Pythian* 4.218; see section 2.2 for full discussion. For the *iunx* as a generalized magic spell, see Lycophron 310, Diogenes Laertius 6.76, and Aeschylus *Persians* 989. Bury (1886) notes that Virgil translates Theocritus' *iunx* with *carmina* ("magic spells").

108. For the terms derived from *stergein*, see Sophocles *Women of Trachis* 1138, Euripides *Hippolytus* 256, and Dioscorides *MM* 4.48. See Winkler (1991) 218–219 for *charitēsia*.

109. See note 88 above. In medical texts, erection-producing drugs are also called *saturika* or "tension-producing drugs" *(entatika);* see Gourevitch (1995) 150.

110. There are three recipes for *philtra*, all in the same handbook: *PGM* VII.405–406 (= 661–663), 459–461, and 462–466. The first is called "a *philtron* for (gaining) affections (or perhaps 'friendships,' *epi philias*)," and the second two have the rubric "an excellent *philtron*."

111. It is formed from the Greek verb *agein*, "to lead" or "to drive." See Eitrem (1925) 49–50.

suggesting that the term was originally borrowed from the vocabulary of marriage or initiatory ritual.[112] The term *agōgē* is first used as a rubric for an erotic spell in third-century C.E. and later handbooks, but the alternate form *agōgimon* was known to both Plutarch and Galen.[113] Like the general term *pharmaka, agōgē* is sometimes qualified by an adjective to identify a more specifc type of spell. Thus one recipe is labeled an *agōgē agrupnētikē* ("a spell that leads by insomnia"),[114] while another handbook qualifies the term *agōgē* by adding in apposition the noun *empuron* (an "in-the-fire spell") in order to indicate a special subset of *agōgē*-spells that attempt by "persuasive analogy" to burn the victim and thereby force her from her home.[115] Other terms are used in a more narrowly defined way. The rubric *potērion* (literally, a "drinking-cup spell") appears thrice as a rubric for spells in which a drink or a cup is enchanted by a verbal incantation or adulterated with magical material, and then given to the victim to drink.[116] These are the technical terms most commonly employed in the papyrus

112. Borgeaud (1988) 32 notes that the word *agōgē* is used for the bride's procession from her father's house to her husband's and also for initiation rites that force young men and women from their parents' homes.

113. The first handbook recipe labeled *agōgē* is *PGM* LXI.39–44 (3d cent. C.E.). Soon thereafter, however, we find several examples in *PGM* VII (3d–4th cent. C.E. handbook): 300a–310 *(agōgimon)*, 593–619 *(agōgē)*; 973–980 *(agōgimon)*. For earlier literary references see Plutarch *Moralia* 1093d and Galen 12.251 (Kühn).

114. *PGM* IV 2943 *(agōgē agrupnētikē)*. The neuter form of the adjective, *agrupnētikon*, is used by itself to mean "insomnia spell," but it refers consistently to erotic spells of the *agōgē* type, e.g., *PGM* VII.374–376 ("Let Ms. So-and-so . . . lie awake because of me"); XII.376–396 ("Let her, Ms. So-and-so . . . lie awake until she consents"); and LII.20–26 (very fragmentary but undoubtedly erotic, e.g., "summoning Eros," "through night and day," "set a flame in the heart"). Insomnia or similar restlessness is also a component of Mesopotamian magic. Leick (1994) 200–201 quotes a spell that encourages a female victim to "be restless at night, find no peace during the day, not sit peacefully at night." See Ortega (1991) 71 for the very similar focus on insomnia in a Spanish love spell.

115. The term *empuron* is used in only one of the late-antique handbooks (*PGM* XXXVI), where we find "*agōgē, empuron*" (68–101), "another *empuron*" (102–133), and "*agōgē, empuron* over unburnt sulfur" (295–311). Other terms are used for this type of spell; see, e.g., "*agōgē* over myrrh" (XXXVI.333–360) and "*agōgē* over myrrh as it is burning on hot coals" (IV.1496–1595). For discussion see Kuhnert (1894) and section 4.1. I use Stanley Tambiah's term "persuasive analogy" throughout this volume as a more precise way of referring to the phenomenon that Frazer called "sympathetic magic"; see Chapter 2, note 4.

116. *PGM* VII.385–389, 619–627, 643–651, 969–971; cf. XIII.319–320 *(potēria)*. The term may be as old as the eighth-century B.C.E. "Nestor's Cup Inscription"; see Faraone (1996b) 104–106.

handbooks; but other clever coinages appear as well, such as *philtrokatades-mos* ("love-binding spell") and *phusikleidion* ("genital-key spell").[117]

What survives, then, of native Greek terminology and taxonomy for love magic is not at first glance very helpful to our analysis, and indeed most scholars implicitly assume that love magic is comprised of a wide variety of charms or magical materials that all aim generally at the same goal. In this study, however, I argue that Greek love magic in fact falls into two distinct categories: those rituals used *generally* by men to instill erotic passion in women and those used *generally* by women to maintain or increase affection in men. (I stress the word "generally" here, for, as we shall see in the final chapter, there are important and illuminating exceptions to these trends, which reveal how the Greeks constructed gender in some interesting ways.) Table 1 summarizes these categories of use. The second column characterizes the types of spells that women traditionally use to induce *philia* and similar affections in men, while the third column characterizes those magic rituals that men usually employ to throw *erōs* into women.[118] Each group of rituals is deployed in a very different social context. The former are generally used within a household or at least within an existing relationship to increase a man's affection and esteem for his partner or associates. The Greeks generally describe such feelings with words connected etymologically with the nouns *philia*[119] and

117. The rubric *philtrokatadesmos* (a combination of *philtron* and *katadesmos*) is first used self-referentially on a second-century C.E. lead tablet from Egypt (*SM* 38), twice as a handbook rubric (*PGM* IV.191–192 and 296–466), and on a series of fourth- and fifth-century C.E. lead tablets from Egypt. For *phusikleidion*, see *PGM* XXXVI.283.

118. Kieckhefer (1991) 31–36 suggests a similar taxonomy of medieval European love spells, which he divides into three categories: "sex-inducing magic," which was used "to induce a person to become a sexual partner" (= my *erōs* magic); "love magic," which was used "to encourage an intimate and lasting amorous relationship" (roughly = my *philia* magic); and "sex-enhancing magic," used "to enhance the sexual experience of partners who were already willing," a category that corresponds to the "self-help" love magic discussed earlier. He does not, however, point to gender as a significant criterion as it is in Greek love magic.

119. Benveniste (1973) 273–278. Dover (1984) 143 provides a succinct contrast between *philia* and *erōs*. The long debate over the affect of *philia*—does it simply designate a relationship (i.e., "friendship") without any comment on human feelings, or does it mean "affection"—has focused primarily on some peculiar uses in Homer. See Konstan (1996) and (1997) 28–31, who champions the latter view. Joly (1968) 15 notes that the verb *philein*, when used (rarely) to indicate erotic passion, is limited to amatory inscriptions, the PGM, and Lucian, esp. his *Dialogues of the Courtesans*, where it appears five times. For a similar development in these same genres of the slang meaning of the Greek verb gamein ("to marry") see note 55 above.

Table 1. A taxonomy of ancient Greek love magic

	Spells for inducing *philia*	Spells for inducing *erōs*
Greek terms	*philtra, charitesia*	*iugges, agōgai, empura, agrupnētika, philtrokatadesmoi*
General description	incantations over amulets, knotted cords, rings, love potions, or ointments	incantations over bound images, tortured animals, burning materials, or apples
Desired action	binds, enervates, or mollifies victims, thereby reducing their anger and making them esteem their companions	burns, tortures, or maddens victims, thereby emboldening them to leave their homes and come to the practitioner
Desired effect	love or affection *(philia, agapē, storgē)*	uncontrollable lust *(erōs, pothos, himeros, oistros)*
Social context	used by an insider within a marriage or an existing relationship to repair or heal it	used by an outsider in courtship or seduction to destroy existing loyalties to natal family, spouse, or community
Typical users	wives or social inferiors	men, courtesans, or whores
Typical victims	husbands, kings, and other male "heads of household"	young women and men, usually living in their natal home
Mythic exempla	Hera against Zeus, Deianeira against Heracles	Hippomenes against Atalanta, Jason against Medea

agapē,[120] both of which in their root meaning refer to "affection" and "love" in a wide range of relationships, including but not limited to family members, friends, and spouses. In the last case (marriage), these terms can be used to signal bodily passions as well, which is precisely what we see in the *Iliad*, where Hera clearly uses an amulet to arouse sexual desire in Zeus. The charms that arouse *erōs*, on the other hand, are almost always used to begin a new relationship by forcing the victims (usually but not always women) from their homes and into the arms of the person who performs the

120. See LSJ s.v. I.1. The basic meanings of the verb are "to hold in great affection," "to love," and "to be content with." Joly (1968) 36–41 surveys the various uses of this verb from the classical to the imperial period and shows how it gradually ousts the verb *philein* in popularity.

spell. In this case the spell is designed explicitly to arouse the victim's sexual desire for the practitioner of the spell, as is abundantly clear from the repeated use of the Greek nouns *erōs* and *pothos* and related verbs and adjectives.

Here I must pause to make the linguistic distinctions between "*erōs* magic" (spells that induce passion) and "*philia* magic" (spells that induce affection) as clear as possible, since modern notions of the meanings of "erotic" and "friendship" may cause problems here. In archaic and classical Greek discourse there is a clear difference between the invasive and dangerous onset of *erōs* and the more benign feelings of *philia*, a term that generally describes a reciprocal relationship based on mutual affection.[121] Thus, from the earliest periods Greeks either describe the onset of *erōs* as an invasive, demonic attack or use a ballistic model in which Aphrodite is said to throw and hit someone with *erōs* or *pothos*.[122] On the other hand, Greeks never personify or demonize *philia* or *agapē*, nor do they ever picture a deity hurling *philia* or *agapē* at mortals in an hostile way. This distinction should not, however, be overdrawn in a way that denies a sexual component to "*philia* magic." Indeed here I am careful to avoid the polar opposition of "erotic magic" to "nonerotic magic,"[123] because in Greek, verbs and nouns related to *philia* and *agapē* describe a wide array of marital, familial, and other relationships, some of which *do* involve—more so in Mediterranean cultures than in northern European ones—intimate personal contact, such as kissing on the lips and cheeks, embracing, caressing, and, in the case of a marriage or a homosexual friendship, sexual intercourse as well.[124]

121. The Greeks understood that *erōs* was basically incompatible with *philia*; see Konstan (1997) 38–39. Jordan apud Versnel (1998) 256 n. 107 seems to anticipate the distinction I make here, when he suggests that the more violent spells should be called "erotic charms" or "lust charms" rather than "love spells."

122. Discussed in detail in section 2.1.

123. As I mistakenly did in Faraone (1992a) and (1994a).

124. The gradual historical development of these terms creates an additional problem. The verbs *philein* and *agapan* (cognates *philia* and *agapē*)—and even the rarer *stergein* (related to *storgē*)—which originally mean "to love" or "to be affectionate" by the Roman period can mean "to fondle" or even "to have sexual intercourse" in an extramarital context, a development that is probably parallel to the evolution of the verb *gamein* (see note 55 above). As a result, beginning in the late second century C.E., we occasionally find these verbs in spells of the erotic type: *philein* first in spells like *PGM* XVI.1–38 (late 2d–early 3d cent. C.E.), LXI.1–38, or *DT* 271 (both 3d cent. C.E.); and then *agapan* and *stergein* in spells like *PGM* VII.862–918 and *SM* 42 (both 3d–4th cent. C.E.).

The real emphasis, then, for understanding these categories lies on the term *erōs,* which for the Greeks was clearly and narrowly defined as a dangerous, unwelcome, and irresistible lust that aims squarely and explicitly at sexual intercourse.

I should also note in passing that the types of magical devices employed in these two genres of love spells accord well with the two larger categories of Greek magical technology: beneficial charms (i.e., "white magic"), which usually aim at warding off or curing an illness; and harmful curses (i.e., "black magic"), which generally seek to harm or destroy an enemy. Thus although some *philia* charms traditionally deployed by women against men—ointments and amulets—can be connected in obvious ways with the adornment of Greek women, they also have (especially when we include love potions in the group) very strong affinities to the Greek corpus of healing and prophylactic lore, a fact that suggests that this whole branch of *philia* magic may aim (at least conceptually) at protecting an existing relationship or curing a sick one.[125] The various types of erotic spells, on the other hand, are clearly related to the large arsenal of rituals used in the more masculine world of interpersonal curses and other invasive techniques, a point to which I shall return in great detail in the next chapter. These commonalties suggest ironically enough that the general category of "love magic" may not in fact have been recognizable to the Greeks themselves, who may have seen *erōs* magic as a specialized extension of cursing rituals and *philia* spells as a subcategory of healing and protective rites.

1.3 The Advantages of a Synchronic and Comparative Approach

This study is unabashedly synchronic and makes comparative use of literary and nonliterary Greek texts from a wide chronological and geographic range to provide as rich a description as possible of an ancient social practice. In my defense I might, of course, invoke Braudel's *longue durée* or

125. Kieckhefer (1991) 34–35 points out that in medieval formularies recipes for increasing marital affection are "often explicitly remedial" and aimed at healing angry rifts or recovering love lost. He also notes that women who used magic to improve their own marriage were much less likely to be persecuted for magic than were women who used magic to facilitate adultery. On this point, see also Ferrante (1988) 218 and Flint (1991) 233–234, who notes the concern of the church fathers that love magic was being used to attack married women.

Lévi-Strauss' *structure* or the important subsequent work on antiquity of their followers, especially Vernant and Detienne,[126] or the similar techniques of the so-called New Cultural Historians;[127] but in fact nearly every modern scholar of ancient Greek religion from Foustel de Coulanges to Burkert and beyond has depended on (1) a mélange of Greek literary sources, inscriptions, and artifacts from different epochs and widely separated localities in and around the Mediterranean; and (2) repeated comparisons between the generally "realistic" ancient poetic tradition (e.g., epic and drama) and ancient life.[128] This method of "historically soft focus"[129] was dictated then—as it is dictated now—primarily by the paucity of evidence in any one city or century, and in the case of ancient magic it can perhaps be further defended by the assumption that rituals, at least in their formal outer manifestations, remain fairly stable in one place over time and even after considerable geographic diffusion.[130]

In this study, however, I regularly make comparative use of two corpora of evidence that until very recently have been generally ignored or overlooked by historians of early Greek religion and which therefore merit specific explanation: fourth- and fifth-century C.E. Greek magical handbooks from Upper Egypt (discussed briefly above) and tenth- and ninth-century B.C.E. cuneiform tablets from Assyria. In the case of the Egyptian documents, I can understand why a skeptical reader might hesitate when I juxtapose, for instance, a hymn of Sappho or a Pindaric ode with a series of much later Greek magical spells from Roman Egypt and North Africa, and then go on to extrapolate a continuous Greek tradition between them.[131]

126. On the subsequent fusion and confusion of the two theories—signaled in the beginning by Braudel's move from "geohistory" to "structural history" and typified by Sahlins' use of *longue durée* to mean Lévi-Strauss' *structure,* see Bierstack (1989) 72–74.

127. Cohen (1991b) and (1992) uses this term to describe the work of Winkler (1990) and several of the essays collected in Halperin, Winkler, and Zeitlin (1990).

128. Rives (1995) and Parker (1996) are exceptions that prove the rule; both have written excellent and detailed histories of the religions of (respectively) Roman Carthage and classical Athens, based on an uncharacteristically huge amount of archaeological, epigraphical, and literary data. For the usual synchronic treatment, see, e.g., Burkert (1985) or Parker's earlier work (1983) on pollution and purification in the Greek world.

129. As Redfield (1982) 182 puts it in his excellent synchronic discussion of Greek wedding ritual.

130. See Faraone (1992c) 114–117 and below in section 4.1.

131. See Finley (1971) 70 for "extrapolation" of a series from fragmentary data as an

My assumption of continuity involves, of course, two imaginative leaps, one of chronology and another of geography and ethnicity, since my juxtiposition of these texts seems, at first glance at least, to straddle a millennium-long interval and to involve questions concerning the assimilation of Greek and Egyptian cultures from Alexander's conquest onward. The chronological gap between classical Greece and these late papyrus handbooks has, however, been cut at least in half in recent years by the discovery in Egypt of papyrus fragments of very similar Greek handbooks dating to the first centuries B.C.E. and C.E.,[132] confirming earlier suggestions that sections of the fourth- and fifth-century C.E. handbooks were in fact copies of collections composed or compiled as early as the Hellenistic period.[133] Recent research has also shown that in the specific case of hexametrical incantations—many of them love spells—there is firm evidence of a continuous Greek tradition stretching from classical Athens to late-antique Egypt.[134]

The Egyptian provenance of the Greek magical papyri also raises questions about the ethnicity of the spells they preserve, since that country is generally thought to be uncharacteristically insular and since the Greeks themselves beginning in the Roman period attribute so much to Egyptian expertise in magic and the occult.[135] But scholars reluctant to treat these papyri as part of a much wider cultural phenomenon in the Greek world ignore at their peril the growing evidence that many similar handbooks were indeed known and used widely throughout the Mediterranean basin, as is borne out by reports of the burning of magical handbooks outside Egypt[136] and by some striking parallels between the papyrus recipes found

---

acceptable form of generalization for historians. But he was talking about much shorter periods.

132. Brashear (1995) 3413–14 surveys these important discoveries of the 1970s.

133. Ibid. 3419 discusses several other features of the fourth- and fifth-century C.E. handbooks that point to original compositions in the first and second centuries C.E. Gow (1952) 35–36 suggests that Theocritus knew of similar recipes, albeit probably not collected in handbooks.

134. Faraone (1995, 1996a, and 1996b) discusses the history of Greek hexametrical incantations generally; see idem (1992b) and sections 2.2 and 4.1 below, where I trace the history of a special coda ("O Lady Cyprogeneia, bring to perfection a perfect incantation") that seems especially popular in erotic incantations.

135. Brashear (1995) 3390–3420 gives a detailed survey of the problem. Ritner (1993) 99–100 argues for a traditional Egyptian basis for nearly all the rituals in the PGM, a greatly overstated claim, as Graf (1997) 5 notes.

136. E.g., thousands of magical handbooks were burned in the first century B.C.E., most

in Egypt and actual incantations on metal tablets and gemstones that have survived in Athens, Cyprus, Rome, Afghanistan, and elsewhere.[137] In several cases, moreover, scribes unwittingly copied handbook instructions onto a metal tablet, thus giving us valuable information about the use of Greek handbooks—during the early first century B.C.E. (Syria and Rome),[138] the second and third century C.E. (Sicily),[139] and the third century C.E. (Athens, Rome, Hadrumentum, Carthage, and Beirut).[140] In short, the fact that favorable climatic conditions have preserved so many magical papyri in Egypt should not be interpreted as proof that such handbooks were designed only for an Egyptian audience and did not exist elsewhere in the Greek-speaking world. Indeed, by such faulty logic we might be tempted to conclude that since all of our papyrus fragments of Homer, Euripides, and Menander come from Egypt, only Egyptians were reading Greek classics in the Hellenistic and Roman periods.

This is not to say, of course, that the ancient Egyptians were uninterested in such technologies or that they had no influence on the spells that

---

spectacularly in Ephesus (Acts of the Apostles 19:19) and in Rome (Suetonius *Augustus* 31.1); see Betz *GMPT* p. xli.

137. Brashear (1995) 3416–19 provides a sizable list but is puzzled that there are not more examples. Jordan (1994a) 123–124, (1994b) 323–331, and (1996) 123–125 gives several more examples, including two late-antique gemstones, one from Rome and the other from Afghanistan, which have virtually identical texts, copied from handbooks, as errors on the Roman text reveal; and a curse tablet with Egyptian themes found in Rome (*DT* 188) that employs a formula found in a contemporary papyrus handbook from Egypt (*PGM* LVIII.6–14).

138. In lines 11–12 of *GMA* 48, an inscribed silver amulet from Emesa in Syria, the scribe mistakenly copied the words "the drawing of the god" instead of inserting the drawing at this point; see Sijpesteijn (1978–79) and Kotansky *GMA* ad loc. Fox (1912) 54–56 published five nearly identical Latin *defixiones* from Rome (dating between 75 and 50 B.C.E.) written by a scribe working with a model that was used three centuries later by the people who inscribed *DT* 134, 135, and 190 (all from Latium).

139. In lines 6–7 of *GMA* 32, an inscribed copper amulet from Sicily, the scribe mistakenly copied directions from the handbook.

140. See Jordan (1985b) for evidence of professional scribes copying spells from handbooks in the Athenian agora; idem (1988d) for similar activity regarding spells against charioteers in Beirut and Carthage; and idem (1994a) 116–123 for very close parallels between a curse found at Corinth (against runners) and those against charioteers found in Hadrumentum. See Bevilacqua (1997) for a Greek *defixio* (from Rome) with a mistakenly copied handbook-rubric "For a hate spell" *(pros miséthron)*. Versnel (1991a) gives a detailed survey of curses from Greece and Italy and suggests that only "sample books or professional formularies" (p. 91) can explain similarities; likewise Tomlin (1988) 63: "oral tradition or the circulation of handbooks."

appear in the Greek magical handbooks discovered there. To the contrary. Although there is almost no extant evidence that the Egyptians practiced love magic prior to Alexander's conquests,[141] it would be churlish to suggest that all or most of the love spells in the Greek magical papyri are solely of Greek origin. Indeed, Roman-era handbooks written in demotic and the Coptic texts from the Christian period suggest a lively native Egyptian interest in love magic, some of whose forms are completely alien to the Greek methods surveyed in this study.[142] The difficulty, then, in dealing with the late Greek handbooks lies in separating, if possible, traditional Greek material from Egyptian, Jewish, and other materials. In some cases, this is not so difficult. Take, for instance, a series of erotic binding spells inscribed on lead tablets in Egypt in the second and third centuries C.E. that begin with a very similar invocation:

> I deposit *(parakatatithemai)* this binding charm *(katadesmon)* with you, chthonic gods, Pluto and Kore Persephone, Ereschigal, and Adonis, also called *Barbaritha,* and chthonic Hermes Thoth *Phōkensepseu erektathou misonktaik* and mighty Anubis *Psēriphtha,* who holds the keys of the gates to Hades, and chthonic demons, gods, men, and women who suffered untimely death, youths and maidens, year after year, month after month, day after day, hour after hour, night after night.[143]

We can begin to parse some of the various ethnic contributions to this spell by noting that inscribing on lead a text that calls itself a *katadesmos* and then depositing it in a grave and invoking Pluto, Kore, and chthonic Hermes and the "untimely dead" *(ahōroi)* are all immediately recognizable as parts of a traditional Greek ritual documented as early as the classical period in Sicily, Athens, and elsewhere.[144] There are, however, some obvi-

---

141. The single example is *AEMT* 1; see Smither (1941) for discussion.

142. For example, they use persuasive analogies drawn from the behavior of animals, e.g., "just as a calf the footsteps of its mother, so too, may X follow my footsteps." See the preceding note.

143. *SM* 46–51. I give the editors' translation of *SM* 47.1–5.

144. See Versnel (1991) 99 n. 68 and Kotansky (1995) 266 n. 50 (for the verb *parakatatithemai* and related terms of deposit in Greek *defixiones*); Faraone (1991a) 3–6 (for invocation to "the chthonic Hermes"), 7–8 (the use of lead), 9–10 (for the idea of a legal deposit or consignment of the victim to the underworld gods), 21 n. 3 (for the word *katadesmos*), and 22

ously foreign elements as well: alongside the usual denizens of the Greek underworld, we find two Semitic deities (Ereschigal and Adonis) and two Egyptian (Thoth and Anubis). Both of these Egyptian deities, moreover, are further identified by "magical names" that are clearly derived from Egyptian divine epithets and by possession of the keys of the underworld, another native Egyptian motif.[145]

From the point of view of a historian of ancient Greek magic, this text, which continues on to adjure a series of Jewish magical names, is very clearly the combination of an originally Greek binding spell—a *katadesmos* ritual performed at a graveside—with a popular exorcistic conjuration of Hellenistic Jewish origin.[146] A recent study has suggested, however, that the origin for this text and others like it is "not Greek but Egyptian, deriving directly from the ancient native custom of private 'letters to the dead.'"[147] This problem of competing claims of ethnic identity derives, of course, from the fact that both Greek and Egyptian—indeed, most Mediterranean—cultures have native traditions of invoking the dead to attack the living, and as a result modern scholars well versed in one or the other of these traditions "see" what is "native" to their own discipline and fail to appreciate what is not. This phenomenon itself has, however, much to teach us, for it suggests that these later spells may have been *purposely* shaped by the professional magicians and scribes in late Roman Egypt to appeal to the widest range of ethnic expectations (not only Greek and Egyptian, but also Semitic), and that the more popular spells are those that could be quickly understood as a natural extension of more than one national tradition. A similar effect is achieved when a formal Egyptian pedigree is given to a patently Greek spell, as in the case of this rubric in a late Hellenistic handbook: "An excerpt . . . from the holy book called 'of Hermes,' found in Heliopolis in the innermost shrine of the temple,

---

n. 6 (for the word *ahōroi*). A recently discovered Greek erotic spell from the late fourth or early third century B.C.E. calls itself a *katadesmos;* see Jordan (1999) no. 3.

145. Martinez (1991) 41–45.

146. Kotansky (1995) discusses this hybrid Jewish-Greek tradition in amulets, and Faraone (forthcoming b) applies his work to this text.

147. Ritner (1993) 178–183; quotation p. 180; he discusses this tablet on p. 181 with n. 842. See also p. 183, where he insists on "a purely Egyptian milieu" for the bound and pierced image that accompanies this text. I argue below, Chapter 2, note 5, that this image can similarly be understood as a development of native Greek traditions. For the difficulty in arguing for "single-source" approaches to the ethnicity of the Greek magical spells of the Hellenistic and Roman periods, see Faraone (1996a).

(written) in Egyptian letters and translated into Greek."[148] The incantation that follows, however, is composed in good Greek hexameters, closes with a traditional appeal to Aphrodite Cyprogeneia, and is used to charm an apple for erotic purposes—a practice that has a long prehistory in Greece but is otherwise unheard of in Egypt.[149] For the purposes of this study, therefore, I do not insist that many, more, or most of the Greek magical texts on Egyptian papyri are purely or primarily "Greek," but only that some of these later international or polyglot erotic spells preserve identifiably Greek images, idioms, media, rites, or ideas that are also reflected in earlier archaic and classical Greek texts, and can therefore be discussed as part of a continuous Greek tradition of erotic magic.

The cautious reader may hesitate again at the points in this study where I use Neo-Assyrian cuneiform recipes dating between 1000 and 800 B.C.E. to elucidate ritual practices in archaic and classical Greece (800–300 B.C.E.). In fact these comparisons are not as outrageous as they would have seemed as recently as two decades ago, before mounting archaeological and linguistic evidence forced classical scholars to admit the existence of close and continual cultural contacts between the Near East and Greece, beginning in the Bronze Age and reaching a zenith in the eighth century, the so-called Greek Renaissance, when numerous eastern technological innovations—for example, the construction of monumental temples and the use of the alphabet—begin to sweep westward into the more rudimentary Greek city-states.[150] More important, however, is the continual east-to-west drift of "religious technology," an extremely useful concept coined by Walter Burkert. Archaeological and linguistic evidence has shown, for example, that incense burning, purificatory rituals, hepatoscopy, and the use of foundation deposits in temples—all well-documented Near Eastern practices—begin to make their first appearance in Greece and Etruria in the eighth and seventh centuries.[151] There is, moreover, the further complication of Mesopotamian recipes arriving in Greece throughout the classical and Hellenistic periods either directly or via Egypt. Indeed, cuneiform ritual texts continue to be copied well into Hellenistic times, and there is evidence for the transmission of some Mesopotamian recipes into

148. *SM* 72 col. i.1–4.
149. See section 2.3.
150. See, e.g., Burkert (1983b) and (1992) and Faraone (1992c) 26–29 and (1993b).
151. Burkert (1992) 41–87.

Greek magical handbooks and Neo-Pythagorean treatises of Hellenistic date.[152] Most astonishing is the case of a second-millennium Mesopotamian curative incantation that apparently finds its way into a magical handbook written in Greek, found in Egypt and bearing the rubric "The [incantation] of . . . , the Syrian woman from Gadara"—a startling attestation of the close proximity of these different magical traditions, especially in highly hellenized and centrally located cities like Gadara in northern Palestine.[153]

Such interplay between East and West is already evident in the earliest Greek references to magic. In the *Odyssey*, Helen claims to have learned about magical *pharmaka* from Egypt (4.220–230), and Hermione, in her angry diatribe against Andromache, accuses her of working spells against her, pointing out that "the minds of Asian women are skilled in such things."[154] In Theocritus' second *Idyll*, Simaetha—a Greek woman probably living on the island of Cos[155]—implies that she has learned her love charms from a "foreign Assyrian man" (line 162), and we hear of a similar rite performed by a Syrian woman living near the Athenian Ceramicus, who performs for a fee.[156] Although the Greeks (as we have seen) sometimes falsely displaced their own home-grown magic onto foreigners to the east, it would be perverse to deny that some of the love charms used by the Greeks have in fact been borrowed at a very early period from Mesopotamia or the Levant.[157] It must be stressed, however, that such cultural transfers quickly become an essential part of Greek culture. Thus Greeks in archaic or classical times who use love charms first attested in the tenth century B.C.E. in Mesopotamia probably would not consciously see them-

152. See section 3.2 for similar Assyrian and Greek recipes for magical rings and facial ointments. For amulets used outside the sphere of love magic, see Barb (1950) and Reiner (1995) 124, who discusses the use of amulet stones "to make a woman talk," an expression that appears in Pliny (*NH* 37.169).

153. Faraone (1996a).

154. Euripides *Andromache* 159–160, translated by D. Kovacs, with "Asia" here meaning Asia Minor.

155. Dover (1971) ad loc. and Sherwin-White (1973) 291 and 321–322.

156. Lucian *Dialogues of the Courtesans* 4.1; see section 4.2 for detailed discussion.

157. Indeed, as we shall see in sections 2.3 and 3.1, close similarities between Greek and Neo-Assyrian love charms suggest that the Greeks borrowed such charms in the geometric or archaic period and made them, like incense burning and the divinatory inspection of entrails, "Greek" for all intents and purposes.

selves as imitating a strange "oriental" rite any more than, say, those who burn incense to a god or examine the entrails of a sacrificial animal to determine the course of future events, even though both of these rites were demonstrably borrowed from the Near East during the eighth century B.C.E., if not earlier.

Finally a short note on my use of literary descriptions or enactments of love magic as evidence for real social practices. Can I in fact safely assume that with regard to magic rituals, at least, art does imitate life? Here the detailed evidence from the Hellenistic and Roman worlds, late antiquity, the Middle Ages, and the Renaissance is especially helpful, for scholars in those fields, armed in some cases with an enviable mass of nonliterary data, can frequently show numerous close correspondences between literary descriptions of magical ceremonies and reports of actual practice. Scholars have argued convincingly, for example, that episodes involving the use or accusation of love magic in Theocritus' *Idyll* 2,[158] in Horace's *Epodes*,[159] in Apuleius' *Metamorphoses*,[160] in Lucian's comic sketches,[161] in the Icelandic sagas,[162] or in Renaissance drama[163] often reflect close and accurate knowledge of contemporary magical spells or handbooks. Indeed, it is most notable that Apuleius himself, when he is put on trial for allegedly having used love magic to induce a wealthy widow to marry him, quotes from a wide variety of Greek and Latin literary texts to show the ubiquity and social acceptance of magic, a strategy that implies the ready understanding of his audience that there is a close correspondence in the ancient world between life and letters in the case of magical rites.[164]

158. Gow (1952) 35–36: "The details of Simaetha's magic have every appearance of being true to contemporary practice." Faraone (1995) argues further that Theocritus consciously imitates the metrical form and some oddities of syntax of traditional hexametric magical incantations.

159. Riess (1893), Manning (1970), Ingallina (1974), and Freudenburg (1995) agree that Horace's poems about the witch Canidia reflect contemporary rites.

160. Winkler (1991) 223–224, discussing the elaborate description of Pamphile's love spell (*Metamorphoses* 2.32 and 3.15–18): "Before the recovery of the rituals in *PGM*, one might have thought that Apuleius' picture was so much fantasy. But everything in it . . . belongs to the regular procedures for drawing one out of one's house."

161. Herzig (1940) 12–19.

162. Pálsson (1991).

163. Wills (1995) 33–76 passim, citing older bibliography, gives numerous examples from Elizabethan drama. See Ruggiero (1993) 247–48 n. 52 for the magic in Ruzzante's comedy *La moschata*.

164. Apuleius *Apology* 30–32, with the detailed commentary of Abt (1967) 167–213.

If, then, other premodern periods of history provide repeated examples of literature closely imitating life with regard to love magic, why should we be reluctant to believe that the same is true of archaic and classical Greek texts? The answer lies, as I have argued elsewhere, in the modern perception of the fifth-century "Greek miracle," which constructs the Greeks—the Athenians really—as an ancient anomaly, a people who as the first rationalists threw aside the tyranny of superstition and religion at least for a few centuries. The evolutionary and teleological underpinnings of such an approach have long been exposed, but the influence of these ideas lingers on.[165] As a result scholars have traditionally had little difficulty using the text of Homer or Sophocles to illustrate Greek beliefs and social practices concerning burial, marriage, or the manufacture of woolen goods, but stop short when it comes to the use of amulets or erotic magic. This prejudice in fact flies in the face of decades of research showing that early Greek poetic texts repeatedly testify to magic rites in contemporary Greek society, for example: the incantations sung over Odysseus' wound by his uncle Autolycus,[166] the necromantic ceremonies performed in book 11 of the *Odyssey* and in Aeschylus' *Persae*,[167] the wind magic performed by Aeolus,[168] and the series of magical statues designed by Hephaestus to protect palaces, cities, and even entire islands.[169] It has, moreover, been pointed out that traditional magical incantations also lie behind the *form* of a number of early poetic texts, for example: Sappho's *Hymn to Aphrodite*,[170] Demeter's boast to knowledge of protective magic in her Homeric *Hymn*,[171] the Erinyes' "binding song" in Aeschylus' *Eumenides*,[172] and Aristophanic parodies of inscriptions found on amuletic rings[173] and of hexametrical love charms.[174] In short, if we lay aside some timeworn ideas

165. See Faraone (1992c) 114–117 for discussion.
166. Kotansky (1991a) 108 and Renehan (1992).
167. Headlam (1902), Eitrem (1928), Lawson (1934) 79–89, and Broadhead (1960) 302–309.
168. *Odyssey* 10.19–27; for the argument that this incident reflects actual magical practices, see Strömberg (1950) 82–84 and Page (1973) 73–78.
169. Faraone (1992c) 18–35.
170. See note 19 above.
171. *Hymn to Demeter* 227–230. For discussion, see Maas (1944) 36–37, Richardson (1974) 229–231, and Scarpi (1976) 159–173.
172. Faraone (1985) 150–154.
173. Aristophanes *Wealth* 883–885, discussed by Bonner (1950) 4–5 and Kotansky (1991a) 110–111.
174. Faraone (1992b).

about the special status of classical Greece as an age of pervasive and (for the ancient world) atypical rationalism, we can see that the literature of this period—generally famous for its thoroughgoing realism—can provide us with extremely useful information about early Greek love spells, just as it has in the past provided crucial details about sacrifice, divination, or the burning of incense.

2

Spells for Inducing
Uncontrollable Passion (Erōs)

A small clay effigy of a woman was discovered in Egypt carefully sealed inside a clay pot with a folded lead tablet that had itself been inscribed with a Greek magic spell of the third or fourth century c.e.[1] The effigy kneels with her feet tied together and her arms bound behind her back, and she has been methodically pierced with thirteen pins: one in the top of the head, one in the mouth, one in each eye and in each ear, one each in the solar plexus, vagina, and anus, and one in the palm of each hand and in the sole of each foot. To look at it you would assume, of course, that this apparatus was designed to torture and harm a lifelong enemy. The accompanying text, however, reveals that in fact a man named Sarapammon made or commissioned this effigy in hopes of forcing a woman named Ptolemais to abandon her apparently haughty demeanor and come to make love to him:

> Rouse yourself for me and go into every place, into every quarter, into every house, and bind Ptolemais, she whom Aias bore, the daughter of Horigenes . . . Lead Ptolemais, whom Aias bore, the daughter of Horigenes, to me. Prevent her from eating and drinking until she comes to me, Sarapammon, whom Area bore, and do not allow her to have experience with another man, except me alone. Drag her by her hair, by her guts, until she does not stand aloof from

1. The person who manufactured the apparatus seems to have followed in part an elaborate recipe like *PGM* IV.296–469; for discussion see du Bourguet (1975) and Kambitsis (1976), Martinez (1991) 6–20, and below, notes 6 and 54.

me . . . and until I hold her obedient for the whole time of my life, loving me, desiring me, and telling me what she is thinking.[2]

Like most Roman-era erotic spells, this one directs a ghost to prevent the female victim from engaging in the joys of everyday life and to drag her to the man who is performing the spell.[3] It also combines two types of over-lapping ritual operations, one that requires supernatural assistance and another that does not: (1) Sarapammon orders the ghost to bind Ptolemais and to force her to come to him; (2) by binding the arms and legs of her effigy and then piercing it, he seeks by a persuasive analogy to bind her and most likely to torture her as well;[4] for although in the Greek tradition the needles would normally be understood as another form of binding,[5] a con-temporary magical recipe for a very similar effigy directs the practitioner to pierce a female effigy in the same thirteen spots while saying: "I pierce the so-and-so member of Ms. So-and-so, in order that she will remember me, Mr. So-and-so." Thus, part of this spell is a performative ritual which is accomplished as soon as the man says "I pierce . . ." and simultaneously pierces the effigy. Here the goal is apparently that the woman feel aches and pains throughout her body that will cause her to remember the man who pierces the effigy.[6]

2. *SM* 47.19–27. This is a later part of the spell (quoted and discussed in section 1.3) that begins: "I deposit this binding charm with you, chthonic gods."

3. The charm was presumably recited in a necropolis. It is addressed to a ghost named Antinoos, raising speculation that he is in fact Hadrian's young lover who drowned in the Nile. See commentary in *SM* ad loc.

4. The usual terms for describing a magical action of this sort ("sympathetic" or "homeo-pathic") are problematic. Tambiah (1973) 199–229 dismisses the common view that so-called sympathetic magic is based on poor observation of empirical analogies. He distinguishes instead between the operation of "empirical analogies" (used in modern scientific discourse to *predict* future actions) and "persuasive analogies" (used in rituals by traditional societies to *encourage* future action). Such rituals do not betray inferior observation skills, but rather reveal a profound belief in the extraordinary power of language. For the application of his work to the ancient world, see Lloyd (1979) 2–3 and 7, Faraone (1991a) 8, and Graf (1997) 206–208.

5. Ritner (1993) 111–113 claims that this rite is the culmination of indigenous Egyptian tradition. See my general criticisms of such exclusive claims in section 1.3. On the long Greek tradition of such "voodoo dolls" generally, see Faraone (1991b) 193–194 and 200–203 nos. 3–7, 9–14, 18, and 21.

6. *PGM* IV.296–469. Graf (1997) 138–143 sees this entirely as a binding spell. The performa-tive verb, however, is "I pierce," not the very common "I bind," and suggests a different

We will do well to keep this magical assemblage in mind throughout this chapter. The apparent psychological stance of Sarapammon is quite striking, of course, but not unimaginable if we summon up the image of a man helplessly in love, who is willing to inflict such suffering on the woman of his dreams.[7] But any interpretation of this effigy as testimony to a bizarre moment in the emotional life of a desperate man is shattered completely when we remember that it has most probably been manufactured by following a recipe in a magical handbook and that other, very similar examples of this apparatus have recently come to light.[8] Thus it would appear that the violence and desire that typify this spell are indeed generic, and that this effigy does not reflect the idiosyncratic state of mind of a deranged individual, but rather the peculiar *mentalité* of the somewhat deranged culture that produced it. Indeed, in what follows I shall argue that the violent images, the immediate goals, and the female gender of victim of this spell are all perfectly consistent with a long Greek tradition of erotic magic.[9]

2.1 If *Erōs* Is a Disease, Then Erotic Magic Is a Curse

Before we can adequately understand why a man would bind and torture an effigy to force a woman to desire him, we need to explore in greater detail how the Greeks perceived the experience of erotic desire as the onset of a pathological disease.[10] Indeed, it is instructive that when Homer wishes to express the feeling of erotic infatuation, he uses epic formulae that

---

motive. See *PGM* IV.2943–66 for an erotic spell that involves piercing the eyes of an effigy to keep the victim awake thinking of the practitioner.

7. So Winkler (1991) 224–228, who posits a general theory of psychological transference for these spells; see some counterarguments in section 2.4 below.

8. See note 1 above for the handbook spell. Brashear (1995) 3416–17 discusses further evidence for a generic spell of this type, including two unpublished pairs of images that are similar to but not identical with those described in the recipe.

9. By my count, of the eighty-one published erotic spells (i.e., those used to compel one person to have passion for another or to come to another for sex), sixty-nine target women (two of these are homoerotic), nine target men (one of these is homoerotic), and three recipes allow for either target.

10. See, most recently, Maehler (1990), Winkler (1991) 222–224, Parry (1992) 270–271, and Martinez (1995) 353–354. Griffiths (1991) 60–67 compares similar Egyptian beliefs with the Greek tradition and contrasts both with the Mesopotamian and biblical tradition.

elsewhere describe dead and wounded warriors whose limbs have been "loosened" or on whose heads a mist has been poured.[11] The earliest Greek lyric poets knew this equation of erotic seizure *(erōs)* and illness *(nosos)* all too well.[12] Archilochus speaks in similar ways of a thick mist over his eyes or pains piercing his bones, and when Anacreon says "Eros struck me with a massive hammer, like a bronze worker, and then doused me (i.e., red-hot) into a frigid stream," he is probably thinking of the alternation of fever and chills that often accompanies severe illness.[13] Indeed, this is an image that Sappho develops in great detail when she speaks in the same sentence of a fire running under skin, her ears buzzing, and a cold sweat pouring over her (frag. 31.9–15). But *erōs* is also treated as a mental disease, which attacks the various inner faculties of thought and emotion, such as the heart (*phrenes* or *thumos*) or the mind *(nous)*. In epic poetry, the magical *kestos himas* of Aphrodite can "steal away the mind of thoughtful men," and Eros can "pour a mist over the stout heart" of Zeus or "subdue the mind and thoughtful counsel in a man's breast."[14] Likewise Ibycus says that Paris caused Helen's heart to flutter in her breast and that she was driven mad, and Sappho speaks of her heart (*phrēn*) burning with desire.[15] This tradition of *erōs* as a disease, moreover, continues into Roman times both as a literary conceit[16] and as a serious topic of medical debate.[17]

Such images have, of course, entered into our own western tradition of describing the sudden onset of love—albeit in watered-down form, such as "my heart is breaking" or "I am on fire"—but we should not underestimate the power and fear that originally motivated much of the ancient discourse on the subject. Thus, modern readers are rather startled by the image of a god physically attacking the lovesick.[18] Sappho, for examples, sings:

11. Taillardet (1962) 159–160, Campbell (1983) 1–27, and Cyrino (1995) 7–43, esp. 8–20.
12. Cyrino (1995) 71–164.
13. Archilochus frags. 191 and 193 (West); Anacreon frag. 413.
14. Homer *Iliad* 14.217 and 294; Hesiod *Theogony* 122.
15. Ibycus frag. 283.3–6 and Sappho frag. 48.
16. See Maehler (1990) for its frequent appearance in the novels and in the *Greek Anthology,* and Keyser (1989) for its role in Horace *Ode* 1.13.
17. Giedke (1983).
18. For detailed discussion of these images, see Carson (1986) and Cyrino (1995), who notes (p. 166) that Eros usually attacks the individual from somewhere outside the body

"Eros shakes my heart *(phrenes)*, as a wind falls upon the trees," a simile that Ibycus picks up and elaborates when he describes the same deity as a "Thracian storm-wind burning with parching fits of madness" that shakes his heart *(phrenes)* violently from its roots.[19] Elsewhere Eros "melts" or "burns" his victims, or "strikes" them with a hammer.[20] Here, too, although modern scholars might be tempted to think that this is merely an idiosyncratic feature of early lyric poetry, it is extremely significant that centuries later Galen, in a very serious refutation of the idea that both epilepsy and erotic infatuation were caused by gods, feels it necessary to address explicitly the apparently popular belief that erotic seizure is caused by a the attack of a "small, young god who holds burning torches."[21] A modern misunderstanding (and alteration) of an early fifth-century vase painting by Douris provides a good lesson in the perils of the sentimental approach. Douris depicts the famous heroine Atalanta running swiftly to the right while glancing back in surprise or fear at the first of three winged Erotes, who pursues her with a wreath in his left hand and a flower in his right. The "flower," however, is the work of a modern restorer, who painted over the poorly preserved remains of a whip, a motif known from other vases by the same painter.[22] Given the serenity and beauty of all the participants in the scene, one can hardly—from a modern perspective, that is—fault the nineteenth-century owner who decided to change the detail, but in fact both literary and iconographic evidence corroborate the impression that Eros began his career as a frighteningly demonic figure. Indeed, his standard weapons—the whip, the torch, and the bow and arrow[23]—all connote violence

---

through the use of violent actions, such as grabbing, seizing, or gripping. Padel (1992) 114–137 sets Eros' hostile behavior into a larger pattern of divine or demonic attacks against mortals.

19. Sappho frag. 47 and Ibycus frag. 286.8–13.

20. See Cyrino (1995) 111–112 ("melts") and 139–140 ("burns"). Anacreon frag. 413 describes Eros hitting him with a hammer.

21. Galen 18.2.19 (Kühn).

22. *LIMC* s.v. "Atalanta" no. 90.

23. Rosenmeyer (1951) and *LIMC* s.v. "Eros" nos. 364–365 (whips), 362–363 (goads), and 366–382 (torches). Magical gemstones show Eros burning Psyche (popular slang for female genitals) with torches; Mouterde (1930) 51–56 and Delatte and Derchain (1964) 233–238. A whip *(mastix)* in a god's hands is equally terrifying, esp. in a context of the bloody rout of an army: *Iliad* 13.812 ("by the evil whip of Zeus") and Euripides *Rhesus* 36–37 ("feeling fear under the whip of Pan").

or torture, and in early vase paintings he is nearly indistinguishable from other hostile figures like the *kēres*,[24] the Harpies, and other winged death-demons.[25]

The god Eros is the primary source of such painful tortures in archaic and classical Greek thought, but some authors also name the god Pan as the source of sudden and uncontrollable erotic seizure.[26] In the *Lysistrata*, for example, the entrance of some uncomfortably ithyphallic Spartan messengers produces the inference that Pan has attacked them.[27] Pan also inspires passion in a young man in a comedy of Menander, and later in the same play the lad's mother has a frightening nightmare that Pan has shackled her son—an ominous dream that she seeks to avert by sacrifices.[28] A man might also pray directly to Pan, the special patron of male homoeroticism, and ask him to force another man to love him.[29] All these attacks, however, carry a deeply negative valence in the Greek world, in which the "panic attack" that routs an army is literally "an attack by Pan" pictured, like Eros, wielding a whip.[30] He is also believed to attack individuals violently and to cause sudden deaths. Thus when Jason's new wife dons Medea's deadly gift and falls down in a dead faint, her servant suspects "the anger of Pan or some other of the gods." An ancient commentator explains that "in the olden days" people who fainted or suffered stroke were thought "to have been struck by Pan most of all and by Hecate."[31]

This repeated image, then, of Eros or Pan violently attacking his victims with torches or whips is best understood in the more general context of popular Greek beliefs about the etiology of disease, especially those like

24. See, e.g., Cook (1925) 315 and Padel (1992) 116.

25. Hesychius and the *Et. Mag.* (both s.v. *harpun*) give Eros as an example of a male harpy. See Cook (1925) 315 n. 3.

26. Borgeaud (1988) 84–85.

27. Aristophanes *Lysistrata* 997–998. The verb is *empiptein*, "to attack," typical of supernatural assault; see LSJ s.v.

28. *Dyscolus* 44–46 and 441, with Photiades (1958) 116–118.

29. Theocritus *Idyll* 7.103–117, with Fantuzzi and Maltomini (1996). Borgeaud (1988) 74–76 discusses Pan as patron of male homosexual love.

30. The Greek words for such an attack, *paneion* or *panikon*, are derived from the god's name. See Euripides *Rhesus* 36–37 for the whip (quoted in note 23 above) and Borgeaud (1988) 88–102 for discussion.

31. Euripides *Medea* 1167–77 with scholiast's comments on line 1172 and Borgeaud (1988) 102–110.

epilepsy, quartan fever, or mental illnesses that manifest themselves in violent agitations, shivering, or feverish outbursts.[32] This close relationship is most obvious in the confused reaction of the chorus of women in Euripides' *Hippolytus*, as they try unsuccessfully to diagnose the illness that has confined the lovesick Phaedra to her bed for three days (141–147): "Are you, princess, raving about in the grips of Pan or Hecate, or the holy Corybantes, or the Mountain Mother (i.e., Kybele)? Or are you wasting away because you failed to offer up the unburnt holy cake to Diktynna?" When faced with such a violent and otherwise inexplicable sickness, their minds naturally turn to wild and hostile gods like Pan, Hecate, or the Corybantes. The chorus then goes on to suggest some more natural causes (Theseus' infidelity, bad news from her Cretan home, or pregnancy). Later in the play the Nurse speculates that they will need to consult a diviner to discover "which one of the gods beats you up *(anaseirazei)* and knocks aside *(parakoptei)* your wits" (236–238).[33]

In some ways this is a set response for a chorus when confronted by a sick or crazy character; the chorus in Sophocles' *Ajax*, for example, wonder aloud if their leader, Ajax, is the victim of Artemis or Enyalios (172–181). In fact, the idea, that the blows of a god cause violent physical or mental disease is common in early Greek thought.[34] Presumably the wild gesticulations of the feverish or mad person were thought to be the body's reaction to blows from some invisible hand. One is reminded, for example, of

---

32. Padel (1992) 114–137.

33. The scholiast ad loc. sees metaphors drawn from riding ("reining in") and falconry ("clipping the wings of your wits"), while Barrett (1964) ad loc. translates "What god it is that pulls you back and sends your mind awry?" but is agnostic on the precise meaning of the metaphor. The problem is with the somewhat rare verb *anaseirazein*, which if derived from *seira* ("rope" or "rein") must mean something other than "to rein in" (here inaptly a metaphor for control, not the loss of it). The only attested simplex form of this verb *(seirazein)*, however, apparently means "to strike"—see Aelius Dionysius frag. 430 (a description of lightning)—a meaning corroborated by Hesychius' gloss of *anaseirazein* as *anakoptein*.

34. This explanation is later ousted by the idea that the god actually enters the person and takes possession of them; see Smith (1966) 405–413, esp. 406, who rightly challenges the long-standing arguments of Tamborino (1909), Pfister (1940), and others by pointing out that here and in other testimony to demons in the classical period the patient is never said or understood to be literally "taken over" by the demon; the language always indicates some kind of physical attack (hitting, biting, etc.), much like the description of the Furies pursuing Orestes. See Faraone (1992c) 36–53 and Padel (1992) 117–119.

Apollo in the *Iliad*, who stands unseen next to Patroclus and stuns him with a blow of his hand, leaving him paralyzed and at the mercy of Hector (16.787–796). Plutarch, writing in a philosophic tradition that is generally embarrassed by the notion that gods directly harm humankind, speaks condescendingly about people who attribute all their misfortunes to the "beatings" *(plegai)* of a god and the "assaults" *(prosbolai)* of a demon, pouring special scorn upon the "superstitious" man, who regularly fears that an angry god "will set his teeth into your body and bite it through, or he will get hold of your little child and beat him to death" (*Moralia* 170a).

The apparently wide popularity of this belief in classical times is underscored by the fierceness with which it is attacked by a late fifth-century B.C.E. Hippocratic writer, who mocks those who claim that the so-called sacred diseases[35] like epilepsy are caused by malevolent gods and unnamed heroes who attack and strike the patient's body and thereby presumably produce the various convulsions and seizures that are associated with such illnesses.[36] It is in this light, too, that we should examine long-standing Greek beliefs about *erōs* as a disease, an idea that is apparently alive and well more than half a millennium later, when Galen feels compelled to refute allegations that both epilepsy and *erōs* are "sacred diseases," that is, pathologies caused by the attacks of the gods.[37] It is, I think, highly instructive that in the *Hippolytus* the Nurse suggests that they use divination to find out which of the gods is the source of Phaedra's discomfort, for this process—divination, presumably followed by purificatory or apotropaic ritual—was the standard response in antiquity to the onset of violent illness.[38] In the case of Phaedra, however, the audience

35. The term covers a wide variety of diseases manifested by seizures, including epilepsy, stroke, and even quartan fever; see Tempkin (1945) 15–20.

36. [Hippocrates] *On the Sacred Disease* 1.38 (Grensemann): "They make a different god responsible for each of the different forms of the complaint. If the sufferer acts like a goat, and if he roars or has convulsions involving the right side, they say the Mother of the gods is responsible. If he utters a higher-pitched and louder cry, they say he is a horse and blame Poseidon, etc." The text is usually dated to the end of the fifth century; see Dodds (1951) 98–99 and Bonner (1943).

37. Martinez (1995) 356–357 cites Galen 18.2.18–19 (Kühn) and connects this idea of *erōs* as a divine disease with the "divine passion" (*erōs theios*) that some later Greek erotic spells call down upon their victims.

38. Faraone (1992c) 36–37.

knows from the very beginning of the play that she "has been struck out of her mind by the goads of Eros."[39]

The ultimate cause of such illnesses is, however, complicated by the Greek belief that mortals might use various rituals to encourage supernatural beings to harm or inflict diseases on other people. As early as the classical period, for instance, Greeks living in Cyrene[40] and Selinous[41] apparently believed that as the result of some ritual action they could send ghosts against their enemies, and Plato has Adeimantos speak of wandering priests and soothsayers who hang about the doors of the rich claiming that for a fee they can persuade the gods by charms (epagōgais) and binding spells (katadesmois) to harm their enemies, clearly a reference to the practices that have produced the scores of lead binding-spells recovered from contemporary Athenian graves.[42] Similar practices must also lie behind the Nurse's question to the lovesick Phaedra: "Have you been harmed by a hostile spell of one of your enemies?"[43] If the ancient Greeks, then, understood erotic seizure to be an unwanted affliction similar in its symptoms and divine causes to a violent disease like epilepsy, it should occasion little surprise that the extant spells for inducing erōs are quite similar in both form and content to traditional Greek cursing techniques. Or to put it the other way around: if erotic passion is an accursed state, it stands to reason that techniques of cursing can be used to instill such a passion in another person.[44]

We find, in fact, that nearly every form of spoken curse or imprecatory ritual used by the Greeks against their enemies also appears in the

39. Hippolytus 38: ekpeplēgmenē kentrois Erōtos. Cf. also line 1303, where she is "bitten by goads as she lusts."

40. SEG 9.72.111–121. The ghosts are referred to as hikesioi epaktoi, "hostile visitants." For full translation, bibliography, dating, and commentary see Parker (1983) 332–351, Burkert (1992) 68–71, and Faraone (1992c) 81–84. Plutarch Moralia frag. 126 (Sandbach) describes Thessalian sorcerors, who have the power to send ghosts (eidōla) against someone or to send them away; see Faraone (1991b) 185–186 and Johnston (1999) 82–123.

41. Jameson, Jordan, and Kotansky (1993) 116–120.

42. Republic 364c with Graf (1997) 22–23. For the use of ghosts in Greek defixio rituals, see Jordan SGD pp. 152–153 and Johnston (1999) 127–160.

43. Euripides, Hippolytus 319, with Maas (1944) and Barrett (1964) ad loc.

44. As has often been noted by scholars, e.g., Eitrem (1933) 34, Martinez (1995) 356–357, and Johnston (1995) 179 n. 3, although there is a tendency to focus on individual psychological motivation (Eitrem, e.g., is discussing Dido) at the expense of the larger historical pattern.

repertoire of their erotic spells. In both curses and erotic magic, for in-stance, Greeks destroyed wax effigies or other special materials in fire in hopes of projecting the pain and discomfort of fire onto the victim. This practice is attested as early as the seventh century B.C.E., when colonists setting out from the island of Thera to found the Greek city of Cyrene in Libya molded wax images and burnt them while they uttered the following imprecation: "May he, who does not abide by this agreement but trans-gresses it, melt away and dissolve like the images, himself, his seed, and his property."[45] Compare how Theocritus' Simaetha burns a variety of house-hold items, including wax and bay leaves, in an effort to burn her perfidi-ous boyfriend—"As with the goddess' aid I melt this wax, so straightway may Delphis of Myndus waste with love"—or how Horace's Canidia melts down the wax image of the victim of her love spell.[46] Many burning spells *(empura)* of this type appear in the Greek magical papyri, in which, for example, the performer of the spell places the spice myrrh on a hot surface in a steambath and addresses it as follows: "Myrrh . . . as you burn, so also will you burn her, Ms. So-and-so,"[47] a pattern found in another incanta-tion that is to be recited while myrrh is burned on an open fire: "Do not enter through her eyes or through her side or through her nails or even through her navel or her frame, but rather through her *psuche.* And remain in her heart and burn her guts, her breast, her liver, her breath, her bones, her marrow, until she comes to me, Mr. So-and-so . . ."[48] Here the practi-tioner, by burning something on a fire, seeks to burn or melt various parts of his female victim's body or mind. Another handbook spell (identified as an erotic spell) directs us to pour burning hot coals on a live lizard

---

Similarities between cursing and erotic magic are well known in other cultures. See, e.g., Leick (1994) 204 (ancient Mesopotamia); Ritner (1995) 3348 (ancient Egypt); Ruggiero (1993) 100 and 110–113 (Renaissance Italy); and Ortega (1991) 89 (during the Spanish Inquisition).

45. See Faraone (1993b) for full discussion of this text and other burning rituals used in oaths.

46. Theocritus *Idyll* 2.24–25; Horace *Satire* 1.8.43–44. Kuhnert (1894) 1 and 54–55 and Gow (1952) ad loc. give a good assessment of Simaetha's ceremony, which I discuss in detail in section 4.2.

47. *PGM* XXXVI.340–341.

48. *PGM* IV.1525–31, with Kuhnert (1894) 41–43. Here and occasionally elsewhere (e.g., note 81) I leave the word *psuche* untranslated, when I feel that I cannot precisely distinguish between the more abstract meaning "soul" (the usual definition) and the slang usage "female genitalia" that occurs in magical love spells. See note 23 and *GMPT* p. 339 s.v. "Soul."

in hopes of projecting a similar state on the female victim.[49] Such ritual actions are, of course, nearly impossible to find in the archaeological record,[50] but at this point it is not difficult to imagine the kind of ceremony that may have accompanied a Greek incantation ordering a ghost to make someone "waste away *(phthinein)* and melt down *(katatēkesthai)* in passion *(erōti)*."[51]

This overlap between curses and erotic spells is, however, most dramatically illustrated in the use of paired effigies to bind enemies and force them into a subservient position. In the first century B.C.E., for example, Apollo's oracle at Claros directed the inhabitants of Syedra, a Greek city on the southern coast of Anatolia, to set up an image of Ares, bound in chains and supplicating the goddess Dike (Justice), in order to prevent brigands or pirates from attacking their city. Here, in a magical binding ritual aimed at the brigands, a statue of Ares (representing their enemy, the brigands) is to be bound and placed in an inferior position to a dominating figure of Justice (who presumably represents the Syedrans).[52] Very similar pairs of images appear in descriptions of private rites used for erotic purposes. Horace, a Roman poet roughly contemporary with this Apolline oracle, describes a pair of dolls used by the witch Canidia in a magical spell that apparently has an erotic conquest in mind: "There was a wax doll and a larger woolen one, which restrained the smaller with punishments *(poenis)*, while it (i.e., the smaller, wax figure) lay there groveling, like a slave about to die." Most commentators build upon the suggestion of a medieval scholiast that the dominant, woolen doll represents the female

49. *PGM* LXI.39–71.

50. Egger (1948) suggests that we have such evidence in a small jug found in Austria in a second-century C.E. Roman shrine located in an area filled with graves. The jug was sealed with a lead tablet inscribed in Latin on both sides with a putative love spell and contained the remains of wood ash, sand, and fibers like human hair. The text, however, is not a love spell per se, but a curse addressed to Pluto and Eracura (identified as Chthonic Jove and Juno) and apparently aimed at someone's husband: "Fetch now, quickly, the name inscribed below and hand him over to the *manes*. Aurelius Sinnianus Caesarianus. Thus, O Silvia, may you see your husband upside down, in the same manner as his name is written." Egger is probably correct to think of some amorous connection; perhaps the practitioner was jealous of Aurelius and had designs on his wife.

51. *PGM* XVI, a lead tablet from Egypt, now dated to the late second or third century C.E.; see Jordan (1988c) 232–233.

52. Faraone (1989b) 296–297 and (1992c) 75–76.

practitioner (Canidia), while the smaller, wax figurine depicts some unfortunate male victim, perhaps even Horace himself.[53] This scenario of domination also appears in this explicitly erotic spell preserved in a later Greek handbook:

> Wondrous "binding love spell *(philtrokatadesmos):* Take wax [or clay] from a potter's wheel and make two figures, a male and a female. Make the male in the form of Ares fully armed, holding a sword in his left hand and threatening to plunge it into the right side of her neck. And make her with her arms behind her back and down on her knees . . .[54]

The recipe continues with directions to insert thirteen needles into the female figure, just as the effigy discussed at the beginning of this chapter has been treated—a fact that leads scholars to infer correctly that the person who created that effigy was working from a handbook tradition very similar to the one quoted here.[55]

This identification of the dominating male image as "Ares fully armed" suggests a Greek narrative that would have identified the bound and tortured female as Aphrodite, since the two appear together in similarly antagonistic fashion on a series of Roman-era gemstones from various parts of the Mediterranean outside Egypt. These gems depict either a fully armed Ares leading a naked Aphrodite whose hands are bound behind her back or the reverse, a fully clothed Aphrodite leading Ares, who is naked (except for his helmet), while Eros stands to the side holding Ares' sword and shield.[56] Since each of these gems carries an inscription of *voces magicae,* or vowels that are typical of other magical texts, it is extremely unlikely that such scenes are simply mimetic of a lost mythic narrative about these two divinities, and it seems prudent to suppose that they, too,

53. *Satire* 1.8.30–33, with Riess (1893), Kuhnert (1894) 44–45, Tupet (1976) 302–305, and Faraone (1989b) 298. The woolen material of the larger doll is also telling, as the Greeks associated female flesh with wool; see Hanson (1990) 317, Carson (1990) 154 n. 39, and Dean-Jones (1994) 55.

54. *PGM* IV.296–303, which has been widely discussed in connection with Horace *Satire* 1.8, beginning with Riess (1893) and Kuhnert (1894) 44–53. See also notes 1 and 6.

55. See note 1. The effigy in the Louvre was, however, found alone, sealed in a ceramic jug, and thus was treated differently from the pair of images described by the *PGM* recipe.

56. Blanchet (1923) and Delatte and Derchain (1964) 239–244.

were used as part of a persuasively magical ritual to bring about the subservient relationships depicted in these scenes.[57] There are, moreover, indications of a specific affinity to erotic magic: one of the stones with Ares triumphant bears a magic word, which also shows up in a series of "binding love charms" aimed at women and in the recipe discussed above for a pair of statuettes depicting Ares threatening a bound female effigy.[58] It would seem, then, that the gems with "Ares fully armed" were designed, like this more elaborate *PGM* recipe, for men seeking to erotically attract and bind a woman.[59] The gems with Aphrodite triumphant, on the other hand, were probably designed for women to use against men. We should also postulate a similar use for the set of thematically opposed magical gemstones that show either Eros torturing a bound Psyche (used by men against women) or Psyche torturing Eros (vice versa).[60] In any event, in each of these paired images—whether it is the tableau of Ares and his naked victim in the *PGM* recipe, the pair of roughly formed effigies of wool and wax described in Horace's poem, or the paired divinities in these finely carved gemstones—the genders of the two figures are clearly marked, and the people who use these images aim both at subjugating their victims erotically and at the same time giving themselves the dominating role (a goal nearly identical with that of the paired images of Dike and Ares bound, which the Syedrans used to curse the brigands who were harassing their city).

One can further illustrate the close affinities of curse and erotic spell in the shared use of the so-called vow of renunciation, which in early Greek

57. Faraone (1992c) 117–123 for a general discussion of "persuasive images" in Greek ritual. For a specific example of such images used in erotic magic, see Mouterde (1930) 51–56, who discusses a gemstone with Eros and Psyche in an erotic embrace on one side and Eros burning Psyche on the other, a design that is described in a recipe (*PGM* IV.1718–1870: "The Sword of Dardanos") for a love spell cast by a man against a woman (lines 1806–09): "Turn the *psuche* of Ms. So-and-so to me Mr. So-and-so, so that she may love me, feel passion for me."

58. The so-called *iaeō logos* appears on, e.g., *SM* 48 and 49, both erotic binding spells aimed at women. Martinez (1991) 105–108, esp. 107–108, discusses the link between the *PGM* recipe and the gemstones.

59. *PGM* IV.376–381: "Drag Ms. So-and-so by her hair, by her heart, by her *psuche*, to me Mr. So-and-so, at every hour of life, day and night, until she comes to me . . . do this, bind her for all the time of her life."

60. Delatte and Derchain (1964) 233–238.

and Semitic cultures appears both in conditional self-curses and in imprecations directed against others.[61] This is the form of Achilles' famous promise: "But until then [i.e., until I take revenge for Patroclus' death], neither drink nor food will pass down my throat," a vow of revenge that is repeated nearly a millennium later by Paul's enemies, who "put themselves under a curse, declaring that they would neither eat nor drink until they killed Paul."[62] This type of cursing formula is also extremely popular in Greek erotic charms, in which this denial of sustenance is inflicted on the victim, as for example in this incantation from a late Hellenistic Greek recipe, which urges a demon or deity (the name is lost) to "go into every [house and lead Ms. So-and-so to me.] If she is sleeping, let her not [sleep], if [she is eating, let her not] eat, if she is drinking, [let her not drink, until she comes to] me, Mr. So-and-so . . . quickly, quickly."[63] Such formulas were apparently used in Greek *erōs* spells much earlier, however, as we have already seen in the late classical binding spell from the city of Acanthus, which asks that the female victim not be able to perform a successful sacrifice to Athena, or have Aphrodite be well disposed to her, *until* she embraces the man who authored the spell.[64] By the third century C.E. such interventions into the personal lives of the victims were extended to in-

61. In this paragraph I closely follow Martinez (1995), who rightly distinguishes (pp. 344–345) "vows of abstinence" (in which someone places himself under a curse *until* he does something) from "self-curses" (in which someone places himself under a curse *after* he does something). Both are in fact conditional curses, the former designed to force a desired action, while the latter aims at preventing an unwanted action.

62. *Iliad* 9.209–210 and Acts of the Apostles 23:12.

63. *SM* 73 (1st cent. C.E.). For a particularly elaborate version, see *PGM* IV.1511–20. This type of love spell remains popular in Europe for centuries. Kieckhefer (1991) 40–41 notes examples from fifteenth-century Holland and Germany (e.g., "So may she burn and not be able to sleep, wake, lie down, sit, or walk"), and Ruggiero (1993) has numerous examples from sixteenth-century Venice, e.g., pp. 45 ("so that one cannot eat drink, sleep"); 88–89 ("so that she will have no content, no repose of her spirit or her body unless she is with me"); and 167–168 ("may she never be happy, neither eating or drinking"). See Ortega (1991) 71–74 for examples collected by the Spanish Inquisition, e.g., "so that he can neither eat or drink until he comes to love me well."

64. Jordan (1999) no. 3. The stipulation that she not touch a sacrificial animal or that a deity be well disposed toward someone is common in later Greek curses; Versnel (1985). They are designed to force the victim to do something by interrupting their harmonious relations with the gods, and thereby (presumably) threatening their health, livelihood, and happiness.

clude the prevention of a wide variety of activities, most notably specific sexual acts expressed in the crudest language.[65]

On a strictly formal basis, then, the techniques of many forms of erotic magic are quite indistinguishable from those of hostile curses used against enemies or of self-curses used in especially fearful oaths. Although this might trouble our own modern and romantic view of the positive and humanizing nature of erotic passion, the regular compatibility of erotic spell and curse is indeed—as we have seen repeatedly—perfectly harmonious with traditional Greek views of erotic seizure as a hostile demonic attack of the sort that results in deadly disease. There is, however, one important difference between common Greek curses and erotic spells: the former torture their victims with fever or pain until they die, while the latter do so only until they yield.[66] This formulation makes sense at two levels. First, in nearly all the ancient Greek discourses on love as a disease, it is clear that the disease is most acute when the beloved is far away or unobtainable and that the disease vanishes as soon as the beloved returns. Thus we find in a line of the feverish Sappho: "I am mad with love, but you cool my burning heart" (frag. 48), a movement not unlike the "in-the-fire spells" that burn a woman *until* she comes and satisfies her desire by making love to the man who performs or commissions the spell. Second, there seems to be a practical short-term goal behind most erotic spells. Whereas most curses use these punishments as an end unto themselves, erotic spells, like the "vows of renunciation," are clearly the means or tools for achieving another, more important goal: forcing the victims to do something against their will, a point to which I shall return in section 2.3, where I discuss what I call the "transitory violence" of erotic magic.[67]

2.2 Jason's *Iunx* and the Greek Tradition of *Agōgē* Spells

Several forms of ancient Greek incantations are designed to induce erotic seizure, and some of them are exceedingly short and simple. A first-century C.E. spell from Carthage, for example, has the wish: "May Successa burn

65. Jocelyn (1980) 20; Bain (1991) 57 and 74–75.

66. This apt formulation is from Kuhnert (1894) 37.

67. Versnel (1994) discusses a series of similar (and perhaps closely related) curses that throw fever into another person in order to force him or her to confess publicly to a crime.

with passion and desire for Successus!"[68] Another, inscribed a century later in Egypt, directs a ghost to "make and force Nike, daughter of Apollonous, to desire Paitous passionately."[69] These spells focus in an almost abstract way on the victim's erotic desire and in a manner that is unbounded by time and space. This is untrue, however, for the most popular Greek erotic charm, the *agōgē* spell, which has a consistent narrative: it "leads" the woman immediately from the house of her father or husband to the practitioner, a movement that mimics in some obvious ways the transfer of a bride from her old home to her husband's home.[70] We shall see, moreover, that the *agōgē* spell was used widely in the Greek-speaking world and has a remarkably long history, first attested in a Pindaric ode of the early fifth century and showing up repeatedly in the historical record well into the Byzantine period. In essence, this type of spell employs a wide variety of means to torture or otherwise discomfort the female victim, until she is forced away from her family and into the arms of the man performing the spell.

The earliest literary description provides a fifth-century charter myth of sorts for the very first *agōgē* spell, one that Aphrodite herself invented and taught to Jason:[71]

> And the queen of sharpest arrows, Cyprogeneia,[72]
> brought down from Olympus the dappled *iunx* bird
> pinned to the four spokes of an inescapable wheel,
> a mad bird, to mankind for the first time,
> and she taught Jason to be skillful in prayers and charms,
> in order that he might strip Medea of reverence for her parents,
> and that desire for Greece might shake[73] her
> with the whip of Persuasion as she was burning in her heart.

68. *DT* 227.

69. *SM* 37A.

70. See Chapter 1, note 112. In fact, according to Hesychius (s.v. *agōgē*), on Rhodes this formal wedding procession was actually called an *agōgē*. For the frequent crossover of female initiation and wedding rituals, see also Seaford (1988) 120–124.

71. Pindar *Pythian* 4.213–219.

72. "She who was born on Cyprus," a special cult name of Aphrodite that appears frequently in later hexametrical erotic spells, beginning with the Hellenistic "apple spell" discussed in the next section; see Faraone (1992b).

73. Some confusion has arisen about the meaning of the verb *donein* here and in a few other passages describing the effects of erotic seizure. Until quite recently the verb was translated

As is true for most magical rites, the ritual described here combines a *praxis,* the binding of the *iunx* bird to a wheel, and a *logos,* the "prayers and incantations" taught by Aphrodite.[74] The immediate goal of this erotic spell is that Medea be whipped and burnt with desire. But since both effects are included in traditional poetic descriptions of the effects of erotic seizure,[75] scholars have traditionally assumed that this section of the ode serves merely as an elaborate poetic device for describing how Medea falls in love with Jason at first sight. Pindar's constellation of images, however, with its dense allusions to burning, flagellation, madness, and bondage, is far more complex than the usual descriptions of erotic seizure; and when he combines these images with the goal of attacking her reverence for her parents, he clearly reflects both the language of torture and the goals that repeatedly appear in Greek incantations of the *agōgē* type, beginning with a first-century B.C.E. papyrus handbook from Egypt and a century later on a lead tablet from Carthage.[76]

In what follows, I offer a detailed discussion of these similarities and argue that Pindar's description of this *iunx* spell reflects the actual use of *agōgē* spells in classical Greece. This argument draws its strength generally from the realism of early Greek narratives, and it is dramatically enhanced by the way in which Pindar presents Aphrodite as the inventor of

---

in its usual meaning "to shake" or "to trouble" (see LSJ), but in the last two decades some scholars have wrongly inferred a circular motion; see Faraone (1993a) 3 n. 6 for detailed discussion. The basic notion of the verb is "to shake, churn, agitate" as when the wind strikes and shakes the leaves of trees. Some suggest plausibly that these are only poetic images of the *iunx*'s effect on Medea's mind—e.g., Sullivan (1983) 19 ("set in a turmoil") or Johnston (1995) 181, who suggests that in an erotic context "arouse" or "excite" might be appropriate. But vase paintings of Eros threatening his victims with a whip suggest a traditional image of physical discomfort and compulsion, as is brought out in the translation of Borgeaud (1988) 85: "driven by Persuasion's whip." See, e.g., the Douris painting discussed in the previous section and *LIMC* s.v. "Eros" with a whip (nos. 364–365) or a goad (nos. 362–363).

74. For the combination of oral spells and rituals, see Faraone (1991a) 6 and 17–20 and Graf (1991) 188–213.

75. See section 2.1.

76. *SM* 71 (= *GMPT* CXVII), tattered fragments of first-century B.C.E. handbook, apparently had a recipe for an *agōgē* spell. The blanks for the names of the female victim and the male agent in a first-century C.E. Latin spell from Carthage (*DT* 230; discussed in great detail in Chapter 1, pages 4–5): "lead [blank] loving, burning on account of her love and desire for me . . . force her to have sex with me [blank] . . . drive [blank] from her parents, from her bedroom."

the *iunx* spell, who brought it to mortals "for the first time" and taught them how to use it. This idea stems, of course, from a popular tradition of Greek speculation about the origins of human culture according to which the gods themselves discover and then teach mortals how to use some practical technology (e.g., Dionysus invents viticulture and Demeter agriculture) or useful device (e.g., Athena invents the bridle) that *is actually being used* in the time of the poet who sings the story.[77] In this case, it would seem that Pindar uses this myth about Aphrodite and the *iunx* spell in part to explain why men in his own day use *iunx* spells to drive women from their homes. Indeed, despite Pindar's very brief and terse description, we can, by making use of a wide array of later evidence, reconstruct the actual procedures employed in these early *iunx* spells: a man binds a small, lascivious bird on a wheel (a common frame for torture in the Greek world) and then tortures it with whips and fire in the hope that he can force his female victim from her family by transferring to her body—by means of persuasive analogy—the bird's natural lubricity and madness, as well as the additional pain and burning brought on by the torture.

The goal of burning the female victim is probably the most popular one found on the extant Greek *agōgē* spells of the later periods. We have seen, of course, how during an "in-the-fire spell" *(empuron)* a practitioner burns various herbs, spices, and other household objects in order to cause the woman to burn with passion.[78] A similar strategy undoubtedly lay behind papyrus charms that were placed in the scalding hot areas of the public bath,[79] and the magical gemstones that depict Eros burning Psyche with a torch.[80] Most extant *agōgē* spells do aim at torturing the victim with fire,[81] but they do so in a much more complicated and diffuse manner, with

77. See Graf (1995) 37 and (1997b) 93 (with 265 n. 20 for bibliography) for this important insight into Pindar's description.

78. See Chapter 1, note 115, and notes 47 and 48 above. For general discussion, see Kuhnert (1894) and Tavenner (1942) 17–37. For similar medieval rites, see, e.g., Kieckhefer (1991) 38–41.

79. Dunbabin (1989) 36–37; Bonner (1932a) suggests the presence of special demons in the public bath itself, but he misses the obvious persuasive analogy that one might draw with the searing heat of the bath.

80. See Nock (1925), Schlam (1976) 14–20, and note 60 above.

81. E.g., *PGM* IV.2767 ("torch her *psuche* with ceaseless fire"), 2932–33 ("melt her"); *PGM* XVI passim ("melt her down"); *PGM* XXXVI.340–341; *PGM* LXI.24 ("burn her heart"); *PGM*

fire only the most prominent among an array of discomforts such as hunger, thirst, and insomnia, as, for instance, in this elaborate spell preserved on a papyrus in Berlin:

> Aye, lord demon, attract, inflame, destroy, burn, cause her to swoon from love as she is being burnt, inflamed. Goad the tortured soul *(psuche)*, the heart of Karosa, whom Thelo bore, until she leaps forth and comes to Apalos, whom Theonilla bore, out of passion and love, in this very hour, immediately, immediately; quickly, quickly. . . . do not allow Karosa herself, whom Thelo bore, to think of her [own] husband, her child, drink, food, but let her come melting for passion and love and intercourse, especially yearning for the intercourse of Apalos, whom Theonilla bore, in this very hour, immediately, immediately; quickly, quickly.[82]

This papyrus is not a fragment from a handbook, but an actual spell used in late antiquity by a man named Apalos to encourage a woman named Karosa to come to him for sex. I have quoted a large portion here to give the reader a sense of how fire and burning, though clearly the central and reiterated images in the spell, are combined with evocations of other forms of torture, much as we see in Pindar's description. Apalos' spell has two other points of special interest that can be illustrated in other erotic spells as well: the peculiar combination of vividly physical torture directed at abstract faculties like Karosa's heart and soul,[83] and the manner in which imperatives and passive participles are combined to give a richly detailed description of the intended effect on the victim, such as "cause her to

---

O[strakon] 2.29–30 ("burn her *psuche*"); SM 40.14 ("burn her liver, her breath, her heart, and her *psuche*"); 45.31–32 ("burn her limbs, her liver, her female body [= pudendum]"); DT 51 ("throw feverish heat into her / burn up her soul [*psuche*] and her heart"); DT 227.2 ("let her burn"); and DT 270.11 ("let her soul [*psuche*] and heart burn") and 18–19 ("let her breath and heart catch fire").

82. PGM XIXa.50–54 (4th or 5th cent. C.E.); the lively translation is that of O'Neil and Kotansky in GMPT, who rightly translate *psuche* as "soul" here (see note 48).

83. The soul *(psuche)* and the heart *(kardia)* appear most frequently as targets of erotic spells (see, e.g., the texts quoted above in note 81). The poetic term for heart *(phrēn)* appears only twice: PGM IV.2489 ("Give her a burning of her soul and a punishment of her *phrēn*") and 2762 ("as she is being subdued in her heart [*en phresi damnomenē*]"); cf. Pindar's expression: "as she is being burnt in her heart [*en phrasi kaiomenēn*]."

swoon *as she is being burnt*" or "goad her soul *as it is being tortured.*"[84] It is not, I think, coincidental that both of these features appear in Pindar's descriptions of the power of the *iunx* spell cast against Medea, which was designed "to shake her with a whip *as she was burning in her heart.*"[85]

In his description of the effects of Jason's spell Pindar says that Medea is to be attacked by "the whip of Persuasion," an image that is consistent with traditional Greek notions of demonic attack[86] and that reflects a rarer and perhaps older understanding of the goddess Peitho (Persuasion) as a violent deity.[87] Goads, whips, and other instruments of torture appear, moreover, several times in later Greek *agōgē* spells and in contexts very similar to this "whip of Persuasion." A hexametrical incantation, for example, invokes Aphrodite to attract a female victim "as she is being driven by frenzy"[88] under compulsion with "violent goads,"[89] and another spell bids the Egyptian god Anubis to attack a woman "until she, as she is being

---

84. The Greek in Apalos' spell is *skotōson [kai]omenēn and kentei <ba>sanizomenēn tēn psuchēn)*; cf. *PGM* IV.1412–13 ("Lead her *as she is being tortured*"); *PGM* VII.471–472 ("lead So-and-so to me . . . *as she is being burnt* in her soul [*psuche*] and in her heart"); *PGM* VII.611–612 ("lead her to me . . . *as she is being burnt*"); *PGM* XVIIa.10 ("*as she is being melted with erotic desire*"); *PGM* XVIIa.16 and 25 (both quoted in note 90 below). See also *PGM* XXXVI.110–111 ; *PGM* XXXVI.200–201; *SM* 48.35–37; and a rare example with a male victim: *DT* 271.12–14.

85. The Greek is *en phrasi kaiomenēn doneoi mastigi.*

86. Whips and goads are common divine weapons; see Padel (1992) 117–119 and my discussion in the previous section. Zeitlin (1986) 145 discusses a vase painting (c. 490 B.C.E.) of Eros prodding Zeus with a goad as he pursues Ganymede.

87. Peitho is usually depicted by the philosophers and the tragedians as a gentle or positive force, often contrasted with violence or trickery. Buxton (1982) 31–67 rightly notes, however, that here in *Pythian* 4 and twice in Aeschylus (*Ag.* 385 and *Ch.* 726) Peitho is closely associated with both of her traditional opposites. For other instances in which the verb "to persuade" *(peithein)* and its cognates seem in a similar manner to embrace violent or deceptive actions, see Buxton pp. 48–51, Bobonich (1991), and Petropoulos (1993) 48.

88. *PGM* IV.2911. Or perhaps "driven with madness" or "passionately driven" (the Greek is *oistrōi elaunomenēn*). The word *oistros* ranges in meaning from "gadfly that infests bovines" or "goad" to "madness or frenzy, often of desire," and eventually the "mating madness" of female mammals in heat (whence the English word "estrus"). See Padel (1992) 120–122.

89. *PGM* IV.2912, in the corrupt middle portion of a rather sophisticated hymn to Aphrodite (*PGM* Hymn 22). Kuster (1911) 66 cites as a parallel Plato's description of an infatuated person "driven by necessity and frenzy" (*Phaedrus* 240d: *hup' anagkēs te kai oistrou elaunetai*). The personification appears twice in Greek erotic spells, *PGM* VII.300a–310 ("bitter Necessity") and *PGM* Hymn 24.1.

whipped by you, comes yearning for me."[90] This image is in fact a common one for the god Eros in Greek art and in the later periods seems to become his defining symbol, as is suggested by a series of late Roman sarcophagi that show the god Pan being flogged by a group of *erōtes*, an image that was—for a Greek-speaking audience at least—a visual pun on the idea that "love conquers all."[91] Other more generalized images of torture appear as well. A fourth-century c.e. Greek incantation from Hermoupolis encourages demons to lead a woman named Gorgonia to the practitioner and "to torture her body night and day,"[92] and Apalos, in the long spell quoted earlier, commands them to "goad the tortured soul, the heart of Karosa, whom Thelo bore, until she leaps forth and comes to Apalos." Here and in the other spells quoted above the connection between the torture and the movement of the victim is quite clear; she is to remain sleepless, hungry, and in pain *until she comes* to the practitioner.[93]

There are two other intriguing correspondences between Pindar's *iunx* spell and later *agōgē* spells. The first is insanity. The sexual desire that is to be generated by Greek erotic spells is often described as a mad frenzy.[94] It can hardly be coincidental, therefore, that Pindar describes the *iunx* bird with great emphasis[95] as a *mainas*, an adjective that means a

---

90. *PGM* XVIIa: *hupo sou mastizomenē*. The spell continues: "and lead her to me under my feet melting with passionate desire at all hours, day and night, serving both my desire and her own, without hesitation or shamefacedness, joining her thigh to my thigh, her belly to my belly, her 'black' (= pubic hair) to my 'black' . . . quickly, quickly, now, now, driven by your whip (*tēi sēi mastigi elaunomenēn*)." Anubis appears in several Greek magic charms to augment or oust the traditional Greek chthonic gods, who often undertake erotic spells; see Jordan (1994c) 138.

91. See note 23 above for the iconography of Eros. The pun works on the close similarity in Greek (only the accent differs) between *pan*, "everything," and Pan the god; see Borgeaud (1988) 73. Given the pun, this Roman image probably derives from a Greek original.

92. *SM* 42.37–38. For other instances of the verb "to torture" *(basanizein)* in erotic spells, see note 84 above. The same verb has been restored at *PGM* XIXa.51–52: "goad her soul as it is being tortured (<*ba*>*sanizomēn*)!"

93. The basic syntax of these incantations is: "Do x, y, and z, until she comes to me" or "in order that she come to me." See Faraone (1993a) 10 n. 28.

94. *PGM* IV.2756, "as she is being driven mad *(mainomenē)*"; *DT* 270.7, *furens*, and 271.6, "as he is being driven mad"—the rare male victim. Sometimes the emotion itself is described as frenzied: *SM* 41.12, "with mad passion" *(erōti manikōi)*, 45.7, and 45.49; and *DT* 265. Cf. Euripides' Medea "with a heart that was being driven mad *(mainomenai)*" *(Med. 431–432)*. For the topos of madness caused by magic, see Mattes (1970) 44–49.

95. Emphatic because of the strophic enjambment; see Braswell (1988) ad loc.

"madwoman"—a detail that suggests to most commentators that the *iunx* charm is to drive Medea insane with desire[96] or to make her act like the maenads (another meaning of this same word), who in Greek myth are driven from their homes by Dionysus.[97] Pindar's description of Aphrodite yoking a mad bird—and, by extension, Medea—to "an inescapable wheel (*en alutôi . . . kuklôi*)" also uses the language that we find in later erotic spells.[98] Pamphile's love charm in Apuleius' *Metamorphoses* is similarly designed to bind a young man in "eternal shackles," and the term "inescapable bonds" appears in three Roman-era binding spells,[99] as well as in a pair of nearly identical late-antique Greek *agōgē* spells from Egypt:[100]

> Seize Euphemia and lead her to me, Theon, loving me with crazy desire, and bind her with inescapable bonds *(desmois alutois)*, strong ones of adamantine, for the love of me, Theon, and do not allow her to eat, drink, obtain sleep, jest, or laugh, but make her leap out . . . and leave behind her father, mother, brothers, sisters, until she comes to me.

The image of a demon both binding and leading the victim is typical of this sort of "binding love spell" *(philtrokatadesmos)* and shows up in a third-century C.E. *agōgē* from Tunisia, which like Pindar uses a verb of yoking: "I adjure you . . . to lead Urbanus, whom Urbana bore, and to yoke him as a

96. Most commentators seem to agree that Medea is to be driven mad by the *iunx* spell, but I disagree with their reasoning. Braswell (1988) ad loc., e.g., suggests that we translate the adjective *mainas* in an active sense (one otherwise unattested in Greek) to mean "maddening," i.e., that the bird/spell was designed to make Medea mad.

97. I discuss this connection further in section 2.4. Some later authors describe the peculiar movements of the *iunx* bird metaphorically as "bacchic dances"; see Capponi (1981) 296.

98. This image of yoking is not (to the Greek mind at least) inconsistent with the idea that Jason seeks to make Medea wild and insane. In fact it is part of a wider pattern of myth that I discuss in section 2.4, e.g., in Bacchylides 11.45–46, where Hera yokes the *phrenes* of the daughters of Proetus who run wildly from their father's house; see Seaford (1988) 120.

99. Apuleius *Metamorphoses* 2.5: "pedicis aeternis"; DT 252 and 253 are both 1st-cent. C.E. Carthaginian curses, but neither is a love charm. But see Chapter 1, note 102, for an unpublished first-century C.E. love spell from Cyprus that uses this same term.

100. Brashear (1992) publishes the fourth-century C.E. version; SM 45, translated here, was inscribed a good century later. Both papyri were, moreover, discovered inside a sealed clay vessel wrapped around a pair of wax puppets held together in an erotic embrace; see Brashear (1992) 80–81 with plate 11 and Wortmann (1968) 85–102.

lifemate to Domitiana, whom Candida bore, desiring her, as he is being tortured and sleepless in his passion and desire for her."[101]

The many correspondences between Pindar's compressed description of Jason's "incantations and prayers" and these later erotic spells suggest a new and somewhat different understanding of the *praxis* of Pindar's spell, especially the role of the wheel to which the *iunx* bird is bound. The traditional interpretation rightly sees the bird as an effigy for Medea, but suggests or implies that the wheel is spinning and thereby disorients Medea by setting her thoughts spinning.[102] However, Pindar never says that Jason's wheel was rotated in the course of the ritual. In fact the wheel that Jason uses would have been more easily recognizable to Pindar's audience as the stationary wheel commonly used in Greek torture as a frame on which criminals or slaves were bound and then racked with pain first by stretching or twisting the limbs with ropes or winches[103] and then by whipping or even burning[104] the contorted body—a combination that Pindar seems to be evoke in his complex allusion to the four-spoked wheel, the whip, and

101. *DT* 271.12–15.

102. This inference depends generally on a mistranslation of the verb *donein* (see note 73 above) and on later descriptions of magical spells in Roman poetry, where there is no mention of a bound bird and where it is clear that poets and scholiasts alike have hopelessly confused three originally different magical devices, perhaps all used in erotic magic: the *iunx* wheel, the *rhombos*, and the top. For general discussion see Bury (1886), Sutphen (1902), Dedo (1904) 18–20, Abt (1967) 178–179, Cook (1914) 253–265, Tavenner (1933), Gow (1934), Eitrem (1942), Nelson (1946), De la Genière (1958), C. Segal (1973), Ingallina (1974) 157–173, Tupet (1976) 50–51, Capponi (1981), Petropoulos (1988) 221, Lo Monaco (1989) 261–271, Johnston (1990) 90–110 and (1995), and Pirenne-Delforge (1993). I agree that (because of this confusion) the word *iunx* can be used from the late Hellenistic period onward to refer to rotating tops and wheels, and that such tops and wheels are used in magic, but I deny that the word *iunx* here in Pindar's fourth *Pythian* refers to a spinning wheel or top; see Faraone (1993a) 11–13 for my view and Johnston (1995) 178–180 for the best defense of the traditional view.

103. Vergote (1972) and Thür (1977). The most common expression in Greek is "to be racked *(streblousthai)* upon the wheel" (Herodotus 2.89, Demosthenes 29.40, Plutarch *Nicias* 30, Aristophanes *Wealth* 875 and *Frogs* 620, and Antiphon 5.32). The basic meaning of *streblousthai* is "to be twisted" or "to be strained tight" as in the case of cables in a windlass (Hdt. 7.36) or strings on a musical instrument (Plato *Republic* 531b). The focus seems to be on the stretching or the tension of the victim's body, e.g., the simile in Aristophanes *Lysistrata* 845–846: "Such is the strain and the stretching that hold me—as if I were being racked *(streblousthai)* upon the wheel"; see Cunningham (1971) 100 and Henderson (1987a) 175.

104. E.g., Aristophanes *Peace* 452: "let him be drawn upon the wheel as he is being whipped *(mastigomenos)*" with the scholia ad loc. See also Anacreon frag. 388 (= Athenaeus

the fire. A similar combination of tortures is evoked by images on a first-century B.C.E. silver bowl and a series of Roman-era gemstones that depict Eros burning or whipping a bound Psyche, while nearby the goddess Nemesis (or her token animal, the griffin) holds or leans upon a four-spoked wheel, a reminder of how Nemesis punishes the hubristic and the recalcitrant.[105] In short, Aphrodite teaches Jason how to use the bird as an effigy of Medea, just as the Greeks pierced and mutilated lead, wax, and clay figurines in their curses and other erotic spells.

But what evidence do we have that the Greeks used live birds or animals for such rituals? As it turns out, Aristophanes, writing a half-century or so after Pindar, parodies what appears to be a very similar kind of erotic spell in a fragment of his lost play the *Amphiaraus:* "Thoroughly shake the old man's butt from its foundations, like a shake-tail bird, and <you> bring to perfection this excellent incantation."[106] This two-line fragment, which quite openly calls itself an "incantation" (*epaoidē*), was most probably the end of masterful parody of an erotic spell. We know this because the meter and the last three words of it closely mimic a popular line that appears at the end of a series of erotic incantations, most of them also in hexameters: "O Lady Cyprogeneia, bring to perfection this perfect incantation." Moreover, this genre of spell that Aristophanes parodies seems somewhat similar to the one that Pindar has in mind when he describes his *iunx* spell. First of all, it is quite telling that Pindar calls Aphrodite "Cyprogeneia" when he describes her as the inventor of the first *agōgē*, the very guise in which she appears in this later tradition of hexametrical incantations that Aristophanes knows. It is noteworthy, too, that both Aristophanes and Pindar connect their erotic spells with very similar

12.533 f.), where whipping is mentioned after the victim's neck has been placed on a wheel. For the combination of wheel, whip, and fire in later Greek literature, see Achilles Tatius 6.21 and Chariton 3.4.7.

105. Most scholars believe that Nemesis' wheel was borrowed in the Roman period from the iconography of Tyche/Fortuna, where it symbolizes the cyclical nature of human luck, and it is clear that late imperial authors understand this to be the case; but in the extant sources Nemesis appears with the wheel about a century before Tyche. Moreover, the recent discovery of a four-spoked bronze wheel of archaic date dedicated at the Nemesis sanctuary at Rhamnous suggests a much longer prehistory for the wheel and one connected (in the Greek world at least) with judicial torture and punishment. See Hornum (1993) 25–27, esp. 26 n. 10.

106. Frag. 29 K-A, with Faraone (1992b).

kinds of birds, the *kigklos* and the *iunx,* for ancient and modern scholiasts are in agreement that these birds were employed in love magic because of the characteristic movements of their necks or tails, which were thought to indicate either their lascivious nature or their madness. In these types of spells, therefore, practitioners apparently hoped that by persuasive analogy they might transfer the natural madness or sex hunger of these birds to the female targets of the spell.[107] This interpretation is correct, as far as it goes, but it fails to appreciate the added importance of the ritual treatment of the bird, which Jason binds to a wheel and apparently tortures with whips and fire. He does so in hopes of compounding the naturally deviant or mad behavior of the bird with the further discomfort and madness caused by torture, and to project the resulting mental turmoil and physical pain onto the victim, in a complex manner similar to the actual magical spells surveyed above.

The very idea that a person might torture or mutilate a live animal in the course of a ritual is, of course, a bizarre idea for a modern reader, but it is in fact fairly well documented in a variety of very old Greek oath ceremonies during which men swearing oaths kill and butcher oxen, sheep, pigs, and dogs and pray that they themselves be treated like these animals if they violate their oaths.[108] These are, of course, large public ceremonies, but similar rites were apparently performed individually by Athenian officials and Olympic athletes, and there is quite a bit of evidence that smaller animals were used in a wide array of interpersonal curses and erotic charms.[109] For example, in one simple erotic spell, an "insomnia spell," the following incantation is painted on the wings of a live bat: "May Ms. So-and-so, whom Ms. So-and-so bore, lie awake until she consents (i.e., to sex)"; the animal is then allowed to fly away into the night while the same incantation is spoken aloud, apparently in the hope that the animal's natural nocturnal restlessness will—by the process of persuasive analogy—be transferred to the victim and thus prevent her from sleep-

107. For the natural salaciousness of the *iunx* bird and the *kigklos* bird, see Tavenner (1933) 110–111, Thompson (1936) 124–128, and Capponi (1981) 295–296, who quote and discuss all the relevant passages in the natural historians and the scholia to Pindar and Theocritus. Capponi stresses the fact that later Greeks noticed the mad behavior of the bird as well as its alleged sexual hunger.

108. Faraone (1993b) 65–72.

109. Faraone (1993b) 68–70.

ing.[110] This spell is uncharacteristically coy regarding the nature of the woman's "consent," but another similar recipe is explicitly erotic: here the eyes of a live bat are removed, placed in the eye-sockets of a clay dog, and pierced with needles in order "that Ms. So-and-so may . . . be unable to sleep, holding no one in her mind except me alone, Mr. So-and-so" and that she "may lie awake for me through all time."[111] This language is in fact quite close to that used in the incantation sung as the female effigy discussed at the beginning of the chapter was pierced with thirteen copper needles: "I pierce . . . in order that she remember me." In this spell, however, the effect is doubled, for the natural nocturnal sleeplessness of the animal is augmented by the piercing pain of the needles.

From other sources we discover that in their cursing rituals Greeks and Romans mutilated chameleons or sewed up the mouths of "crazy-fish" in hopes of silencing their enemies,[112] and burned lizards on hot coals in erotic spells.[113] In these rites, too, the choice of animal was sometimes dictated by some special quality of the animal, as in the ritual that apparently accompanied this curse designed to prevent a group of men from defending themselves in a lawsuit: "Just as the mother of this puppy is unable to defend it, so too may the legal advocates of these men be unable to defend them . . . Just as this puppy is unable to get up, so too may they be unable (to get up). May they be transfixed, just as this one is."[114] Here

110. *PGM* XII.376–379. Another incantation inscribed on a seashell uses a similar kind of persuasive analogy: "Let her, Ms. So-and-so, daughter of Ms. So-and-so, lie awake because of me" (*PGM* VII.374–375); the shell, taken from the always restless sea, is presumably thought to induce a similar state of disquiet in the victim (cf. *PGM* IV.3274, where the restlessness of the sea is connected with insomnia).

111. *PGM* IV.2943–66.

112. Chameleon: Libanius *Oration* 1.245–249, with Bonner (1932b) 34–44 and Graf (1997) 137. "Crazy-fish": Ovid *Fasti* 2.577–578 and 581, with Bömer (1958) 572–573 and LoMonaco (1989) 259–260. The fish presumably gets its name from some peculiarly frenzied or erratic behavior (in Greek, the same fish is called a *mainē* or *mainomenē*; see LSJ s.v.). Thus, probably like Pindar's use of a "mad" (*mainas) iunx* bird to drive Medea insane, Ovid's spell may have been designed to project both the natural inclinations of the "crazy-fish" and the state that results from the ritual manipulation, in this case the sewing of the mouth.

113. *PGM* LXI.39–44. Ruggiero (1993) 120 describes a similar sixteenth-century Venetian ritual used in love magic and curses: stick live eels in the head and heart with needles and then pour hot coals on top of them.

114. *DT* 111–112, two nearly identical second-century C.E. Latin texts from Aquitania.

the effect of the curse is doubled, since the ritual aims first at making the victims like a defenseless puppy that has been removed from its mother, and then at transfixing them so they cannot get up, just as (we assume) the puppy was brutally transfixed at the scene of the ritual. Closest to Pindar's *iunx* ritual, however, are two first-century C.E. binding spells from Carthage, in which the torture of a bird is the focus of a curse. The first reads (in Latin): "[Just] as I have ripped out the tongue from this rooster while it was still alive and pierced it, so too may they (i.e., the ghosts of the dead) silence the tongues of my enemies."[115] The second is in Greek "Just as this rooster has been bound feet and hands and head, so too you (i.e., the demons addressed earlier in the text) bind the legs, hands, head, and heart of Victoricus."[116] In all these texts the emphatic use of the deictic pronoun "this" must refer to the animal that had been used in the ritual and then (presumably) buried with the tablet.[117] In light of such practices, we should probably consider seriously the remarks of an ancient commentator who, in a discussion of Jason's *iunx,* remarks that some people claim that during the performance of an erotic spell sorceresses would bind a *iunx* bird to a wheel and then drag out its guts and attach them to the wheel as well.[118]

Foregrounded against this apparently widespread Mediterranean practice of manipulating and mutilating small animals in curses and erotic-magic rituals, Pindar's *iunx* spell begins to make more sense. As in the case of the bats, the *iunx* is an effigy in two ways. First the spell is to transfer the "natural" qualities of a mad and salacious bird[119] to Medea, just as, for example, the spells discussed above aim to project onto the victim

115. *DT* 222.A13–B5.

116. *DT* 241.16–17.

117. The word "deictic" refers to Greek pronouns like *hode, hēde,* and *tode,* which usually indicate something close at hand that can be pointed to, i.e., "this thing here."

118. Scholiast on *Pythian* 4.381a (Drachmann). The verb used by the scholiast, "to drag out" *(exhelkein),* may perhaps be connected to the demand found on *agōgē* charms that a demon draw or drag *(helkein)* the female victim "by her guts and by her hair" (e.g., *SM* 46.23, 47.23, and 50.64).

119. See note 107 above. For another possible example of this kind of transfer, see Freudenburg (1995) 212–214, discussion of Nasidienus' perplexing feast at the end of *Satire* 2.8. Ruggiero (1993) notes two sixteenth-century Venetian love spells involving the mutilation of small birds, which apparently stand as effigies for the victim: a bird is skinned and then stuck with four needles (pp. 92 and 124–125); and the heart of a bird is scorched to heat up the heart of the victim (pp. 121–122).

the natural wakefulness of a bat or the defenselessness of a puppy. But these spells also manipulate animal effigies in ways that will augment or intensify their natural attributes. Thus the normal insomnia of the bat is increased by piercing its eyes, and the helplessness of the puppy is augmented by transfixing and killing it. The symbolic impact of a bird bound to the wheel and tortured would, moreover, be quite dramatic, for such ignominious treatment was generally reserved for slaves and disreputable noncitizens, while the whip and goad were primarily tools used to drive recalcitrant animals to and from their pens.[120] In the semiotics of erotic magic, more-over, such abuses, usually reserved for the subjected and helpless, are—like the nudity that accompanied whippings[121]—obvious markers that distinguish the social categories of free and subjugated. This is perhaps more obvious in the use of paired images (discussed above), especially in the love spell described by Horace, in which the female practitioner sets up two effigies—a larger one of wool and a smaller of wax—and then places them in a tableau in which the larger image "restrained the smaller with punishments, while it (i.e., the smaller, wax figure) lay there groveling, like a slave about to die."[122] Thus when Jason binds an effigy to a wheel and then tortures it, he clearly delivers a double blow: he hurts Medea's body, of course, but he also hurts her prestige and standing by marking her symbolically as a member of a servile and unprotected class.[123] This element of subjugating a person of lower social class is, perhaps, to be expected in a patriarchal culture like the ancient Greek, in which women were often treated, legally and otherwise, as chattels owned by and transferred from one man to another, and it is most clearly illustrated by the same ritual shower of nuts that greeted both the new bride and the newly bought slave at their new home.[124] In fact, as I shall argue in section 2.4, Greek wedding

120. On legal torture, see Hunter (1994) 91–94 and Borgeaud (1988) 125–126, who adds the point about herd animals. Borgeaud must be right that shame and loss of freedom are the focus here, not any broader concern with criminality or moral wrong, as Johnston (1995) 179–180 suggests.

121. Saller (1994) 136 notes the shame of being exposed naked and then beaten. In the spells that use paired images of Ares and Aphrodite, the submissive partner is usually naked and bound while the dominant is clothed. See section 2.1 above.

122. *Satire* 1.8.30–33. See above, note 53. For similar reference to slavery, see *DT* 271: "Grant that he, like a slave, be subordinated (*hupotetachthēnai*) to her."

123. Hunter (1994) 154–184; Saller (1994) 132–153.

124. Keuls (1985) 6–7.

ceremonies, especially the less reputable form known as "bridal theft," offer a provocative model for understanding the transitory violence of these *agōgē* spells, which are—at least at the symbolic level—likewise designed to move a woman from the home of one man to that of another.[125]

2.3 Apples for Atalanta and Pomegranates for Persephone

A second type of erotic magic, though neither as popular nor as violent as Jason's *iunx* and the other *agōgē* spells discussed above, appears often in the context of traditional courtship and marriage: the throwing or presentation of enchanted "apples" (*mēla*) or other kinds of similarly seeded fruit.[126] The earliest testimony to such a ritual is a papyrus scrap of Hesiod's lost epic poem the *Catalogue of Women,* which preserves part of the story of Atalanta, a young woman who vowed that she would marry only the man who could defeat her in a footrace. In Hesiod's version of the tale, Hippomenes—acting, like Jason, on the advice of Aphrodite—carried three apples onto the racetrack, and threw them at various intervals during the contest. Only one small papyrus fragment actually mentions the apples: "And she, quick as a harpy [. . .] snatched it. And he threw the second one to the ground with his hand [. . .] swift-footed Atalanta held two apples (*mēla*), and she was near the end of the race. But he threw the third to the ground, and with it he fled death and dark destruction."[127] In their interpretation of this strange scene, scholars have in the past rightly pointed out the frequent appearance of apples as love tokens in elegy, amatory epi-

125. This is not to say that all Greek women were treated in this manner. Foxhall (1989) and Hunter (1989) have, for instance, questioned the idea that Athenian women were unable to control their own dowries, and they have shown that some wealthier women (esp. *epikleroi* and widows, like Demosthenes' mother) could and did exercise power in their household.

126. I use "apple" throughout to translate the Greek word *mēlon* when it appears without qualification. *Mēlon* actually designates the entire class of fruit that grows on trees; thus the word frequently refers to apples and quinces but can also designate tree-fruit with stones, such as peaches and apricots. When a writer wishes to be more specific the word is modified by an ethnic; thus, e.g., a *mēlon persikon* ("Persian apple") = a peach, and a *mēlon kudonian* ("Cydonian apple") = a quince. The specific type of fruit is rarely indicated. A parallel in painting and sculpture seems to be the generic round fruits, said to be pomegranates or apples, held in the hands of archaic statues of Hera and Persephone, the two best-known Greek patronesses of marriage.

127. Hesiod frag. 76.18–23 M-W.

grams, and romances, and they have repeatedly suggested that fruits designated by the term *mēla* originally played a role as engagement or wedding gifts.[128] This practice is, in turn, usually compared with ancient Greek fertility rites such as the throwing of nuts or the dedication of seeds at agrarian festivals, since, it is argued, apples, quinces, pomegranates, and other fruits designated by the term *mēlon* contain many small pips, and thus are suitably many-seeded symbols for fecundity.[129] In fact a closer look at the use of apples in marriage rites and seduction scenes reveals that they were designed to produce sexual desire in the female, not fertility, and as such merit a close discussion as a form of erotic magic.[130]

In an etiological myth preserved by Pherecydes, the goddess Earth originally caused apple trees to spring up at the wedding of Zeus and Hera as her gift to the new couple, and later versions report that the trees were in fact a gift from one of the pair to the other.[131] In either case, from their very first appearance this class of fruit was connected with weddings. Stesichorus describes how presumably friendly onlookers pelted the wedding chariot of Menelaus and Helen with "Cydonian apples" (quinces) and flowers.[132] None of these early fragments, however, provides any obvious explanation for the custom, and vase paintings that depict mythical brides holding apples are similarly mute.[133] Later accounts of Greek wedding ceremonies suggest, however, that the appearance of such fruit in myth reflects its use in actual ritual. Strabo, a native of Pontus, tells us in

128. This is a much-discussed topic: Foster (1899), Trumpf (1960), Littlewood (1967), Lugauer (1967), and Brazda (1977). Trumpf gives a particularly good discussion of apples, pomegranates, and quinces in early Greek love poetry.

129. McCartney (1925); Brazda (1977) 42–45.

130. Detienne (1979) 41–44 anticipates some of my arguments here about the predominantly erotic nature of the apple in Atalanta's story and the pomegranate in Persephone's (see note 155 below). Obviously, in heterosexual relationships in a culture with primitive contraception, an aphrodisiac is inevitably a source of fertility.

131. Pherecydes, *FGrHist* 3 F17. The mythographer Apollodorus (2.5.11) is the first to mention the variant version, and he is followed by several Byzantine authors. Littlewood (1974) 40 argues somewhat unsuccessfully (see his concession in n. 40) that this later tradition arises from a corruption in the manuscript tradition of Apollodorus.

132. Stesichorus frag. 187.

133. Brazda (1977) mentions, e.g., a depiction of Theseus offering an apple to Ariadne (36 n. 1) and describes a vase painting of the wedding of Jason and Creusa, who holds an apple (43 n. 1).

passing that among the Persians a girl on her wedding day was allowed to eat only apples and camel marrow (15.3.17). We might hasten to dismiss this information, were it not for evidence of a similar custom among the Athenians. Indeed, Plutarch describes a special set of Athenian laws allegedly handed down by Solon,[134] which concerned the marriage of *epikleroi*, or heiresses:

> It is a good provision, too, that the heiress may not choose her consort at large, but only from the kinsmen of her husband, that the children may be of his family and lineage. Conformable to this, also, is the requirement that as a bride she eat a quince (*kudonian mēlon*) and then be shut up in the bridal chamber with the bridegroom; and that the husband of an heiress shall approach her thrice a month without fail. For even if no children are born, still, this is a mark of esteem and affection which a man should pay to a chaste wife; it removes many of the annoyances that develop in all such cases, and prevents their being altogether estranged by their differences.[135]

Although this law is ultimately concerned with the production of legitimate heirs, Plutarch clearly saw another benefit; along with the thrice-monthly conjugal visit, the eating of the apple was somehow supposed to encourage sexual intimacy between the couple.[136]

I suggest that this custom was perhaps borrowed from folk tradition to deal with the special awkwardness of this forced type of marriage, in which the *epikleros* bride could in theory be forced against her will to

134. Most scholars have accepted Plutarch's repeated assertion that this law was attributed to Solon, e.g., Lacey (1968) 29–30.

135. *Solon* 20.3; cf. *Moralia* 138d and 279f, where Plutarch cites the law (in both texts saying simply "bride" and not restricting the provision—as he does here—to the marriage of *epikleroi*) in two completely different contexts. For the *epikleros*, see Katz (1992b).

136. Some may question the use of this testimony as support for the erotic intent of the law, as Plutarch is generally thought to reflect a new epoch of Greek sexuality, in which heterosexual love within matrimony is given precedence over the traditionally privileged male homosexual relationship. See most recently, e.g., Foucault (1986) 176–192 or Veyne (1987) 33–49. Although sex in marriage is clearly more emphasized in Plutarch and other writers of his time, it is an exaggeration to suggest that it was unimportant in the earlier periods; it simply was not expressed publicly in the texts that have survived. For a more

marry a close and considerably older male relative, in some cases even an uncle.[137] It may also have been useful in allaying the perception—undoubtedly threatening in a patriarchal culture—that such a marriage gave the wife an "unnatural" superiority in the relationship, because she was for a time thought to be the heiress of the fortune and thereby to have greater financial power than the husband. This view is clearly expressed in a fragment of Menander's lost play *Plokion*, in which the wife Creoboule, who was married as an *epikleros* to an older, poorer relation, is criticized for acting like the head of the household *(kurios)*.[138] Thus, at the heart of the Solonian custom in Athens probably lies the belief or the hope that a quince offered by the groom in a ritual context would cause the bride to be less hostile to the sexual advances of her new husband, and would lessen the possibility that she might misuse her special position to gain dominance over him.

In certain parts of Greece, then, the presentation and consumption of *mēla* seem to have been customary prerequisites for the wedding night. There is, moreover, further evidence that the fruit was often "delivered" by throwing it at or near the bride, as we find both in the myth of Atalanta and in Stesichorus' description of the wedding procession of Helen, mentioned above. Noteworthy in this regard is the Athenian custom of throwing *mēla* for explicitly erotic purposes, which is widely attested by the peculiar expression "to be hit with an apple." In his speech in Aristophanes' *Clouds*, for example, "Right Argument"—the upholder of traditional Athenian values—gives Pheidippides a series of banal moral maxims, which include the following (996–997): "And don't run after dancing girls, so that as a conse-

---

balanced view, see Redfield (1995) 153–183, who reminds us (p. 159) of Achilles' plaintive question at *Iliad* 9.340–341 ("Are the sons of Atreus the only ones who love their wives?") and points to the great number of early Greek myths that focus on elopement and marriage with a strong emphasis on the erotic elements. This sea change in Greek society is also exaggerated on the other side; Patterson (1991b) 1415–16 and Cohen and Saller (1994) 45–49 rightly criticize both Veyne and Foucault for their unbalanced use of Plutarch and other later sources, which are marked by equally strong patriarchal assumptions and asymmetrical relations within marriage.

137. Gould (1980) 43–44; Katz (1992b).

138. Menander frag. 334.2–4, with Fantham (1975) 74. Hunter (1989) 45–47 shows that in the case of *epikleroi*, widows, or wealthy metic women there seems to have been a popular (albeit nonlegal) sense in which a woman could be a "*kurios* of herself"; i.e., she could be the head of a household and make decisions concerning her property and her estate.

quence you don't, while foolishly gaping, get hit by an apple thrown by a prostitute and wreck your good name completely." The scholiast on the passage and all the later lexicographers mention that the expression "get hit by an apple" means "to become enamored or sexually excited,"[139] from which it is usually inferred that "Right Argument" is using the expression metaphorically to mean: "don't be a fool and fall in love with hooker!" This is a convenient argument for modern scholars, and indeed a similar one has been used traditionally to assert that the *iunx* spell in Pindar is merely a poetic device for describeing Medea's sudden infatuation with Jason. In fact, Aristophanes is most likely referring to a popular fear that Athenian prostitutes actually used such rituals to attract customers,[140] and that the popular saying "so-and-so got hit by an apple" originally voiced suspicions of an attack of erotic magic. Indeed, I hope to show that this ballistic use of apples as aphrodisiacs lies as well behind the scene from the Atalanta myth, in which apples are apparently thrown in the hope of filling the girl with sexual desire for Hippomenes. The tattered papyrus fragments of the Hesiodic poem quoted above do not, unfortunately, describe the effect of the apples on the maiden, and although later Roman versions of the story suggest that the apples were made of gold and thus distracted her by their beauty or monetary worth,[141] Hellenistic writers (the earliest testimony after Hesiod) leave no doubt that the apples, recommended by Aphrodite, stimulated Atalanta's erotic desire for Hippomenes:[142] Theocritus, for instance, says that the girl "went mad and plunged deep into desire"; and Philetas, his slightly older contemporary, apparently maintained in a lost poem that "the apples moved Atalanta to erotic desire."[143]

A large fragment of a Greek magical handbook dating to the time of Augustus provides us with our best evidence for the use of apples in actual erotic spells:

139. Aristophanes *Clouds* 997 with scholia. For the various lexicographers, see Littlewood (1967) 154–155.

140. See section 4.2 for evidence that prostitutes and courtesans regularly employed erotic magic.

141. E.g., Ovid *Met.* 10.666.

142. Lugauer (1967) 93–96.

143. Theocritus *Idyll* 3.40–43 and Philetas frag. 18 (Powell) *apud* scholion to Theocritus *Idyll* 2.120. Byzantine writers describe Atalanta's apple as an *aphrodision* and a *pharmakon*; see Littlewood (1974) 48.

Incantation over an apple (*mēlon*). (Say it) three times: I shall strike
with apples ... I shall give this *pharmakon*—always timely <and?>
edible—to mortal men and immortal gods. To whichever woman I
give or at whichever woman I throw the apple or hit with it, setting
everything aside, may she be mad for my love—whether she takes it
in her hand and eats it ... or sets it in her bosom—and may she not
stop loving me. O Lady Cyprogeneia, bring to perfection this perfect
incantation.[144]

This spell, ending as it does with the traditional coda asking Aphrodite to
bring the spell to fulfillment, is another important witness to the same
tradition of hexametrical erotic charms that is attested by Pindar and
Aristophanes.[145] It also describes a ritual that seems to include both of the
traditional variations discussed above for the use of apples in Greek wedding ceremonies and in myths concerned with courtship, in which the fruit
may be either presented to the woman or thrown at her. A similar variation
is permitted in the girl's reaction; she can either take and eat the fruit or
merely hold it in her bosom. And as in the case of the *agōgē* spells discussed
in the previous section, the "apple spell" survives well into the Christian
period. In a ninth-century Coptic papyrus, the male practitioner asks that
some fruit be charmed, so that when a woman eats them, she may "desire
him with endless desire" and come to him to "satisfy all his desires."[146] An
even later Byzantine handbook describes how an apple inscribed with
magical signs will force a woman to submit sexually to a man if she eats
it,[147] and in a contemporary chronicle we hear how an astrologer named
Seth Skleros, when his sexual advances were scorned by a young woman,
sent her a peach (a "Persian apple," *mēlon persikon*), which she placed in
her bosom; as a result she was struck with "insane lust" and allowed Seth to
deflower her.[148]

There is, moreover, good evidence that this type of magic spell existed
at a much earlier period as well—albeit just beyond the borders of the

144. *SM* 72 col. i.5–14.

145. Faraone (1992a and 1995) discusses this venerable tradition of hexametrical charms.
See Section 2.2 for the Pindaric and Aristophanic allusions.

146. *ACM* 76. The word for "pieces of fruit" is the partially restored word *op[ōr]ai*.

147. Greenfield (1995) 139–140.

148. The girl's parents complained to the emperor, and Seth was blinded as a punishment;
Littlewood (1974) 48; Kazhdam (1995) 81.

Greek world. A cuneiform collection of Neo-Assyrian ritual texts dating to the ninth century B.C.E. provides a startling parallel: "Its ritual: either <to> an apple or to a pomegranate you recite the incantation three times. You give (the fruit) to the woman (and) have her suck the juices. That woman will come to you; you can make love to her."[149] This recipe is part of a short collection of magical rituals all used by men to attract and seduce women.[150] The parallels with the Greek rituals under discussion are obvious: an incantation is spoken thrice over the fruit, which is then given to the victim to eat. In the incantation that precedes this apple spell, moreover, Inanna (Sumerian for Ishtar, often equated with Aphrodite) is invoked as the goddess "who loves apples and pomegranates." As we have seen, in Greek myth it is Aphrodite who suggests that Hippomenes and others use apples to obtain their brides-to-be, and the Berlin papyrus likewise ends with an appeal to Cyprogeneia. Given the general agreement among scholars that important aspects of Aphrodite—especially those concerned with sexual love and her worship on Cyprus—were borrowed or otherwise adapted from the complex of beliefs surrounding the Near Eastern goddesses Inanna and Ishtar,[151] it is not difficult to suppose that this ritual use of "apples" also made its way into the Greek world connected in some way with the worship of Ishtar.

The mention of pomegranates as an alternate fruit in the Assyrian spell also elucidates an obscure detail of the Greek myth of Persephone: in our oldest extant version, the Homeric *Hymn to Demeter,* Hades gives the kidnapped girl a pomegranate seed to eat, and thereafter she must remain with him as his wife. The event is described twice in the hymn. In the omniscient narrative of the action, the poet reports the following after Hades agrees to let Persephone return to her mother: "Thus he (sc. Hades) spoke, and wise Persephone rejoiced and quickly leaped up in happiness.

149. *KAR* 61.8–10; for this translation and commentary, see Biggs (1967) 70–74, who also reports the existence of another fragmentary spell, *KAR* 69.4–5: "Its ritual: over either a pomegranate or an apple you recite the incantation seven times, then give it to the woman." For the most recent discussion, see Leick (1994) 202–203. Ebeling (1925) 9 n. 3 long ago pointed to the parallels between this incantation and the Greek tradition of tossed apples.

150. The other spells in this series involve making effigies inscribed with the name of the desired women (*KAR* 61.11–21, 69.6–19, and 20 rev. 1) or burning incense and libating beer, while reciting an incantation (*KAR* 69 rev. 2–9 and rev. 10–12)

151. Burkert (1985) 152–153 and (1992) 97–99; Mondi (1990).

But he on his part gave her a honey-sweet pomegranate seed to eat, having secretly consecrated it in order that she might not remain continually at the side of grave Demeter of the dark *peplos*."[152] Later in the same poem, when Persephone is closely interrogated by her mother, she gives a somewhat different version of the incident (411–413): "Immediately I leaped up with joy, but he secretly threw me a pomegranate seed, sweet food, and forced me to taste it against my will."[153] This incident has traditionally been interpreted as an example of a widespread folk belief that if one eats the food of the dead, one must remain with them; Demeter herself is thought to express this very concern a few lines earlier in the poem (393–400), but this is far from certain, as the unique manuscript of the poem is torn away at precisely this point.[154] The relationship between Hades and Persephone is, moreover, much closer than simply that of a host and his guest, and most commentators agree that there is some special erotic character of the pomegranate which leads to its appearance here.[155]

152. *Hymn to Demeter* 371–374. My translation follows Myres (1938) 51–52 and Bonner (1939) 3–4, both of whom argue that Hades performs some kind of circular motion or similar consecration ritual connected with "binding magic" that binds Persephone to Hades. Although I see no specific reference in the Greek to "binding magic" per se, this approach makes much better sense of the placement of the purpose clause, i.e. (paraphrase): "having secretly consecrated (the seed) in order that she not remain continually at the side of grave Demeter of the dark *peplos*."

153. *Hymn to Demeter* 411–413. The Greek expression *embale moi* is extremely odd. Richardson (1974) ad loc. translates "put in my mouth" with obvious discomfort, admitting that "the use of *embale moi* without further specification (e.g., *stomati*) is unusual for early epic." Eitrem (1940) 146 calls the action "le jet ritual" without further argument. The meaning of the phrase remains a mystery, but since it is a compound of the Greek verb *ballein* ("to throw") used repeatedly to describe throwing of the erotic *mēla* discussed above, it seems likely that the reference is to throwing the pomegranate seed at or to Persephone.

154. Only the beginnings of the lines remain. The standard interpretation depends tenuously on the word *bromēs* in line 394, which could easily refer (as does *edodē* in 412) specifically to the pomegranate and not to food in general. Allen's supplements in his very influential Oxford text were apparently the work of Goodwin and "were proposed by him *cum magna diffidentia*"; see Richardson (1974) 282, who wisely ventures no restorations to the section.

155. Richardson (1974) ad loc. Allen, Halliday, and Sikes (1936) ad loc. suggest that the pomegranate served either as a fertility charm or as an aphrodisiac. Detienne (1979) 42 discusses the evidence for pomegranates used as gifts for newlyweds, and rightly suggests that they and other kinds of *mēla* "act directly, like a drug or an incantation," although he is evidently unaware of the evidence compiled above for their actual use in magical rituals.

It is interesting, moreover, how easily the setting of this scene—bride and groom at a wedding banquet of sorts—recalls the wedding ceremony of Athenian *epikleros* at which the quince was publicly presented and accepted. A plaintive speech addressed by one of Lucian's courtesans to her faithless boyfriend provides another nice parallel, and gives us some further insight into the symbolic nature of such aphrodisiacs when they are presented and accepted in a public setting: "And finally . . . you took a bite from the apple (*mēlon*) and, leaning forward, you somehow shot it into her lap—without even trying to hide it from me! And she, for her part, kissed it and stuffed it between her breasts under her girdle."[156] As in the story of Persephone or in the magical spell preserved in the Berlin papyrus, the etiquette of the activity described here is indeed bizarre: an amorous young man takes a bite from an apple and then pitches it into the lap of a woman he wishes to seduce. But in fact Lucian's version of this rite reveals precisely how the presentation of a traditional aphrodisiac might indeed evolve into a symbolic act, for by hitting the girl with a piece of fruit, a man indicates his intent to seduce her, and by willingly putting the apple to her lips or hiding it away in her bosom—the same two possibilities anticipated in the Berlin apple spell—the woman knowingly subjects herself to the power of the charm, and by doing so returns a message of her willingness to be seduced. A similar set of messages is clearly understood in a Hellenistic epigram addressed to a young girl: "I hit you with an apple. And you yourself, if you willingly love me, receive it and give me a share of your virginity." [157] Here, as in many of the other examples of *mēla* presented in an erotic context, the female victim seems to be aware that the apple is indeed an aphrodisiac, for her active role in taking it apparently will signal her consent ("if you willingly love me"). This expectation is, of course, in marked contrast to the more popular *agōgē* spells, in which the victim is assumed to be hostile to the practitioner.

This two-step process—presentation and acceptance—is in fact a shared characteristic of several of the texts under discussion, and can be conveniently summarized as shown in Table 2. The second step, the willing acceptance of the aphrodisiac by the female, could help explain the use of

156. Lucian, *Dialogues of the Courtesans* 12.1.

157. *AP* 5.79.1–2, where it is attributed to Plato. Page (1981) 163 describes it as "unmistakably Hellenistic in style and spirit."

Table 2. Gendered actions and reactions in apple spells

Text	Male action	Female reaction
KAR 61 (10th cent. B.C.E.)	recite charm give apple	suck its juices
Hom. *Hym. Dem.* (6th cent. B.C.E.)	give seed	eat it willingly or unwillingly taste it
AP 5.79 (Hellenistic)	throw apple	accept it willingly
Berlin papyrus (1st cent. B.C.E.)	recite charm throw apple	take it in hand and eat it or place it in bosom
Lucian, *Dial. Court.* 12.1 (2d cent. C.E.)	throw apple	kiss it and place in bosom

the *mēlon* aphrodisiac in wedding ceremonies, where it may have functioned as a sign of the bride's consent.[158] The quince legislated for the Athenian *epikleros* certainly provided the bride with a public forum in which to accept the fruit willingly and thus, like the courtesan described by Lucian, display her consent to the seduction that is always implicit in marriage. Atalanta, too, publicly accepts the apples, and in so doing signals her consent to seduction and marriage; in this way the plot of her story is wonderfully streamlined, for by the very same act she loses the race and publicly agrees to become the wife of Hippomenes.

2.4 The Transitory Violence of Greek Weddings and Erotic Magic

The connections and parallels between Greek erotic magic and Greek marriage are pervasive, and we can make much more sense of the spells discussed in this chapter if we recognize that the two principal forms of *erōs* magic—apple spells and *agōgē* spells—correspond somewhat generally to the two types of Greek marriage:[159] the better-known betrothal marriage,

158. Compare, e.g., Patterson (1991) 55, who suggests that the gesture of *anakalupsis* (the uncovering of the bride for the first time) symbolized the bride's consent to the marriage. For female consent in Greek marriage generally, see Redfield (1995) 181.

159. By using the social dynamics of Greek marriage to shed light on these more obscure erotic spells discussed in this passage, I am not asserting that erotic magic was a form of

which is the result of a formal contract between the two families; and a second, less popular form, commonly known in the ethnologies of modern Balkan and Mediterranean societies as "bridal theft" or "abduction marriage," an apparently legitimate form of marriage that was employed by the Greeks for most periods of their history, ancient and modern.[160] The differences between these two forms of Greek marriage can be summed up as follows: a prearranged betrothal marriage generally reinforces familial and community structures, while bridal theft can be more socially divisive in that it subverts the authority of those men who in a patriarchial society are responsible for marriage. Indeed, at its worst bridal theft can be quite violent, as the young girl is forcibly seized and occasionally brutalized; if her family stoutly resists her abduction, members of both families may be injured or killed. More often than not, however, abduction marriage is socially acceptable and provides a face-saving fiction to hide an elopement necessitated most typically by pregnancy or the inability of one side or the other to pay the requisite bride-price or dowry. In this situation, the bride-to-be, sometimes with her family's blessing, conspires with the man, and the successful abduction leads to a stable and enduring marriage.

The crucial difference between these two forms of marriage is the *public* consent or willingness of the bride, which is important in a betrothal

---

marriage or that it was used to facilitate marriages. Although erotic spells do appear rather frequently in Greek myths about marriage, these are usually cases (as I shall discuss below) in which the women or their families "unnaturally" resist sexuality and marriage. Solon's quince (see note 135 above) is the only explicit case I know of in which a device of erotic magic is used in an actual marriage ceremony.

160. Sourvinou-Inwood (1973) and (1987) 136–141, Jenkins (1983), and esp. Evans Grubbs (1989), who marshals evidence from early Greek art and mythology (e.g., Theseus, Hades), historical anecdotes (e.g., the Spartan Demaratus stole a bride betrothed to another; Hdt. 6.65.2), detailed descriptions by the second-century C.E. physiognomist Polemo of bridal thefts in Smyrna and Samos, Roman declamations (which frequently turned on points of Greek law or custom), Roman secular and early Christian ecclesiastical laws, and modern Balkan and Aegean ethnography. For abduction marriage in modern-day rural societies, see Lockwood (1974), Bates (1974), and Herzfeld (1985). In modern ethnographic accounts, the stolen bride is expected to preserve family honor by publicly asserting afterward that she was unwilling and forcibly abducted, although in many cases this is manifestly untrue. For what follows I am indebted to the discussion of Evans Grubbs, who summarizes several ethnographic discussions.

marriage[161] but not so in bridal theft, where the opposite is true: in fact, whether the kidnapped girl is willing or not, she usually pretends (like Persephone) to be unwilling and afterward maintains this story, for she must be careful to save face for herself (regarding her own chastity) and for her family. Apple spells differ from *agōgē* spells precisely on the question of implied consent, especially when they are presented in a public setting by the man, and when the efficacy of the charm depends on the woman's acceptance of the fruit, a gesture that usually indicates her consent. Thus the apples that Aphrodite gives to Hippomenes will work only if Atalanta stops of her own accord and picks them up. Likewise, in the presentation of the Solonian quince, in the hexametrical apple charm, and in Lucian's anecdote, the woman must take up the fruit and either eat it or carry it, if the spell is to take effect. This notion of consent is, however, quite slippery, for it is clear that some of these women—for example, Atalanta or the girl seduced by Seth Skleros—are not fully aware of the consequences of accepting or eating the apple. Nonetheless, the presentation of such fruit at the wedding feasts of Persephone or the Athenian *epikleros* suggests that such a device could function as an emblem for the bride's consent, and that such wedding rituals can in fact provide us with useful model for understanding these magic apples as part of a wider cultural phenomenon.

The social dynamics and symbolic repertoire of an abduction marriage provide an equally useful model for explaining the most problematic aspects of *agōgē* spells: the violent imagery, the assumed unwillingness of the victim, and the repeated focus on her forcible removal from her home. On a general taxonomic level, of course, the cruelty and violence of the *agōgē* spells make perfect sense, given the close formal affinities between these spells and other Greek cursing techniques. A common genealogy does not, however, explain the millennium-long popularity of such images and suggests that we should probe the question more deeply. In the past, scholars have attempted to soften the sadistic tone and images in the *agōgē* spells by appealing to psychological or functional explanations of cursing generally as a cathartic outpouring of venom and frustration that has a primarily therapeutic effect on the agent and perhaps might even operate as a safety valve of sorts which deflects real violence from the proposed human target.[162] In this scenario, the practitioner, by venting his or her

161. Patterson (1991a).
162. See Graf (1997) 146–147 for a summary.

frustration or hatred on an effigy of an enemy, is "cured" of it, and the potential threat of real violence is avoided. This cure, moreover, was thought to lie in the passionate performance of the rite. Malinowski, for instance, reported that the Melanesian sorcerer filled himself with anger and hatred when he enacted a curse, and that even when performing love magic, he "reproduced the behavior of a heartsick lover who has lost his common sense and is overwhelmed by passion."[163] He was, of course, talking about a professional imitating the emotional state of his client, but one could very well imagine a cathartic effect on the client as he watched.[164] Wittgenstein used similar insights to argue against Frazer's influential theory that the popularity of curses, such as the burning of an effigy, was based on a belief that such acts actually harmed the victim; he suggested instead that the real goal is a change in the inner psychic world of the performer, who experiences some kind of emotional satisfaction.[165]

To my mind such an approach is applicable to only one type of ancient Greek curse, the "revenge curse" or "judicial prayer," in which an angry and aggrieved person, acting much like a plaintiff in a divine court, claims that he or she has suffered an injustice and demands the punishment of the victim. Such curses employ highly emotive language, often malign or accuse the victim, and beg the god to help the practitioner, who is allegedly a victim of injustice. All in all, such curses have a fierce emotional edge and tend to be the most idiosyncratic, suggesting a higher level of on-the-spot improvisation.[166] In contrast, such emotional engagement and improvisation are extremely rare in the two other important types of Greek curse, conditional curses and binding curses. This is understandable, perhaps, since neither of these rituals focuses on avenging a past humiliation: to the contrary the conditional curses used in oaths, tombstones, and other proprietary inscriptions aim at preventing future misconduct, while the binding curses aim at inhibiting a rival in some future

163. Malinowski (1948) 71–72.

164. For simplicity's sake here, as elsewhere, I consider the professional magician to be an extension or tool of the client and therefore indistinguishable from him.

165. Wittgenstein (1965), cited with approval by Gager *CTBS* p. 82, and with disapproval by Graf (1997) 146–147, both in discussions of erotic magic. Brooten (1996) 97–101 gives a good critique of Gager's arguments.

166. For general discussion, see Versnel (1991a) and (1994). For improvisation, see Versnel (1996) for Roman-era curses and Ortega (1991) 79 for those used by women accused during the Spanish Inquisition.

competition.[167] Neither betrays any personal animosity or anger, but their very existence does imply a certain level of nervousness that without the aid of the curse some future disaster may in fact come to pass. Thus in the case of the binding spell, the psychological benefit is in all likelihood not the catharsis of anger or hatred, but rather enhanced self-confidence: for if a competitor knows his rival has been attacked by a secret binding curse, he will understandably perform more confidently in the next round of competition.[168] Likewise, the owner of a tomb inscribed with a curse "may he be destroyed, whosoever removes this body" will presumably rest easier.

Given the wide similarities between *agōgē* spells and curses, it is understandable that scholars have taken up psychological explanations of cursing rituals and applied them to erotic spells. Indeed, Winkler seems to have something like Wittgenstein's cathartic or therapeutic model in mind when he argues that *agōgē* spells represent a form of double psychological projection, whereby lovesick persons try to project their own terrible symptoms of pain, madness, and irresistible yearning onto the object of their own helpless desire, and at the same time take on the beloved victim's previous aloofness and imperviousness to such pains.[169] This formulation is certainly helpful in some of its individual parts. The theme of "table-turning," for instance, certainly plays an important role in the two most famous literary enactments of love magic, Sappho's *Hymn to Aphrodite* (frag. 1) and Theocritus' *Idyll* 2; and the idea that erotic magic can affect both practitioner and victim is vital to our understanding of the popular type of erotic spell, which employs a *pair* of effigies, a stronger image that dominates and threatens a servile, bound image. Here, of course, we must

---

167. Oaths: Faraone (1993b); tombstone curses: Strubbe (1991) and Faraone (1996b) 80–82.

168. Faraone (1989a) and (1991a).

169. Winkler (1991) 225–226, speaking of the "curious transference" between the agent and the victim, the former of which "is suffering in that unfortunate and desperate state known as *erōs.*" This assumption is implicit in earlier studies as well, e.g., Dedo (1904) 2, who assumes generally that love charms were deployed by rejected lovers (*amantes repudiati*). Ortega (1991) 66–67 also pursues a "psychoanalysis of love magic" which assumes (wrongly, in my view) that in each case the female practitioner is "enamoured" of the victim and that the spells have therapeutic value for the user. She does, however, admit (pp. 84–87) that many of the spells reveal a commercial aspect to the relationship—they often end: "until he seeks me out, giving me all he has"—a fact suggesting that the woman may be a prostitute or a mistress who is financially rather than emotionally dependent on the victim. For very similar expressions in some *agōgē* spells, see page 85 below.

imagine an expectation that the spell will both weaken and hurt the victim and at the same time strengthen the practitioner. Winkler's arguments have been influential,[170] but they are erroneous to the degree that they imply a standardized lovesick performer or client. He suggests, for instance, that we should "imagine the typical client for such a rite was not a Don Juan who wanted to increase the sheer number of his conquests, but rather some young male who needed it rather desperately."[171] Although he demonstrates that this is probably true in a small number of literary texts, the vast majority of extant erotic spells give us no clue at all to the frame of mind or motives of the individual agent.

In fact I suggest that there were two different types of erotic spells, conforming to the differing styles of Greek curse discussed above. Winkler's literary examples, for example, since they focus on some past humiliation and demand reciprocal justice, clearly take the form of "revenge curses."[172] In her *Hymn,* for example, Sappho complains to Aphrodite that she has been wronged in love and argues that by a kind of erotic *lex talionis* the goddess should afflict the wrongdoer with the *erōs* that she now feels.[173] Likewise, Simaetha in Theocritus' second *Idyll* indicts the perfidious youth Delphis for bringing her grief (line 23), and by the end of the poem we see that the performance of the spell has indeed had some therapeutic effect on her: she seems to have rid herself of the crippling effects of *erōs* and regained her composure[174]—precisely the beneficial effects imagined by Wittgenstein and Winkler. However, only one of the roughly eighty extant erotic spells explicitly takes the stance of a lovesick person seeking redress: a fourth-century C.E. recipe book preserves the following iambic incantation addressed to ghosts: "Grant success to Mr.

170. See, e.g., Faraone (1989), Johnston (1995) 179 n. 3, and Martinez (1995) 354–355. Versnel (1998) 257–258 also assumes a generalized model of a lovesick or jealous practitioner and finds attractive Winkler's idea of transference.

171. Winkler (1991) 226.

172. For the best treatment, see Versnel (1998) 247–257.

173. Levi (1975) 215 n. 21 points out that Aphrodite's query in line 20 ("Who does you wrong?") implies that the poet's previous prayers contained an argument such as we find in the "judicial prayers", e.g., *DTA* 98 or a Cnidian curse that asks Demeter to punish a thief with fever and ends with the argument "for I have been wronged, Lady Demeter" (*DT* 2). See Faraone (1992b) 324 n. 20 and Versnel (1998), esp. 263.

174. Segal (1974) and esp. Griffiths (1979).

So-and-so, who suffers in his heart on account of Ms. So-and-so, the irreverent and the unholy. Therefore, lead her quickly as she is being tortured."[175] Here, like the "judicial prayers" discussed above, we find the combined emphasis on the past or current suffering of the petitioner and the injustice or irreverence perpetrated by the object of his affections.

The majority of extant *agōgē* spells, however, seem closely related in spirit to the Greek tradition of dispassionate cursing, in which we have seen few if any allusions to the agitated psychic state of the practitioner or to some past misdeed of the victim. Instead these spells are normally tightly focused on the future benefit: the prospect of the female victim eagerly making love to the man who performs or commissions the spell. Here, too, we need not imagine that the effect of the performance on the agent is one of healing or catharsis, but rather one of increased self-confidence, since knowledge of the spell will presumably make the suitor or seducer more confident as he competes for the favors of the victim. Indeed, understanding a broadly competitive context for these erotic spells removes one of the central impediments to Winkler's cathartic model: that the user must actually be lovesick. In what follows, I seek to explain the violence of *agōgē* magic not as some universally recognizable feature of a lovesick or jealous practitioner, but rather as a traditional and practical response to problems of access to woman of marriageable age—problems brought on not by the alleged physical seclusion of women,[176] but rather by parental interference or disapproval, by betrothal to another man, or by the unwillingness or haughtiness of the woman herself. In this reading, I take the social practice of bridal theft as a model for explaining the violence of *agōgē* spells as a necessary but transitory step—like the forcible abduction of a bride—in creating a new social alliance that is not altogether welcomed by the woman's family.[177]

---

175. *PGM* IV.1410–14. A third- or fourth-century c.e. *defixio* from Cumae (*DT* 198) invokes the gods of the underworld to subject Quadratilla to the "ultimate punishments, because she was the first to break her loyalty[?] to her husband Felix." Here, however, we have a judicial prayer of sorts—see Versnel (1998) 247—but this hardly qualifies as an erotic spell, since there is no request (as in, e.g., Simaetha's spell) to lead the woman back to Felix; the goal is simply to punish her.

176. Women and men in ancient Greece were separated from each other, but there is little evidence for the seclusion of women as in a harem. See section 4.3.

177. This peculiar notion of "stealing to make friends" is well documented in Mediterra-

I begin with the evidence for the dispassionate use of *agōgē* spells by men who hardly seem to be helpless victims of erotic infatuation. Most notably, the recent appearance of a spell written by one man with the goal of seducing four different women suggests that Winkler's hypothetical "Don Juan" could indeed avail himself of this technology for the purpose of multiple conquests.[178] More typically, however, we find hints that a man might use erotic magic to arrange a socially or financially beneficial match that might otherwise be beyond his reach,[179] a feature already implicit in the charter myth of the first *agōgē* spell: Jason, we should remember, elopes with Medea as part of his long-range plan to seize the Golden Fleece, win great renown, and thereby reclaim his father's kingdom. Given the importance of marriage to social advancement in the ancient world, one can easily imagine other scenarios in which a cool-headed social climber might use erotic magic to secure a profitable alliance. This is in fact precisely what his prosecutors suspect when they charge that the orator and writer Apuleius used erotic magic to seduce and marry an extremely wealthy widow.[180] Nor are such practical considerations absent from the surviving *agōgē* spells, where we sometimes see odd stipulations that the woman be forced to come to the practitioner "so she will give whatever I tell her to give" or so that she come "surrendered like a slave, giving herself and all her possessions," or "in order that she will give me what she has in her hands." Such wording seems to reflect an active interest in the dowry and property that such a woman might bring with her.[181] It would appear from the start, then, that although Winkler's "lovesick practitioner" may provide a useful model for a few erotic spells of the "judicial prayer" type, the great bulk of the

---

nean countries, where talented but socially disadvantaged young men abduct women or herd animals and consume them (sexually or gustatorily) as an initial step in forcing new relationships with powerful families. See the excellent discussion of the social meaning of sheep rustling in Herzfeld (1985) 163–205, who draws the obvious parallel to bridal theft (p. 180).

178. The tablet, described briefly by Robert (1981) 35 n. 1 and Jordan SGD pp. 186–187, is in the Getty Museum and will be published by Roy Kotansky. On the basis of its formulae Robert suggested that the tablet came from Carthage or Hadrumentum.

179. Graf (1997a) 104.

180. See Fantham (1995) on Pudentilla's wealth; Graf (1997) 65–88 gives a detailed discussion of the trial and the issues involved. Ortega (1991) 89–92 notes similar stipulations in Spanish love charms.

181. *SM* 39, *DT* 230, and *PGM* IV.1806. I owe this insight to an unpublished paper by David Jordan and am grateful to the author for the opportunity to read it.

extant erotic spells may have been much closer to dispassionate types of Greek curses and could be used by males either for sexual conquest or to advance their social position by arranging profitable marriages for themselves.

Another important similarity between *agōgē* spells and bridal theft is the short duration of the violent treatment of the women. In most *agōgē* spells, the various forms of torture and deprivation are applied for a limited time only to force the desired woman to shake off the many social constraints and obligations that anchor her to home and family. In the earliest Greek references to erotic spells, this aim is expressed simply as an attack on the victims' reverence for their parents (such as Medea in Pindar's poem) or their mindfulness of their families.[182] But in the late Hellenistic period we see signs of other targets: "abandoning her husband . . . to sleep very sweetly with me";[183] and again in a second-century C.E. ostrakon from Oxyrhynchus: "burn, ignite the *psuche* of Allous, her 'female body,' her limbs, until she comes away from the household of Apollonius."[184] Indeed, as we have seen, many later spells exhibit this same close relationship between torture and the woman's rejection of her family, for example in the *agōgē* spell that Apalos deploys against Karosa, in which he asks that the demon "not allow her . . . to think of her [own] husband, her child . . . but let her come melting with passion" for Apalos himself.[185] The peculiar insistence a few lines earlier in the same spell that the torture must continue until she "leaps forth and comes" to him (line 51) also seems to be traditional; a later recipe for an *agōgē* spell boasts the power to "make virgins leap forth from their homes."[186]

At first glance, such spells seem to focus rather exclusively on liberating the girl from the control of her male guardian. Seen in this light, *agōgē*

182. As is perhaps reflected in Homer's description of Calypso, who with "soft and wheedling words charmed *(thelgei)* Odysseus" in order that he might forget Ithaca (*Od.* 1.56–57), or as is clear in a late-classical Athenian spell that binds Charias so that he will be forgetful of the bed *(koitēs)* of Theodora, "the very woman whom he desires *(erāi)*" (*DT* 68). See Petropoulos (1988) 219–220 for discussion.

183. *SM* 71 frags. 2 and 21i (1st cent. B.C.E.).

184. *PGM* O[strakon] 2.25–34. Apollonius is identified as the victim's husband at the end of the spell (lines 40–41).

185. *PGM* XIXa.53–54, quoted extensively above in section 2.2.

186. *PGM* XXXVI.70–71, quoted in section 2.2 . For other examples of this vivid verb "to leap out," see *PGM* XXXVI.359; *SM* 40.18, 42.17, and 45.46.

spells appear quite similar to other magical techniques used surreptitiously to steal the property of others, be it crops from a neighbor's field or animals from his herd.[187] In fact Apuleius tells a hilarious story in which an incorrectly executed *agōgē* spell inadvertently results in a theft rather than a seduction,[188] and the overlap between the two is especially noticeable in a prayer for revenge from the island of Amorgos, in which a man complains how a fellow named Epaphroditos ("Mr. Charming") had talked his slaves into running away and had also "cast a spell *(sunepithelgesthai)* on my handmaid, even though I was unwilling, so that he could take her as his wife, and for this reason he had her flee together with the others."[189] Whether or not we take this charge of "spell-casting" seriously, we see here how these two different events—a minor slave rebellion and the elopement of a servant girl without the permission of the male head of the household—blend together easily into a general panic about the overthrow of patriarchal order.

But this general parallel to theft greatly oversimplifies the imagined effects of an *agōgē* spell, which often aims at much more than subverting another man's claim to ownership. Several spells indeed try to alienate the female victim from a much larger web of important relationships that emanate from the home. For example, in the spell that he casts against Euphemia, Theon commands the demons to "make her leap out . . . and leave behind her father, mother, brothers, sisters, until she comes to me";

187. The Twelve Tables at Rome prohibited people from "chanting away the crops *(fruges excantare)* of another"; see Graf (1997) 41–43 and 62–65. A similar belief may have existed concerning herds; in Longus' *Daphne and Chloe* 1.27.3, a handsome young singer lures livestock from the herd of his neighbor, a young girl: "he charmed *(thelksas)* her best eight cows, and rustled them off *(apoboukolēsen)* into his own herd."

188. In the *Metamorphoses*, Pamphile's servant girl is sent to fetch some hairs of a handsome Boeotian youth to be used in an *agōgē* spell, but the vigilance of his barber stymies her; rather than admit failure she plucks hairs from some inflated goatskins that had been hung up to dry in the neighborhood and gives them to her mistress (2.32). Later that night, when Pamphile knots and burns these hairs in her magic spell, these inflated skins are drawn magically by her spell and come rushing toward her house and pound on the door (3.15–18). This folktale persists in modern Algeria (Jansen [1987] 113) and Bolivia (Scobie [1983] 303–306).

189. SGD 60 = *CTBS* 75. The tablet has been dated as early as the second century B.C.E. and as late as the second century C.E.; see Pleket (1981) 189–192 and Versnel (1985) 252–254. The crucial verb here is *sunepithelgein*, a compound of *thelgein*, "to charm."

and elsewhere a male practitioner prays to Hecate that the desired woman "in a frenzy . . . come quickly to my doors, forgetting her daily life with her children and her parents."[190] Yet another *agōgē* spell from the second century C.E. reveals the wide range of important relationships that an erotic spell could undermine: ". . . in order that she may forget her mother, her father, her neighbors, and all her friends."[191] This wider pattern of effect with its attendant shift in loyalties is reflected even in an Athenian courtesan's humorous recollection of how a hired sorceress successfully used an erotic spell to lead her former boyfriend away from a tight-knit circle of drinking partners—a close "family" of sorts—centered at the house of a rival courtesan; we are told specifically that the young man returned to her, even though his male friends rebuked him and the rival courtesan begged him many times not to go.[192] Here, a successful attack of erotic magic is evidenced not only by the arrival of the victim at the practitioner's house, but also by the manner in which he ignores the repeated pleas of his peculiar demimondaine "wife" and "family."

And yet, despite the threatening images of a daughter unwillingly thrust from her home and alienated from her family and friends, we find in the Greek anecdotes and myths about erotic magic a peculiar ambivalence, one quite similar to that expressed about abduction marriage. This ambivalence is best illustrated by a contrast to later, Christian views on the subject. Jerome, for example, writing near or at the end of the fourth century C.E., records how a young man in Gaza is spurned by a young Christian woman, who chooses instead the life of a "virgin of God." The lovesick young man inscribes copper tablets with magic incantations and drawings and buries them under the threshold of the woman's house, with the result that the virgin instantly goes crazy, whirling her hair about, hissing through her teeth, and calling the youth's name. Her parents bring her to a saint, who sagely diagnoses the source of the attack and brings the

190. *SM* 45 and *PGM* IV.2756–64, for which see Cameron (1939) 9 n. 45 and Sutphen (1902) 317.

191. *DT* 266.15–16. For provisions with a similarly wide cast, see, e.g., *PGM* XV.4–5 ("let her forget parents, children, friends"); *PGM* LXI.29–30 ("let her forget father and mother, brothers, and her own husband"); *SM* 48.47–48 ("Abandon your father, mother, brothers, and sisters").

192. Lucian *Dialogues of the Courtesans* 4.1–4, discussed in detail in section 4.2.

girl back to sanity and chastity.[193] In a tenth-century hagiography, we hear of a Cappadocian novice whom a former suitor also attacks with an erotic spell:

> the girl was unexpectedly attacked by a seething passion which maddened her with a frantic lust for her former suitor and did not allow her to control herself. Violently leaping, screaming, moaning, crying and calling out his name in a loud voice, she assured with fearful oaths that unless someone let her see him with her eyes and enjoy in excess his sight and conversation, she would hang herself. Then one could see her continually running to the gateway, urging her escape and with inarticulate screams and shameless gestures ordering the gatekeeper to let her out.[194]

A little while later, the nuns miraculously uncover the magical device that is apparently causing the girl's insanity: two lead effigies in an erotic embrace (a *sumplegma*), presumably like the pair of wax images that accompanied the similar erotic spell cast against Euphemia. Such a detailed description of the effect of an erotic spell is quite rare, and allows us to see how closely the novice's violent symptoms—frantic lust, leaping, madness, and shamelessness—match up with the desired effects of the *agōgē* spells discussed above.

In contrast to these two later Christian accounts, pagan Greek myths

193. Jerome *Life of St. Hilarion the Hermit* 21 (= *PL* 23 cols. 39–40 = *CTBS* 163), with Graf (1997a) 93–96. For erotic spells buried at the victim's doorway, see the tenth-century B.C.E. Mesopotamian recipe that involves the burying of a woman's effigy at the city gate. If an incantation is recited thrice as she passes over the spot, "that woman will come to you (and) you can make love to her." See Biggs (1967) 70–72 and Leick (1994) 202–203. In the Middle Ages, a Carmelite friar allegedly seduced three women by burying pierced effigies under their doorways; see Kieckhefer (1991) 41.

194. For text and commentary, see Rosenqvist (1986) 52–65. For wider discussion, see Abrahamse (1982) 13–14 and Kazhdem (1995) 78–79. Flint (1991) 299 records an early modern instance of the reverse situation: a disappointed suitor accuses St. Lonoghyl of using magic to persuade his fiancée Agnofleda, to take up the religious life. Such social tension about devotion may have had earlier antecedents; Martinez (1995) 358 points out that Jesus' description of religious devotion as exclusively overriding traditional emotional attachments to family and friends (Luke 14:26: "If anyone comes to me and does not hate his father and mother and wife and children and brothers and sisters. . . he cannot be my disciple") seems to echo the language of contemporary love spells.

and anecdotes regularly seem to valorize the clever men who use erotic magic to seduce the daughters of other men—precisely the reverse of the Christian narratives, which demonize similarly resourceful and persistent suitors. Thus Hippomenes and Jason, instead of being vilified for using magical charms, appear instead as heroic men of an Odyssean stripe who follow the advice of Aphrodite and use the magical devices she provides to further their suit. In fact these approving narratives about the use of *erōs* magic fit rather well in a popular pattern of Greek myth in which the unmarried women who resist marriage are generally cast as impious villains, while gods or clever young men who overcome this resistance are cast as legitimate punishers or heroes. The daughters of Proetus are the paradigmatic example: they mock Hera, the patroness of marriage, or act haughtily to their suitors; in retaliation the goddess drives them from their father's house insane and forces them to run through the forest acting like wild cows. In some versions, moreover, their punishment is explicitly eroticized: they are struck with lewdness *(machlosune),* and they run through the woods in various stages of suggestive undress.[195] There are alternate versions of their rescue—the girls are cured either by the seer Melampus or by their father's dedication of an altar to Artemis[196]—but in each case the story ends with their marriage. The Greeks apparently told similar tales about the young maiden Io, who in one version is turned into a cow, goaded by a gadfly (*oistros,* a word with strong erotic connotations), and forced to flee her father's home;[197] and about the daughters of Pandareus, who are struck mad by Zeus and run from their house like wild bitches, animals that have strong associations in the Greek mind with shamelessness and lubricity.[198] Such stories seem to reflect a common discourse in

195. Burkert (1983a) 169 n. 4 and Seaford (1988).

196. Burkert (1983a) 168–173 and Gantz (1993) 312–313. There are some conflicting Dionysian versions of the myth, but the earliest ones (e.g., Hesiod) focus on marriage, not maenadism; see Seaford (1988) and Redfield (1995) 161–162.

197. Gantz (1993) 199–202 discusses various versions; the one in [Aesch.] *Prom. Bound* comes closest to the pattern discussed here.

198. In the extant sources the story is truncated and contaminated with another version in which they die; see Burkert (1983a) 169–170 and Johnston (1994). Roscher (1898) discusses their bitchlike behavior; for the connotations of shamelessness, see LSJ s.v.; of lubricity, Loraux (1995) 199–200 and 342.

the archaic and classical periods regarding the divine etiology of mental disturbance in adolescent females. The Hippocratic tradition, which elsewhere vigorously denounces the divine causation of epilepsy, provides a similarly mechanistic explanation for adolescent hysteria in a late-fifth-century B.C.E. treatise known as *On the Maladies of Unmarried Women*, which briefly describes bizarre fits of madness during which young women see frightful visions that compel them to leap, to throw themselves down wells, or to strangle themselves[199]—violent and frightening behavior that recalls the bewitched Cappadocian nun, who also leapt about and threatened to kill herself.

No matter how differently they explain the cause of the disease, all of these early Greek stories end happily with marriage, and although they admit rather wide variations, they all follow a narrative pattern that is similar to the myths and stories connected with *agōgē* spells, a pattern that is summarized in Table 3. On the surface, we can see many obvious similarities in the insane, wild, and sometimes lascivious behavior of the young women and their intense desire to escape from the house.[200] But these narratives are also concerned in one way or another with tensions over marriage in Greek culture and over the timely transfer of women from one home to another. Indeed, the "deep structure" of these narratives is fairly clear: in the normal order of things, a disease (*erōs*) strikes a young girl in order to facilitate her movement from her father's house to another household. In myth, as so often happens, the "normal" process is resisted, and disaster strikes: thus the stories of Io and the daughters of Proetus and Pandareus all appear as cautionary tales of young women who resist marriage and are nonetheless forced out into the open, and in a particularly shameful fashion: by exhibiting the behavior of wild animals in heat. All these pre-Christian stories end with marriage, and even the Hippocratic doctor, who strongly contests the divine etiology of such diseases, seeks the

---

199. King (1983) 113–115. Dean-Jones (1992) 76–78 discusses similar ideas about and cures for female depression and madness associated with the "wandering womb."

200. These stories, moreover, have obvious parallels with those of the married daughters of Cadmus of Thebes or of Minyas of Orchomenos, who insult Dionysus. For possible connections see Bremmer (1984) 282–286, who argues for the "pre-matrimonial origin" (I would say "character" and leave the question of origins to the side) of the maenadic tales. Seaford (1988) 130–133 emphasizes the differences.

Table 3. Explanations and cures for female adolescent hysteria

Victims	Cause	Symptoms	Cure	Aftermath
Daughters of Proetus (see notes 196, 197)	Hera (or Artemis)	go mad, escape house, act like wild cows, lewdness	purification, dedication to Artemis	marriage
Daughters of Pandareus (see note 199)	Zeus	go mad, escape house, act like wild bitches	(not extant)	(not extant)
Io, daughter of Inachus (see note 198)	Zeus	driven by *oistros*, goes mad, escapes house, acts like a wild cow	intercourse with Zeus in Egypt	birth of Epaphus
Patients in Hippocratic *On the Maladies of Unmarried Women*	delay of menarch leads to excess blood in internal organs	go mad, leap, have visions, attempt suicide	dedication to Artemis or marriage and pregnancy	marriage
Medea in Pindar *Pythian* 4	*iunx* bird bound to wheel, spoken charms	goes mad, (escapes house?) loses reverence for parents, acts like a mad bird	runs away with Jason	marriage
Intended victims of *agōgē* spells	burning and binding rites, spoken charms	goes mad, suffers pain, leaps from house, forgets her family	"until she comes to me . . . "	sex and sometimes marriage
Cappadocian nun in Byzantine *Life of St. Irene* (see note 194)	erotic spell (*sumplegma*)	attacked by mad lust, loses sense of shame, leaps, threatens suicide	prayers and exorcism, destruction of *sumplegma*	[marriage avoided]

same cure: he "commands" his mentally ill female patients to marry and get pregnant as soon as possible.[201] In the light, then, of this wider Greek discourse on marriage, we can perhaps understand why myth narrates the

201. He believes the cause of insanity is a delay in menarche and a buildup of excess blood in the internal organs; see King (1983) 113–115.

invention and first use of both apple spells and *agōgē* spells in a very positive manner, and (in the case of the latter) treats Aphrodite's gifts as if they were as valuable to human culture as the divine gifts of wine-making, agriculture, or horse-taming. Indeed, both Jason and Hippomenes, when they use erotic magic to seduce their wives-to-be, seem to act much like Hera and Zeus, who also force reluctant virgins away from their parents and into the wider world of sexuality, marriage, and motherhood. Again the contrast with the later Christian stories could not be greater; there the male suitor is demonized, the attack of the erotic magic is overcome, and the virgin is never forced to marry.

These various Greek discourses about marriage and the dangers of female adolescence can, moreover, suggest useful ways for extending even further our understanding of the wider social context of *agōgē* magic, especially regarding the sadism and violence that pervades some forms of it. I noted earlier that the term *agōgē* itself is used by the Greeks to describe the normal procession of the betrothed bride to her husband's house. The extant *agōgē* spells, however, seem closer in many ways to the mythic stories of delayed and eventually violent transition (for example, the daughters of Proetus) and to the equally violent form of marriage known as bridal theft. Both are replete with images of the pain, humiliation, and subjugation of women; both assume the unwillingness of the victim; and both offer up the apparent paradox that such transitory violence can and does lead to a permanent and happy marriage. Or to put it differently: the images of pain and torture in the extant *agōgē* spells are equivalent to the divine punishments and humiliation meted out in myth and the brute force employed in the course of an actual abduction marriage. In all three situations the violence can perhaps be defended culturally on the grounds that the girl or her family is being unnaturally resistant to marriage, and on the grounds that the violence is supposed to stop when the girl is safely out of her parents' house and under the sexual control of another man.

Some of the extant spells reveal just such a two-step process: madness, passion, and pain will force the girl to come, but a calmer relationship is to follow. Thus one handbook advertises a spell that "leads a woman to a man" and then "makes her steadfast and faithful."[202] The incantation from

202. *PGM* LXXVIII.

another handbook spell ends: ". . . so that you may lead and tame (sc. her) on this very day, on this very night . . . until she comes to me, Mr. So-and-so, and <remains> satisfying me fully, loving me, and cherishing me, Mr. So-and-so." [203] We see a similar request in one of the very rare extant *agōgē* spells used by a woman against a man: "Melt away his heart and suck out his blood in his love, in his passion, in his pain, until Serapion comes to Dioskorous and performs all my wishes and continues loving me, until he goes off to Hades." [204] Here the melting and bloodsucking are to persist only until he comes and performs all her wishes, but afterward he is to continue loving her for the rest of his life. These texts and other stipulations suggest that such spells could be used, like Jason's *iunx*, to form a marriage bond or some long-term relationship. [205]

These broad similarities between bridal theft and *agōgē* spells allow us to abandon the apparent *odi et amo* paradox that has troubled so many commentators and has led to therapeutic or cathartic theories, which are ultimately designed to explain (and I think justify) why a man would torture the woman he desires and wants to have as his companion. This paradox disappears, however, when we recall the two-step sequence of the *agōgē* spell and realize that the practitioner does not love and hate the woman *at the same time*. The initial violence of the *agōgē* spells—like the rough handling in an abduction marriage—seems to be a prelude to a settled and even happy relationship. In both cases violence, torture, and subjugation are clearly part of a traditional (and to our minds admittedly perverse) pattern of thought that viewed the bride-to-be as a member of a hostile tribe of sorts who had to be violently raped—in both its original meaning of "kidnapped" and its later connotations of sexual penetration[206]—to ensure that she sever her loyalty to her natal family and irrevocably cast her lot with her new husband. Similar tensions appear, moreover, in the use of apple spells, from which the images of torture and pain are absent, but not the madness, the lust, and the (eventual) acquiescence in a new life outside the natal home. Here, too, we get a sense of the peculiar

203. *PGM* VII.911–913, with Priesendanz' addition <remains>.

204. *PGM* XVI.

205. Winkler (1991) 232–233. Boll (1910) 9–11 and Eitrem (1925) 33 n. 1 discuss two texts that say that the victim should love the man for five months (*PGM* CI.36–37) and ten months (*SM* 37).

206. See Evans-Grubbs (1989) 59–62.

legitimation and usefulness of erotic magic, for in the case of the particularly difficult marriage of an *epikleros,* the famously wise Solon putatively legislated the use of a quince, to ensure that this potentially reluctant bride might quickly conceive a passion for her husband and thereby enter into a happy and fruitful marriage with him.

3

~

SPELLS FOR INDUCING
AFFECTION (PHILIA)

Males were not the sole users of love magic in ancient Greece, although, as we have seen, they did have a monopoly of sorts over spells used to induce erotic infatuation. As it turns out, women were equally adept, but the types of magic they used and contexts in which they used them are all quite different, for they were designed to retain or regain *philia* or *agapē*, words that generally connote affection in a spouse, a lover, or some other person to whom the practitioner is already well known.[1] Although these spells do from time to time aim at arousing the victim's sexual desire, the images of mad, burning passion and torture are entirely absent, and in general the desired results of *philia* magic are docility and amiability. Indeed, this type of magic is often employed to heal a broken or dysfunctional relationship or to protect a working but fragile one, a fact that fits well with the magical techniques employed, such as amulets, ointments, and potions—all of which are popular in healing magic. We must take care, however, not to idealize *philia* spells, for like the erotic spells described in the previous chapter, these magical rites are also clearly designed to dominate and control others by binding or otherwise debilitating them. This is most apparent in the *philia* spells that use binding techniques or narcotics to control their male victims, practices that do not go unremarked by male writers, who continually voice suspicions that their wives and concubines

1. In Faraone (1992a) and (1994a) I suggested wrongly that *philia* magic was entirely nonerotic. See section 1.2 for a detailed discussion of these terms.

are using magic spells to control them and to undermine their much-prized autonomy.

3.1 Aphrodite's *Kestos Himas* and Other Amuletic Love Charms

In the fourteenth book of the *Iliad,* Hera calls Aphrodite aside and makes an urgent but mendacious request (197–210):

> Now give me affection *(philotēs)*[2] and desire *(himeros),* with which you subdue all the gods and mortal men, since I am about to go to the ends of the generous earth to see Oceanus, the source of the gods, and mother Tethys . . . I shall go to visit them and shall stop their ceaseless quarrels, since now for a long time they have stayed apart from each other and from their marriage bed, since bitter anger *(cholos)* has fallen upon their hearts. If I could with words persuade their dear hearts and bring them back to their bed to be merged in love *(philotēti)* with each other, forever would I be called dear by them and compassionate.

And so Hera, pretending to be worried over the broken marriage of her parents, asks Aphrodite for help in bringing them back together in their bridal bed. Aphrodite agrees to help and gives Hera a specially charmed belt or strap (214–217): "She spoke and from her breasts unbound an elaborate *kestos himas,* on which had been wrought all enchantments *(thelktēria)*: love *(philotēs),* desire *(himeros),* and the whispered endearment that steals away good sense, even from the thoughtful." Despite this detailed description there has been little agreement as to the nature of this magical strap, what it looked like, where it was worn or carried, or what was its intended effect. Early commentators thought it was an amulet of

---

2. LSJ s.v. 4 and 5 admit that the word *philia* is the common prose equivalent for *philotēs,* but claim that *philotēs* in Homer regularly refers to sexual love. This seems to be a mistaken inference, for the word most regularly appears in the dative with a verb of sexual congress *(misgein),* where it may simply describe the emotional state of the person during intercourse, e.g., "she lay with him *affectionately*" (i.e., she was not raped), rather than "she lay with him *passionately.*" Empedocles famously contrasted *philotēs* (= *philia,* "friendship", not lust) with *neikos* ("strife").

sorts carried in the fold of Hera's garment,[3] but more recently scholars have argued that the *kestos himas* was an article of clothing, worn either about the breasts or on the waist.[4]

Scholars do agree, however, that the adjective *kestos* refers to a pattern of perforations used to decorate the *himas*, which was probably a rather narrow strap of leather, like the chinstrap of a helmet.[5] But the precise nature of this perforated decoration is extremely vague; drawing parallels from Homeric descriptions of shields, some envision anthropomorphic representations of the triad Affection, Desirability, and Whispered Endearment.[6] One should, however, exercise caution here in assuming that Homer is simply describing superficial decorations. Hesiod's treatment of the adornment of Pandora clearly reveals the ambiguities inherent in early Greek concepts of abstract qualities such as *philotēs* or *himeros*. In the *Works and Days*, Zeus orders Hephaestus to fashion a life-size clay statue, and as one would expect he turns to Aphrodite for the provision of sexual attractiveness (65–66): "and he ordered golden Aphrodite to pour charm *(charis)* about her head and painful longing *(pothos)*." This process of pouring or draping abstract gifts, such as "longing"[7] and "charm" *(charis)*,

3. See *kolpos* at lines 219 and 223 and Faraone (1990) 220 n. 1 for bibliography. As in the case of most long and hotly contested questions, there are insufficient data on which to base a secure conclusion.

4. LSJ s.v. defines it as a "girdle" in this passage. Bonner (1949) 1–6 suggests that it was a "saltire" (a kind of cross-your-heart brassiere) of the type worn by eastern goddesses. Brenk (1977) 17–20 alters Bonner's theory slightly: the *kestos himas* is an embroidered square or loose collar that joins the saltire together at the breast. Onians (1951) 368–369 compares it to the magical veil worn by Leukothea and given to Odysseus (*Od.* 5.333–335). The word *kestos* may be related to Hebrew *keset* (Ezekiel 13:18 and 20), which seems to mean "magical band" and is apparently transliterated onto a late Greek amulet (*GMA* 32.9) as *kastu*. See Kotansky *GMA* pp. 148–149.

5. Chantraine s.v. *kenteo*.

6. Shapiro (1993) 18–20 points out that there are close formulaic parallels elsewhere in the *Iliad* for three abstract figures appearing together in a single hexametrical line, e.g., Strife *(Eris)*, Battle Din *(Kudoimos)*, and Doom *(Kēr)*, depicted on Achilles' shield (18.535); and Strife *(Eris)*, Strength *(Alkē)*, and Onslaught *(Iokē)*, on Athena's aegis (5.740). These parallels to defensive armor are understandable given that the overall structure of Hera's preparations reflect the standard arming type-scenes; see Golden (1989) 5–6 and note 12 below for the *kestos himas* as a protective amulet.

7. I.e., objective desire like the *himeros* on the *kestos himas*: it is desire to be felt by men for Pandora not Pandora's desire for men.

about the head[8] is enacted a few lines later in Hesiod's description of the actual creation of Pandora, where the commands given to Aphrodite are carried out by her surrogates Peitho (Persuasion) and the Charites (the Graces), who place golden necklaces about the statue's neck (73–74). Thus, as in Homer's treatment of the *kestos himas,* Hesiod depicts abstract, seductive powers in very concrete terms. Although it is unclear in both the Pandora story and the *kestos himas* episode whether qualities such as "charm" or "desire" are by some magical ritual implanted in the strap or necklace, it is an obvious point of both stories that the gifts were meant to infuse magically the person who donned them.[9]

There is also some confusion in the Homeric scene about the expected effects of the strap. From Hera's story quoted above, we know it could be used to heal a marital rift by stopping quarrels and anger. If Hera the would-be marriage counselor had kept her word, she would probably have given the *kestos himas* to her mother, Tethys, to wear, presumably to attract her husband or to calm his anger in similar fashion.[10] But Homer never makes explicit how the device was supposed to help Hera's parents. As it turns out, Hera's real object is to divert Zeus's attention from the battle that rages around Troy, and then (with the help of the god Sleep) to immobilize him[11] so that he will not hinder her from her own strategic objectives with regard to the Trojan War. Indeed, her motivation for the seduction is

8. The former interpretation depends on the use of the same verb to describe similar actions of Athena in the *Odyssey* (e.g., 6.235 and 23.156), where she is said to "pour" either "charm" or "beauty" over Odysseus' head. The verb *amphichein,* however, can be used to mean "drape over" (cf. the *desmata* with which Hephaestus entraps Ares and Aphrodite, *Od.* 8.278).

9. It has long been known that Hesiod's descriptions of the adornment of Pandora (in both the *Works and Days* and the *Theogony*) contain numerous echoes of the Homeric "Deception of Zeus" episode, leading many scholars to conclude that Hesiod has used the episode as a model of sorts. For the large bibliography and renewed debate, see Neitzel (1975) 20–34. Like the *kestos himas,* these necklaces may have also been part of Aphrodite's regular wardrobe; cf. the Homeric *Hymn to Aphrodite* 61 ff. and 86 ff. for her own preparations to seduce Anchises. Henrichs (1972) 22 points to the East as the source for these rich ornaments—especially in traditional descriptions of Astarte and Inanna.

10. Gantz (1993) 101; but see Redfield (1982) 196, who suggests in passing that Hera herself would have worn it and beguiled both her parents.

11. The Homeric account is complicated by the addition of the god Hypnos, who is to put Zeus to sleep after the lovemaking session. Some might argue that sleep after coitus is a

loathing, not love, as she herself readily admits (14.158). Finally, it is clear from Zeus's reaction at lines 313–328 that like Pandora's necklaces, the *kestos himas* makes Hera appear more beautiful and more desirable. We can thus infer the following constellation of effects associated with the use of the Homeric *kestos himas* and the necklaces given to Pandora: they were carried or worn by women; they made them sexually attractive to males; and the *kestos himas*, at least, could be used to stop anger and quarrels between a husband and wife.[12] They are, moreover, similarly deployed within the context of marriage: Aphrodite's magic belt is used to renew affection in an existing but dysfunctional relationship (Zeus and Hera; Oceanus and Tethys), while Pandora's necklace is a bridal gift in anticipation of a new marriage. In fact there seems to have been a tradition in Greek myth (only dimly apparent from surviving literature) according to which Aphrodite or the Graces give famous brides special clothing that will impart beauty or charm to them. Thus Aphrodite gives a *peplos* to Hypsipyle, a special veil to Hector's wife, Andromache, and a wreath woven with roses—Aphrodite's special flower—to Amphitrite.[13]

But to what extent does the story in *Iliad* 14 reflect actual magical practices in the ancient world? One could, of course, dismiss Aphrodite's magical belt as the fantastic invention of an imaginative folk tradition, but an epigram by Asclepiades, a poet who lived in the third century B.C.E.— some five centuries after the composition of the Homeric poems—suggests that Greek women might in fact have worn similar devices: "I myself once

---

"natural" phenomenon in males, and that the poet has simply added the role of Hypnos as a humorous double motivation of sorts, but the sequence of sexual attraction followed by enervation is one common to many *philia* spells (see below, section 3.3).

12. Here, too, there is some ambiguity. In the context of the *Iliad*, in which Hera is often threatened by her angry husband with physical abuse, marital discord seems to be caused by male anger and is especially dangerous for women. In this context, the *kestos himas* does operate like a protective amulet. Du Boulay (1986) 149–152 notes the widely held modern Greek belief that the wife's task is to placate a naturally irritable husband. Ortega (1991) 67–68 connects clauses in Spanish love spells aimed at placating male anger with repeated testimony about male violence against the women who use these spells.

13. *Iliad* 22.469–472 and Bacchylides 17.115–116. See Scodel (1984) 141–142, Ieranò (1989) 164–168, and C. G. Brown (1991) 332–333, who suggests plausibly that the robe of Hypsipyle at Apollonius *Argonautica* 4.423–434 serves a similar purpose. Scodel (1984) 141 suggests that Amphitrite gives her own wedding wreath to Theseus to help him seduce Ariadne when he gets to Crete.

played with easy Hermione, who wore a variegated girdle of flowers, O Paphian one, which had a golden inscription: 'Keep loving me *(philei me)* forever and do not get angry *(mē lupēthēis)* if another man holds me.'"[14] Scholars usually assume that the text on the girdle is designed to communicate with others and that it is Hermione's blunt warning to her boyfriends that they must not get too proprietary about her.[15] The first part of the exhortation—*philei me*—is, however, identical with a brief inscription on a magic gemstone of Roman date that depicts Eros with his hands bound behind his back,[16] suggesting that Hermione's girdle may have been a magical device designed to *ensure* that her boyfriends love her and do not get angry with her, precisely the effects of the Homeric *kestos himas.*

There is in fact evidence that such devices were used much earlier in the ancient world. As in the case of the apple spells, we find that cords or straps very similar to Aphrodite's were employed as magical charms in the Near East at a time and place not very far removed from the eastern edge of the Homeric world: a cuneiform tablet from Ashur[17] dating to about 1000 B.C.E. contains some purification rites for women and then a ritual with the rubric "Incantation to be recited when the husband of a women is angry with her":

> The rite is accomplished (as follows): You weave together into a single strand the tendons of a gazelle, [hemp,] and red wool; you tie it into fourteen knots. Each time you tie a knot, you recite the (i.e., preceding) incantation. The woman places this cord around her waist, and she will be loved.[18]

14. Gow and Page (1965) 45 no. IV (= *AP* 5.158). "Paphian one" is another Cyprian epithet for Aphrodite.

15. Gow and Page (1965) ad loc.

16. *BM* no. 1468. It seems fairly clear that gemstones with Eros binding Psyche are aimed at females and those with Psyche binding Eros (or with Eros bound and alone) are aimed at controlling men; see section 2.1.

17. Ashur lies on the Tigris River in northern Iraq, some 350 miles from the important Greek emporium at Al Mina; Burkert (1992) 11–12.

18. Scheil (1921) 21–27 no. 17 col. iii.10'–14'. I translate the French rendition by my colleague Erica Reiner (1966) 93, who kindly checked the English for me to ensure that no distortions have crept in. Professor Reiner informs me that the word for "love" used in this text encompasses both affection and sexual desire.

The incantation to be used with this recipe is very fragmentary, but we can make out that it invokes Ishtar, just as the Mesopotamian apple spells invoke Inanna, Ishtar's Sumerian counterpart. A different recipe with the very same rubric preserves a prayer to Ishtar as the Morning Star, a prayer that ends with the plea: "I call on you, O Ishtar . . . because he does not tell me the words of his heart, because he is angry and does not talk to me."[19] It would appear, then, that these Assyrian procedures were designed to remedy a situation quite similar to that of Hera's parents in the *Iliad;* a specially made strap or cord is worn by a woman to heal a marital rift by assuaging the anger of her husband and making him more loving.

The underlying magical activity in the Near Eastern spell is the tying of knots, presumably as a form of binding magic aimed at inhibiting the husband's anger. As such, it is clearly related to another, much larger class of Neo-Assyrian magical spells, the so-called *egalkura* spells, which often involve the use of knotted or beaded cords to enhance one's attractiveness in the eyes of a superior:

> You chant this spell seven times over a three-stranded cord of lapis-colored wool, you knot it (and) you bind it in your hem. And when you enter into the presence of the prince, he will welcome you (variant: "whoever looks upon you will be glad to see you").

> You thread *ianibu* stone and carnelian on a cord, (and) you repeat the spell three times. You place it on the teaseled side of your cloak. And when you enter into the presence of the prince, he will welcome you.[20]

Unlike the case of the Homeric *kestos himas,* neither of these recipes even hints at the prospect of increasing the bodily desire of the prince; here the cords are simply designed to make a superior male better disposed toward

---

19. Gurney and Finkelstein (1957) no. 257 rev. 2–9, translated for me by E. Reiner. In the prayer, Ishtar is addressed as she "who makes (men?) love, who brings back an angry man to the house of the bride's family." This recipe has the same rubric as the recipe for the cord, but an entirely different ritual; the text is very fragmentary, but Prof. Reiner was able to make out references to an altar, loaves, incense, and an oil that is anointed.

20. *KAR* 71.21–25 and 71.1–11, translated by E. Reiner. For a discussion of the ambiguous nature of these spells, which are often found in collections that range from explicitly erotic purposes to purely political or economic ones, see Scurlock (1989–90).

one of his subjects or underlings. These *egalkura* recipes do, nonetheless, have much in common with the Homeric strap and the amuletic cord used by an Assyrian wife against her angry husband (described in the cuneiform spell from Ashur). In each case social or political inferiors armed with a magically enchanted cord face their "princes" with hopes of being made more welcome or attractive. A somewhat similar form of this kind of Assyrian "political" magic seems to survive in this short Greek recipe, most probably of Jewish origin: "To restrain anger: Enter the presence of a king or magnate, and while you have your hands inside your garment say the name of the sun disk, while tying a knot in your pallium or shawl. You will marvel at the results."[21] Here the rubric suggests that the binding effects of the knot are focused directly on the anger of the superior, but the result will be the same: his increased goodwill and affection.

Two other forms of *egalkura* spells—special rings and facial ointments—also show up in the Greek magical tradition and seem to be used for very similar purposes. Both the Greeks and Assyrians, for instance, apparently employed magical rings to increase their personal charisma, especially in the eyes of their kings and masters:

> *Neo-Assyrian Recipe:* "Over a copper ring chant the spell three times. You place it on your finger. And when you enter into the presence of the prince, he will welcome you."[22]

> *Greek Recipe:* "A little ring for success and for charm *(charis)* and for victory . . . The world has nothing better than this. For when you have it with you, you will always get whatever you ask from anybody. Besides, it calms the angers *(orgai)* of kings and masters. Wearing it, whatever you may say to anyone, you will be believed, and you will be pleasing to everybody"[23]

21. *PGM* XIII.251–252, as translated and interpreted by M. Smith in *GMPT.* The spell is alleged to be from the "Eighth Book of Moses." Such hoary eastern antecedents are usually fabricated by later magicians in order to make the spell more mysterious, and therefore more valuable to the customer; Betz (1982). There are, however, indications of real Jewish influence here; see M. Smith (1984) and his comments ad loc. in *GMPT.*

22. *KAR* 71 rev. 9–11, translated for me by E. Reiner.

23. *PGM* XII.270–273 and 277–280, as translated by M. Smith in *GMPT.* There follows a long incantation that is to be repeated thrice daily.

The Greek recipe is preserved in a fourth-century c.e. magical handbook, but the *Cyranides,* which dates two or three centuries earlier, boasts similar powers for a number of gemstones; for example, if a man wears a *dendrites* stone, "he will be loved (*ēgapēmenos*) and well heeded by all gods and mortals and he will be successful in whatever he wants"; or if a man wears a sapphire engraved with Aphrodite, "he will be charming, famous, and victorious in every lawsuit."[24] Another late Greek magical recipe claims that when *aerizōn,* a special kind of jasper, is set in a small gold ring, it is "especially effective before kings and leaders," a belief that seems to have been known to Pliny the Elder more than three centuries earlier.[25]

There is, then, a long-standing Greek tradition of such devices, one that is only partially visible in our extant evidence and one that may perhaps be traced back directly to Mesopotamia. Indeed, the Assyrians similarly noted the special qualities of stones, including those that were effective for "entering the palace and not being confronted with calumny" or for "being received with favor by the ruler."[26] Pliny may even have had direct access to such Assyrian lore through intermediaries such as Zachalias of Babylon, whom he cites (with disapproval) for the claim that the stone hematite was useful to litigants or petitioners appearing before the king.[27] There is, however, a hint that such rings were known in the Greek world much earlier than Pliny, for in Plato's *Republic* we learn about the gold ring that magically turned the Lydian usurper Gyges "invisible," allowing him to enter the royal palace unharmed, seduce the royal queen, and kill the king himself (2.359d–360a). But regardless of their ultimate source, I should underscore the fact that most of these devices are worn by men[28] to influence the behavior of a male superior, either to ensure that they will "welcome" the petitioner or (in the Greek example) to calm their anger (*orgē*) and replace it with friendship (*philia*).

24. *Cyranides* 1.4.45–51 and 1.10.39–42.

25. *PGM* XII.201–202. According to Pliny *NH* 37.118, sorcerers claim that a kind of jasper call *aerizousa* is "useful for those who harangue the assembly." See Riess (1896a) 76 for discussion.

26. Reiner (1995) 121.

27. Pliny *NH* 37.169; see Reiner (1995) 124.

28. This is made clear in the *PGM* recipe and the *Cyranides* recipes cited in note 24, which use masculine participles throughout. One recipe, however, supplies a variant recipe if a woman is going to use it (*Cyr.* 1.10.39–42), suggesting that a male user was the norm.

The recipes for Neo-Assyrian *egalkura* rituals also include facial ointments to be applied to the faces of petitioners in anticipation of a meeting
with a superior:

> You chant this spell three times over good oil. You smear your face
> and your hands. And when you enter into the presence of the
> prince, he will welcome you (variant text reads: ". . . and then he
> who looks upon you will be glad to see you").[29]

Here, too, we find a very similar tradition in a fourth-century C.E. Greek
magical recipe titled "Prayer to Helios: A charm to restrain anger and for
victory and for securing charm (none is greater)." The recipe directs us to
say the prayer seven times to Helios and then to anoint our hand with oil
and wipe it on our head and face. The prayer that follows asks for a variety
of abstract benefits: "I ask to obtain and receive from you life, health,
reputation, wealth, influence, strength, success, sexiness (*epaphrodisian*),
and charm (*charis*) with all men and all women, victory over all men and
all women."[30] This recipe, like the jasper gemstone discussed above, can be
traced back much earlier in the Greek tradition: the same Hellenistic handbook that holds the "apple incantation" discussed in the preceding chapter
also contains a short recipe for smearing myrrh on one's face and then
chanting an incantation designed to bring charm (*charis*) to a woman in
the eyes of her husband or lover: "Take myrrh and chant (the following)
and anoint your face: 'You are the myrrh with which Isis anointed herself
when she went to the bosom of Osiris, her own husband and brother, and
on that day you gave her charm (*charis*). Give to me . . .'"[31]

This particular recipe shows reveals the influence of a popular Isis and
Osiris legend, but the technique itself was apparently known to the Greeks
much earlier. In his discussion of plants used as amulets, Theophrastus

29. *KAR* 237.13–17, translated for me by E. Reiner. The variant is *KAR* 237.18–23.

30. *PGM* XXXVI.211–230, translated by R. F. Hock in *GMPT*.

31. *SM* 72 col. ii.4–8. The incantation breaks off here, and although the most likely
restoration is *tas e[paphrodisia]s*, "sexiness," the plural is otherwise unattested; see the editors
of *SM* ad loc. Brashear (1979) ad loc. suggested another plausible restoration, *ta se[autēs . . .]*
(paraphrase): "what you (i.e., Isis) yourself have," which amounts to the same thing, i.e.,
charm and attractiveness. In any event, the logic of the story about Isis suggests that the user
is female and is requesting that *charis* or some other similar benefit also be given to her,
presumably for an effect on her husband.

cites Hesiod and Musaeus for the popular belief that the herb tripolion is useful for "every good thing" and then continues:

> In agreement are the things that are said regarding good fame *(eukleia)* and good reputation *(eudoxia)*. For they claim that the plant called snapdragon produces good fame . . . and that the man who anoints himself with (sc. the essence of) this plant will win good reputation. And they say that a man will also win good reputation if he crowns himself with the flower of the plant goldflower, sprinkling it with myrrh from a vessel of unfired gold.[32]

Theophrastus clearly distances himself from these claims, especially at the end of this section, where he goes on to scoff at the boastful men "who wish to glorify their own areas of expertise"—a reference no doubt to the professional root-cutters and drug-sellers whom he quotes elsewhere. This passage nonetheless gives us a rare view of popular fourth-century Greek beliefs about the charismatic power of herbal essences and myrrh.

Pindar tells us that Jason anointed himself with a magical oil to protect himself against danger and to ensure his victory in the deadly trials arranged for him by Medea's father.[33] This story suggests that such oils could be used for protective purposes as well, and it reminds us that all three of the devices discussed in this section (knotted cords, rings, and ointments) are also used in protective magic. Why is it, then, that they show up repeatedly in the realm of love magic? There is in fact a remarkable fluidity in the later Greek categories of amulets and *philia* magic.[34] For example, although we are accustomed to think of an amulet as self-induced "protective" magic and of an aphrodisiac as invasive magic aimed at another, the passages quoted above from Theophrastus, Pliny, the *Cyranides*, and the Greek magical papyri reveal a continuous tradition of belief that such devices could also be used to affect the way other people perceive and interact with the person who wears or carries the amulet. Thus, instead of

---

32. *HP* 9.19.2–3.

33. *Pythian* 4.221–223.

34. Winkler (1991) 218–220. Much of the following two paragraphs is indebted to this ground-breaking study. Although there are many detailed recipes for such "charm" or "victory" amulets in the Greek magical papyri, there are surprisingly few extant examples, presumably because a valuable material like silver or gold was constantly recycled. For a survey, see Jordan (1985b) 164–165.

simply asking that some evil be turned away, the invocations inscribed on these amulets often request that some abstract benefit be granted. For instance, a second- or third-century C.E. silver amulet from Oxyrhynchus reads: "Grant charm *(charin)*, friendship *(philian)*, success, and sexiness *(epaphrodisian)* to the man wearing this amulet *(phulaktērion)*."[35] Here the spell in a self-referential manner uses the Greek word *phulaktērion* (literally, "a thing that protects") to describe a device that is primarily concerned with increasing the charisma of the owner and the affection of others toward him. In fact the rubrics for such spells vary considerably. Recipes called "victory spells" *(nikētika)*, for instance, were thought to ensure the defeat of a rival, but their effect was far more diffuse; one simple prayer reads: "Give me success, charm, reputation, glory in the stadium"; and another asks a god to "grant victory, strength, and influence to the man who wears (this amulet)."[36] Other spells, sometimes designated as "charm spells" *(charitēsia)*, are used to help public speakers gain the sympathy of their audience, or are flagrantly commercial and ask that the profits of a shop owner be increased; but even in this case, they demand personal benefits such as beauty, sexiness, and charm.[37]

For our purposes, it is significant that these two interrelated categories of "good-luck charms" are often combined and blurred with still another genre, the "charm to restrain anger" *(thumokatochon)*.[38] These spells survive on a variety of media in the Greek tradition (lead, papyri, and gemstones) and can often be very simple, as in the case of a second- or third-century C.E. gemstone from Syria whose underside is inscribed in Greek: "Let all anger *(thumos)* toward me, Cassianus, be restrained *(katechesthō)*"; or another of similar date but unknown provenance which asks a god to

---

35. *SM* 64 = *GMA* 60. The rare Greek word *epaphrodisia* appears only on charms from Egypt and is apparently a calque for Demotic *mr.t*, a charismatic quality that Egyptians asked the gods to grant them when they were about to appear before the pharaoh; see Kotansky's "Excursus" in *GMA* (pp. 356–360).

36. *PGM* VII.390–393 and VIII.923–925.

37. For public speaking: *PGM* XXXVI.275. For good business there are two prayers: "Therefore, give me charm and work for my business. Bring me silver, gold, clothing, and much wealth for the good of it" (*PGM* IV.2440–41); and "Come to me, Mr. So-and so, lord Hermes, and give me charm, sustenance, victory, prosperity, sexiness, beauty of face, power over all men and women" (*PGM* VIII.4–5). A similar prayer is given a few lines later (26): "give me charm, shapeliness, and physical beauty."

38. See Hopfner (1938) and Winkler (1991) 219.

"restrain the angers *(tous thumous)* of Taso."[39] What is most significant about these spells, however, is the ease with which they are combined with the good-luck charms discussed above, as in this recipe for a silver amulet:

> A charm to restrain anger *(thumokatochon)* and a charm to se-
> cure favor *(charitēsion)* and the best charm for gaining victory
> *(nikētikon)* in the law courts—it even works against kings; no charm
> is greater! Take a silver tablet and inscribe with a bronze stylus
> the following . . . and wear it under your garment and you will
> be victorious.[40]

The prayer to be inscribed on the tablet reads: "Give to me, Mr. So-and-so, whom Ms. So-and-so bore, victory, charm, reputation, advantage over all men and women, especially over Mr. So-and-so, whom Ms. So-and-so bore, forever and all time." This is a recipe for a general charm that will bring success over *all* men and women, but the mention of kings and law courts and the place to insert the name of a single man as the primary target ("especially over Mr. So-and-so") suggest that here too we have a spell aimed originally at a male at the apex of some social group. A second-century C.E. gold amulet from Thessalonika includes a similar stipulation: "Grant favor *(epicharin)*, success with all men and women, but especially with him, whomever she herself wishes."[41] Indeed, these spells (like the Assyrian amulets discussed above) are often designed for political situations such as an appearance in a royal audience or a court of law, where the petitioner finds himself in "the presence of a king or magnate."[42] An elaborate inscribed Greek amulet from Arabia gives us some sense of how

39. Mouterde (1930) 77–80 no. 11 and Bonner *SMA* 149. The plural *(thumous)* is odd; Roy Kotansky has suggested in a letter that we translate "outbursts."

40. *PGM* XXXVI.35–68. For similar combinations of these three types of spells, see *PGM* XX 270–273 (all three); XXXVI.161–177 (an anger-binding spell and a victory spell) and 211–230 (all three).

41. *GMA* 40. The text refers to itself or the magical names it carries as "Aphrodite's name." A much later papyrus charm (*PGM* XXXV) has a long general formula, "grant charm, power, victory, strength, before all men, small and large, also gladiators, soldiers, civilians, women, girls, children, and everyone," but at the bottom of the papyrus we see who the specific targets are, for there are three rough drawings of men, two of which are labeled "Paulus" and "Julianus."

42. *PGM* XIII.250.

such charms worked in the practical world of a Roman provincial capital: "Give charm, glory, and victory to Proclus, whom Salvina bore, before Diogenianus, the military governor of Bostra in Arabia and before Pelagius the assessor, and before all men small and great . . . in order that he might win, justly or unjustly, every lawsuit before every judge and adjudicator."[43]

These later Greek magical charms may seem rather distant from the Homeric kestos himas, but in their directness and simplicity they quite readily call to mind Hera's request to Aphrodite in Iliad 14.198–199: "Give me affection and desire, with which you subdue all the gods and mortal men." This is also true for spells inscribed on Roman-era gemstones commissioned by women for apparently amorous purposes, such as "Give charm (charin) to Hieronyma before all men" or "Keep me young and charming,"[44] but especially the end of this early third-century C.E. papyrus spell that invokes Aphrodite for a similar array of benefits: "O Cypris, (come) hither to me every day of (my) life. If your hidden name, Thoathoēthathoouthaethōousthoaithithēthointhō, has pleased you (i.e., on previous occasions), then grant me (i.e., now) victory, reputation, good looks before all men and women."[45] Despite the cryptic magical name inserted in its midst, this short prayer reveals its ancestry in its poeticisms as well as a familiar form of argument found in Greek prayers (i.e., "you have helped in the past, so help me now").[46] Scholars have suggested that the religious overtones of the Homeric seduction scene on Mt. Ida probably reflect aspects of the sacred marriage of Zeus and Hera.[47] In this light, we might speculate that a request similar to Hera's prayer to Aphrodite in the Iliad and used in conjunction with a device like the kestos himas may have constituted a traditional ritual performed by new brides to ward off any future discord in their marriage. There is, moreover, evidence that this whole tradition may itself have been borrowed in quite early times from

43. *GMA* 58.12–19; see Kotansky (1991b) for an excellent discussion.

44. Blanchet (1923) 233. The second text is perhaps addressed to Aphrodite, who was elsewhere addressed with the famous prayer "O beautiful Aphrodite, throw off my old age!" (Plutarch *Moralia* 654).

45. *SM* 63.

46. The poeticisms include *deuro* ("hither") and the address to the goddess as "Cypris," both very common in Greek hymns, as is the argument "help me, because you have in the past." See Graf (1991).

47. Janko (1992) 171–172.

the Near East, for scholars have long suspected Near Eastern influence on the sacred-marriage rites of Greece;[48] and they have also argued that Hera's tale about the anger of Tethys and Oceanus reflects the Near Eastern myth of Tiamat and Apsu preserved in the Babylonian epic *Enuma Elish*, where they, too, appear as the parents of the gods, who were originally united in love but later separated by anger.[49] In any event, it need not surprise us to find *philia* magic with clear Near Eastern parallels in a section of the *Iliad* that betrays other important hallmarks of such influence.

There is, then, abundant evidence for three types of magical devices— a special ring, a knotted cord, or an ointment—that people might use in hopes of increasing their own personal charm and beauty in the eyes of a husband or a male superior. Many of the Near Eastern and the Greek examples are also designed to curtail the anger of such men and to replace it with friendship or affection, although erotic contact is never quite ruled out. Thus, although Hera's immediate goal with Zeus is frankly sexual, she asks Aphrodite for both desire *(himeros)* and friendly affection (*philotēs,* the poetic equivalent of *philia*)[50] We shall see a similar mixture of goals in the ensuing discussion of love potions.

3.2 Deianeira's Mistake:
The Confusion of Love Potions and Poisons

In the early action of Sophocles' tragedy *The Women of Trachis,* Heracles, on his way back from a victorious military campaign, stops to make an important sacrifice, but sends ahead to his home in Trachis a beautiful young captive named Iole, who is to become Heracle's new favorite. His wife, Deianeira, had in the past endured many of her husband's affairs with other women, but he had never brought one home with him, an act that even by the patriarchal standards of Sophocles' audience was obnoxious and threatening.[51] Deianeira, understandably concerned that she may be

48. Burkert (1985) 108 and 132, for discussion and pertinent bibliography.
49. See Burkert (1992) 88–96 for a summary.
50. See above, note 2.
51. Kitto (1966) 168–169 and Hester (1980) 3 n. 3 discuss the significance of Iole's presence in the house, adducing several examples in which husbands are criticized for housing their concubines in the same house as their wives. To their lists add [Demosthenes] 59.22, where an Athenian husband out of respect for his mother and wife refuses to "lead in" *(eisagein)* his

supplanted in her own home, recalls a love charm that she has kept hidden away for many years: the poisoned blood of a centaur, which will allegedly ensure that Heracles will never look at another woman or love *(sterxai)* her more than he loves Deianeira (576–577). She takes this potion, smears it on a robe, and sends it to her husband. The centaur's blood does not in fact have its intended effect; instead it dissipates and eventually kills Heracles. Toward the end of the play Hyllus, the bewildered son of Deianeira and Heracles, speaks to his dying father and defends his mother's actions (1136–39):

HYLLUS: Although her intentions were good, she botched the whole enterprise.[52]

HERACLES: Does she do *good* by killing your father?

HYLLUS: Well, when she saw that marriage (i.e., with Iole) in her house, she was determined to cast a love charm *(stergēma)* on you, but she failed utterly.

Father and son are the first to argue about Deianeira's culpability in this play, but they are certainly not the last.

In fact this has long been a sore point for modern commentators. In the past, the most popular inclination was to see her as an ideal wife who brings destruction on her husband by a tragic miscalculation[53] that stems from innate foolishness,[54] skittishness,[55] or an uncontrollable passion for

---

Corinthian concubine to his own home at Athens while she is being inducted into the Mysteries, preferring to send her off to stay with a friend. An anonymous referee also points out that the earliest of the Greco-Egyptian marriage contracts (*P. Eleph.* 1, dated to 311 B.C.E.) clearly stipulates that the husband is not allowed to "lead in" *(epeisagesthai)* another wife.

52. I follow many editors, e.g., Easterling (1982) ad loc., in taking *hapan to chrēma* as an internal accusative. Davies (1991) ad loc. follows Campbell and others who place a comma after *chrēma*: "The whole thing is, she erred with good intent." Either way, Hyllus is asserting Deianeira's innocence of the charge of homicide, on account of her good intent, as the chorus does earlier in the play (lines 727–728).

53. E.g., Jebb (1892), Whitman (1951) 103–121, and Kamerbeek (1959). For a close analysis of this early trend in the interpretation of the *Trachiniae*, see Johansen (1962).

54. Kitto (1966) 173 nicely sums up the *communis opinio* of his day: "it is natural for us to think of it (i.e., Deianeira's mistake) as Aristotelian *hamartia*. Sophocles has given her many virtues, but not shrewdness; it is her simple-mindedness that now brings her to ruin; one error destroys her." March (1987) 50 describes the Sophoclean Deianeira as "well intentioned but foolish."

55. McCall (1972), Gellie (1972) 55, Hester (1980) 8, and March (1987) 67.

Heracles that clouds her otherwise good judgment.[56] A small minority of scholars have, on the other hand, kept alive the argument that Sophocles is using a somewhat sanitized version of the original myth in which Deianeira allegedly appeared as a wild, man-killing Amazon who—true to the popular etymology of her name Dei-aneira, "Slayer-of-her-husband"—purposely kills Heracles in a fit of jealousy.[57] By most accounts, this well-known story of a loving wife "accidentally" murdering her husband is indeed baffling, but we can begin to make better sense of it once we realize that Greek women apparently *did* give poisons to their husbands, albeit in very small amounts, in the belief that these substances would make the men love them more or become more affectionate toward them. Thus, we shall see that Deianeira errs not in using a powerful poison to win back her husband's love, but rather in misjudging the power of the poison and giving Heracles too strong a dose.[58] Moreover, I shall argue that here, as in the case of the *agōgē* spells, we need not seek out any specific psychological reasons for Deianeira's actions or construct a model of a deranged lovesick user of magic. Indeed, as we shall see, her actions are part of a

56. Most notably Easterling (1968) and Winnington-Ingram (1980) 80–90. Holt (1981) 69, aware of some inconsistencies, speaks of "a fierce erotic passion which Deianeira clearly feels *but only occasionally mentions*" (my emphasis).

57. Errondonea (1927), La Rue (1965) 216–233, and March (1987) 49–77, who gives the most detailed argument, one rebutted by Davies (1989). Errondonea claims that Deianeira, caught in the grip of *erōs*, purposely murders Heracles even in Sophocles' version, and he suggests that either Sophocles or Bacchylides is guilty of a fifth-century whitewash of the character of Deianeira—a drastic revision that inevitably results in certain inconsistencies in her motivation, as well as the survival of dissonant details in the plot, such as the poisoned robe and Deianeira's manly method of suicide.

58. Faraone (1994a). As most of the parallels that follow involve love potions, not ointments such as the one deployed by Deianeira, it will be useful at this point to show that the manner in which a *pharmakon* was delivered to the victim—i.e., by ingestion or contact with the skin—is an insignificant variant. Phaedra, for instance, responds to the Nurse's suggestion of a love spell with the question (Euripides *Hippolytus* 516): "Is the *pharmakon* one that is drunk or anointed?" and a fourth-century B.C.E. lead amulet—discussed by Maas (1944) and Jordan (1992)—bars attack by hostile magic in three forms (lines S–T): "shall not harm me with ointment or with application [so Maas; Jordan suggests 'ghost'] or with drink." As a parallel, Maas cites a second-century B.C.E. curse text from Cnidus: "If he has prepared a *pharmakon* for me, either a drink or an ointment." PGM XXXIV.1–24 mentions an *erōtikon pharmakon* that is either drunk or anointed.

widespread pattern in which wives use love magic as they jockey among their competitors for the support and favor of their husbands.

The correlation between debilitating poisons and love potions is alluded to several times in earlier literary sources, but its social context and significance are most clearly spelled out in Plutarch's "Marital Advice" (*Moralia* 139a):

> Fishing with *pharmaka* is a quick and easy way to catch fish, but it renders them inedible and paltry. In the same way, women who use love potions *(philtra)* and sorcery *(goēteia)* against their husbands, and who gain mastery over them through pleasure, end up living with stunned, senseless, crippled men. The men bewitched[59] by Circe were of no service to her, nor did she have any "use" at all for them after they had become swine and asses. But Odysseus, who kept his senses and behaved prudently, she loved in excess.

The first comparison here is to a type of fishing done by stunning the prey with poison, a method still employed in the Far East. The point is, of course, that by capturing and controlling your husband in this way, you weaken his manliness. This is why Plutarch alludes to the Circe episode in the *Odyssey*, where the ship's crew, once they have been "domesticated" by her magic potions,[60] are no longer of any "use" to Circe, a veiled reference to sexual intercourse.[61] The bottom line of the argument is that using drugs or magic to increase your husband's affection is counterproductive, since it leads paradoxically to a loss in his virility.

Plutarch's advice suggests a real concern that such incidents were occurring in his own day in the second century C.E., and a variety of sources suggest that in the Hellenistic period this concern was shared by other men as well.[62] Sometime in the first or second century B.C.E., for example, a woman set up a curse tablet in the Demeter sanctuary at Cnidus

59. Or perhaps "poisoned" or "drugged"; the Greek participle is *katapharmakeuthentes*.

60. Circe turns the men into *domesticated* animals, not noble, wild ones.

61. The expression used here *(chrēsthai tini)* is probably a euphemism (like Latin *uti familiariter*) for sexual relations with a man. See LSJ s.v. iii 3.

62. See Juvenal 6.610–611, Plutarch *Moralia* 126a, and below for other examples from the Roman period. Roy Kotansky points out in a letter that Josephus *Jewish Antiquities* 25.223–224 and 27.61–64 reports two such accusations in the 30s B.C.E. in the heavily Hellenized court of the Jewish king Herod.

and asked the goddess to punish "the man who accused me of making *pharmaka* for my husband";[63] and in a roughly contemporaneous Greek marriage contract from Egypt Thais promises her betrothed that "she will sleep with no other person except you and that she will not prepare any *pharmaka* against you . . . neither love potions *(philtra)* nor those that cause harm *(kakopoiea)*, neither in your drink nor in your food, nor plot with anyone who is about to do so."[64] So when a Menandrian character says that "a noble character is the one true *philtron* to conquer *(katakratein)* one's husband," we must surely assume that there were other kinds of *philtra* available for the less noble.[65]

There is in fact good evidence that anxiety over wives' using such aphrodisiacs dates back as early as the classical period.[66] The first speech of Antiphon, written in the mid-fifth century B.C.E., deals directly with this issue. One part of this somewhat complicated lawsuit involves a man named Philoneus, who had apparently grown tired of his mistress and was trying to get rid of her by placing her in a brothel. His mistress was convinced by a second woman to give Philoneus an unnamed *pharmakon* to make him affectionate toward her.[67] According to Antiphon's speech for the prosecution, this mistress tampered with the wine as Philoneus was drinking with the husband of this second woman (1.19):

> As she was pouring the wine for the libation, Philoneus' mistress . . . slipped in the *pharmakon*. And at the same time, thinking that she was acting shrewdly, she gave Philoneus a larger dose, imagining,

63. *DT* 4 (= *CTBS* 89). This curse is part of an intriguing cache of thirteen lead tablets all written by or on behalf of women. For bibliography and discussion see Versnel (1991a) 72–73 and (1994).

64. *PSI* 1.42. This papyrus was kindly brought to my attention by Dr. G. Schwendner.

65. Frag. 646 (Kock).

66. Bowra (1944) 147–148 and Kamerbeek (1959) 233 are to my knowledge the only scholars who have examined these passages with an eye toward interpreting the *Trachiniae*. Sealey (1990) 48–49, in his discussion of where and by whom women were tried in Athens, points out the parallels between the chorus' mitigation of Deianeira's guilt (lines 727–728: Deianeira "erred involuntarily") and the acquittal of the women in the Antiphon and *Magna Moralia* passages discussed below. In any event, both of these important texts seem to have fallen out of the current debate and appear nowhere in the most recent commentaries of the play, e.g., Easterling (1968) or Davies (1991).

67. Antiphon 1.14: *philon . . . poiēsai*.

perhaps, that if she gave him more, she would be all the more loved *(mallon philēsomenē)* by him.

As a result of this increased dosage, Philoneus died instantly, while his friend became ill and died twenty days later. Philoneus' mistress, apparently of foreign or servile origin, was summarily tortured and killed for her involvement, but the second woman who advised her to use the *pharmakon* apparently escaped indictment until the trial at which this speech was recited.

The unnamed speaker of Antiphon's speech—the son of Philoneus' friend—argues that this is an open-and-shut case of homicide, but in the course of his pleading he inadvertently reveals that another interpretation of these events was possible and was probably used by the second woman in her defense. For earlier in the speech he tells us that the accused woman's slave could testify that "this woman . . . had contrived to kill our father with *pharmaka* on a previous occasion as well, and that our father caught her red-handed and that she admitted everything—save that her action was aimed not at his death, but at procuring his affections" (1.9.2). We do not know whether this second woman was acquitted or found guilty, but there is a good possibility that if she used this rhetorical strategy in her defense, she may have gone free, for this same argument wins the day in an anecdote preserved by the author of the Aristotelian *Magna Moralia*, where it is adduced as an example of a defense on the grounds of involuntary or accidental homicide:

> For instance, it is said that on one occasion a woman gave a man a *philtron* to drink, and afterward he died from the *philtron*, but she was acquitted on the Areopagus, where they let off the accused woman for no other reason than that she did not do it deliberately. For she gave it to him for affection *(philia)*, but missed her mark; so they decided it was not intentional, because she did not give him the *philtron* with the thought of killing him.[68]

---

68. *Magna Moralia* 16 (= [Arist.] 1188b30–38). This anecdote is regularly used by modern legal scholars to prove the existence of the concept of unintentional homicide in Athenian law of the classical period; see MacDowell (1978) 114–15 (whose translation I use) and Sealey (1990) 48–49. Kamerbeek (1959) 233 points out the verbal similarities between this passage and Hyllus' defense of Deianeira, quoted near the beginning of this section.

In both passages a defense is mounted on the grounds of motive not ignorance; apparently both women knowingly gave their husbands powerful *pharmaka* that killed them. Their culpability lies, therefore, neither in their use of poisons nor in their goal to increase the men's *philia,* but simply in their having misunderstood the precise dosage or power of the poison.

More detailed anecdotes from later Greek literature provide a wider social context for understanding this practice. In his essay "On the Bravery of Women," Plutarch tells the story of Aretaphila, who was accused of *pharmakeia*—poisoning or casting a spell[69]—against her husband, the hated tyrant of Cyrene during the first century c.e. (*Moralia* 256c):

> But when she was apprehended by the proofs, and saw that her preparations for the *pharmakeia* admitted no denial, she confessed, but said that she had prepared no fatal *pharmakeia:* "No, my dear," she said, "my striving is for very important things: your goodwill *(eunoia)* for me, and the repute and influence that I enjoy because of you. It is because of these that I am an object of envy to bad women. It was fear of their *pharmaka* and devices that led me to invent some devices to counteract them. It was foolish and feminine, perhaps, but not deserving of death, unless you as judge decide to put to death, because of love spells *(philtra)* and sorcery *(goēteia),* a woman who yearns for more affection *(pleon . . . phileisthai)* than you are willing to grant her.

We would not be too far off the mark if we imagine that the speech that Plutarch puts here into the mouth of the tyrant's wife is one much like that used by the woman in Antiphon's case to quell the suspicions of her husband after she tried to poison him the first time. It is, moreover, an excellent illustration of the more complicated motivations that lie behind the use of love magic by the wives (like Deianeira) of very powerful men, whose personal reputation and power are closely tied to the goodwill *(eunoia)* that their husband holds for them. Here Aretaphila implies that it was in fact fear for her own social standing which led her to gamble on the use of a potentially lethal type of magic.

69. The term *pharmakeia* in this passage is, like the related word *pharmakon,* ambiguous and can mean either "poisoning" or "bewitching"; see Chapter 1, note 24.

Indeed, outside of the Athenian examples, nearly all of the extant anecdotes about love potions concern famous and powerful men. In addition to Plutarch's anecdote about the tyrant of Cyrene, we have Suetonius' claim that both the emperor Caligula and the poet Lucretius were driven mad and then killed by love potions.[70] The most interesting case, however, concerns the Roman general Lucullus, whose demise was reported by the first-century B.C.E. Roman biographer Nepos:

> Cornelius Nepos says that Lucullus was affected neither by old age or sickness, but rather that he was crippled by drugs (*pharmaka*) given to him by Callisthenes, his freedman. The drugs were given in order that Callisthenes might be loved more (*hōs agapōito mallon*) by him—they were supposed to have that sort of power—but they diverted and overwhelmed Lucullus' mind to such a degree that while he was still alive his brother took charge of his affairs.[71]

One might in this case assume that Lucullus' Greek freedman was motivated by jealousy arising out of an erotic relationship; this may be true, although the verb used here (*agapasthai*) is an impediment to such an argument, as it almost never connotes sexual love.[72] It is perhaps more important to point out that there is here a clearly discernible political dimension to the act: like the wife of a tyrant or king, Callisthenes, a socially inferior freedman, may have feared for his powerful position in the general's retinue—in other words, he had a concern about his personal prestige much like those underlying many of the narratives discussed above, in which wives like Aretaphila or Philoneus' mistress in Antiphon 1 attack their spouses with *pharmaka*.

What, then, are the wider ramifications for our reading of Sophocles' *Women of Trachis?* First and foremost, knowledge of this bit of traditional Greek folklore is of great help in unraveling some ticklish questions about

70. Suetonius *Caligula* 50 and *De poetis* 16 (Rostagni).

71. Cornelius Nepos frag. 52 (Marshall) = Plutarch *Lucullus* 43.1–2.

72. See LSJ I.1, where the basic meanings are "to hold in great affection," "to love," and "to be content with." Joly (1968) 36–41 surveys the various uses of this verb from the classical to the imperial period, stressing that it gradually ousts the verb *philein* as the most popular word for love. This development is discernible in the texts discussed here: Antiphon and [Aristotle] use *philein* and its cognates, while Diodorus Siculus and Plutarch prefer *agapan*.

Deianeira's motivations and about her culpability. If the Athenians in the audience understood that poisons were commonly given in small doses to men as love potions, then her guilt in knowingly employing the centaur's poisonous blood is somewhat mitigated, for Deianeira seems to be using a traditional remedy for lost love in a manner that was not itself illegal in classical Athens.[73] The question of Deianeira's motivation can also be clarified. Her concern is probably one of personal prestige for herself and her children,[74] and not erotic jealousy, although desire might play some role.[75] In fact the main motivation for all her actions is fear—a fear of being ignored or abandoned, a fear that haunts her throughout the play.[76] Indeed, Diodorus' summary of the story confirms our suspicion that Deianeira's erotic passion and jealousy for Heracles were not a standard part of the mythographical tradition: "But Deianeira learned from Lichas of the affection *(philostorgia)* that Heracles had for Iole, and, wishing that she herself might be loved more *(pleon . . . agapasthai)*, she anointed the tunic with the *philtron* that had been given to her by the centaur."[77] The terms used here to describe the emotional ties are once again strangely void of

73. This is clearest in the passage from the *Magna Moralia* discussed above; see MacDowell (1978) 114–116. On the other hand, Philoneus' *pallakē* was executed, and there is a reference to a similar sentence given to a priestess because she made *philtra* for youths (see Chapter 1, note 39), although there is no mention of a murder prosecution in the latter case.

74. Deianeira spells this out clearly to Hyllus very early in the play when she warns that their safety depends on Heracles (83–85). A similar worry apparently leads Phaedra in the *Hippolytus* to leave behind her notorious letter in order to protect the reputation of her children (lines 717–718).

75. For a detailed argument against those who see Deianeira as a lovesick woman filled with sexual jealousy, see Faraone (1994a). In part this misunderstanding of Deianeira springs from modern assumptions that sexual desire is a fundamental part of a good marriage. In ancient Greece, however, there was a greater emphasis on like-mindedness *(homonoia)* and friendship *(philia)*. Xenophon, e.g., says (*Hiero* 3.3) that adultery destroys the *philia* between a husband and wife—he makes no mention of *erōs* or jealousy; and Aristotle *NE* 1161a and 1162a15 describes marriage as a partnership based on *philia*. Cohen (1991a) 98–109 suggests that the core notion of adultery is "a violation of marital *philia* or . . . of the husband's claim to exclusive sexual access to his wife." The later part of his definition applies only to adultery by the wife, for in ancient Greece women had no exclusive sexual claim on their husbands.

76. Brilliantly discussed by Winnington-Ingram (1980) 75–78.

77. Diodorus Siculus 4.38.1. Unfortunately, the oldest extant versions of the myth give no real insight into Deianeira's motivation. March (1987) 49–50 and Davies (1991) discuss Hesiod frag. 25 M-W, which is lacunose at the points where Deianera's emotional state is described.

any erotic sense: Deianeira simply desires to be more loved *(agapasthai)* by her husband.

In fact similarly muted language appears in Sophocles' *Women of Trachis;* in the first mention of the love charm (line 577) Deianeira reports the promise of the dying centaur that if she uses the poison, Heracles will love no other woman more than her (575–576: *mētina sterxai . . . gunaika . . . pleon).* The verb *stergein* here is strikingly devoid of erotic associations, as it is used primarily to describe the love of family members for one another.[78] In a similar way, Hyllus when he defends his mother (quoted at the beginning of this section) describes the love charm as a *stergēma,* perhaps a Sophoclean coinage from the same verb *stergein.* In fact this emphasis on affection and friendship between a man and his wife is typical of the historical anecdotes discussed above. The woman tried and acquitted on the Areopagus claimed that she gave the poison to gain her husband's affection *(philia).* Callisthenes, the freedman of Lucullus, gave his patron the love potion because he wanted to be more loved by him *(agapasthai mallon).* Aretaphila, the wife of the Cyrenean tyrant, speaks not of *erōs* or *pothos,* but rather of losing her husband's *eunoia* and its attendant repute and influence. In nearly all of these situations, moreover, the high social status and personal power of the individual employing the aphrodisiac depend solely on the esteem and goodwill of the victim, usually a powerful king or his counterpart in the microcosm of the Greek family: the male head of the household.

3.3 Narcotics and Knotted Cords: The Subversive Cast of *Philia* Magic

In ancient Greek culture, women and other culturally defined subordinates seem to employ amulets, facial ointments, and potions for very similar goals: to increase the affection or to lessen the anger of a husband or a male superior.[79] Both techniques, moreover, appear to be rooted in traditional

---

In Bacchylides' version (16.25–29) it is the announcement of Iole's arrival as a "sleek wife" *(alochon liparon)* that sets the tragic events in motion, but here, too, Deianeira's emotional state is not revealed.

78. See LSJ s.v.: "seldom of sexual love."

79. This crossover is implicit in the use of the same *logos* (called the "names of Aphrodite") in a *potērion* spell to charm a cup of wine to force someone to love *(philein)* another

female spheres of activity: amulets, rings, and facial ointments are obvious components of a women's adornment, and potions given to men to drink or ointments spread on their bodies or their clothes are part of the traditional Greek role of women as preparers of food, medicine, and clothing.[80] Both technologies also show up in popular protective or healing rites, which were traditionally mastered and passed on by the female members of the family.[81] These *philia* charms, moreover, aim at emotional and endocrinal responses in their male targets that are quite different from the *agōgē* spells and "apple spells," which are clearly designed to provoke mad, erotic lust in their female victims. Erotic magic is, in addition, usually performed from afar and focuses tightly on the name of a single victim, while the imagined effect of *philia* magic seems oddly diffuse. The *philia* amulets, for instance, aim generally at increasing a person's charm to all men and women, and the love potions also seem to be designed to change the victim's mood, friendliness, and affection toward all who come in contact with him. Thus if a wife should successfully perform *philia* magic on her angry husband, she has in fact performed a service for the whole family and perhaps even the whole nieghborhood.

These very clear differences between erotic magic and *philia* magic probably arise from their very different origins: the former, as we have seen, in the arts of cursing, where the precise identity of the target is crucial; and the latter in the arts of healing and protection, where it is in the practitioner's best interest that a magic spell have as diffuse and as universal an effect as possible. But despite the curative stance and the nonviolent

---

(*PGM* VII.385–386) and on a gemstone used for amorous purposes; see Schmidt (1934) 172–173 and Sijpesteijn (1980) 154 no. 154.

80. Compare, e.g., a North African form of magic that involves a prayer addressed to the popular eye shadow kohl, or the widespread belief that women put their menstrual blood and other materials in the food and drink of their husbands. See Janson (1987) 108 (kohl) and 111–112 (tampering with food).

81. See Hanson (1990) 309–311 for a female oral tradition concerned with "women's diseases." Bremmer (1987) 204–206 discusses the traditional belief that old women were knowledgeable about magic. Where we have more detailed testimony, we can see that magical spells are generally disseminated and handed down by two systems: older women pass down an oral tradition to women in their kinship group or neighborhood, while men seem to use written handbooks circulated by marginal and peripatetic men (e.g., friars in Renaissance Italy); see Ruggiero (1993) 171–175 (Renaissance Italy), Ortega (1991) 58–59 (15th- to 17th-cent. Spain), and Pitt-Rivers (1977) 75–77 (modern Andalusia).

quality of these types of *philia* spells, much of the male Greek discourse about them has a distinctly sinister ring. Plutarch, we recall, explicitly cautions brides not to use such devices; and the outcome of Sophocles' *Women of Trachis* can certainly be read, on one level at least, as a cautionary tale along these same general lines. Indeed, this kind of love magic frequently appears in situations that involve what Greek males, at least, would call a worrisome and "unnatural" usurpation of male power, for example Hera's intervention in the *Iliad*, where for a time at least she subverts Zeus's control over the war at Troy. Shocking, too, were the reports (probably circulated by Octavian and his supporters) that Cleopatra controlled both Julius Caesar and Mark Antony with *pharmaka* and sorcery (*goēteia*)[82] and had tried to do so with Octavian, but failed.[83] Thus despite its apparent origins in or affinities with curative or prophylactic techniques, *philia* magic was a source of anxiety for Greek males because it was deployed by social inferiors against their unknowing superiors, most notably by women against their husbands.

This subversive cast to *philia*-producing magic is most strikingly illustrated by a recipe for a magical amulet preserved in the first-century C.E. *Cyranides,* a kind of encyclopedia of amulets; collected under the letter *kappa,* we find a detailed description of a plant, a fish, a rock, and a bird, all of which are described as *kinaidios,* an adjective formed from the Greek noun *kinaidos,* a traditional term of abuse for effeminate males usually translated as "catamite" or "bugger."[84] The *kinaidios* bird is identified as the *iunx* bird, and the well-known refrain from Theocritus' *Idyll* 2 is cited as proof of its efficacy as an aphrodisiac. The *kinaidios* fish and plant, however, have no apparent connection with love magic; taken individually they simply cause a man to become weak and effeminate. At the end of this chapter devoted to *kappa,* there is a detailed recipe for "the first and most

---

82. Plutarch *Antony* 37: "He was not the master of his own faculties, but under the influence of certain drugs *(pharmaka)* or sorcery *(goēteia)*." Compare ibid. 25.4 and 60.1. The *hōs* at *Antony* 37 in Nabor's influential text is the editor's addition (the Loeb translation, which follows Nabor, reads: "*as if* he were under the influence") and does not appear in the manuscripts. I have used Ziegler's revised Teubner text (1971), which is also used by Pelling (1988) as the basis for his recent commentary.

83. Aelian frag. 57 and Suda s.v. *iunx* report that she tried magic on all three Roman leaders but failed in the final attempt; see Johnston (1995) 187 n. 21.

84. Winkler (1990) 46–54.

formidable *kestos* of the great goddess Aphrodite," an amulet that employs each of the four items described as *kinaidios* earlier in the chapter:[85]

> Engrave into the obsidian stone a castrated man with his genitals lying alongside his feet and his hands extended downward, as he gazes at his genitals. And inscribe Aphrodite behind his back . . . turning her face and looking at him. Enclose the "stone" of the *kinaidios*-fish beneath it. And if you do not have one of the "stones" in its head, set a small root from the *kinaidios* plant under it and the left top wing of the *kinaidios* bird, and enclose it in a very flat golden box. And you will place this within a strap *(himas)* of sinew from the body cavity of a falcon to make it soft, sewing it shut along the middle of the strap so that the box is invisible. This is the strap, like the diadem which is seen in paintings and in statues around the head of Aphrodite, which is called the *kestos*. If any male, then, touches the strap, he will not become erect. And if he unwittingly carries it, he will become effeminate. And if he tastes some of the "stone" of the *kinaidios* fish, he will become a complete *kinaidos*, never returning to natural intercourse. And if a woman bears this strap, no man will have sexual intercourse with her, for he will not get erect. The strap measures two fingers wide and five palms long.

The list of effects of this magical strap and the engraved image of a castrated man gazing ruefully at his lost genitals reveal quite graphically that this *kestos* is designed to emasculate men, and that it is probably related only in name to the Homeric *kestos himas,* which Hera does in fact use to kindle desire in her husband.

But even in Homer's tale, Hera ends up sedating Zeus and subverting his political authority, and I propose that we use this startling image of the castrated man as a radical model of sorts for the implied male victim of all the *philia* spells discussed in this chapter, and that we return to the conundrum voiced by Plutarch in his "Marital Advice": Why would sensible wives ever consider using magic devices or potions that might *weaken* their husband's sexual vigor? The explanation lies, I think, in the repeated focus—in the Homeric episode and in many of the recipes for amulets, ointments, and rings—on binding or controlling a man's anger, for in

---

85. *Cyranides* 1.10.49–69; see Waegemann (1987) 195–222 and Montserrat (1996) 149–150 for discussion.

Greek thought, at least, anger is closely linked to the cultural construction of masculinity. This connection is best illustrated in the range of meanings for Greek words for anger. The noun *thumos,* for instance, which eventually gives rise to the handbook rubric "anger-restraint spell" *(thumokato-chon),* derives from the verb *thuein,* "to rage" or "to swell," a verb used to describe swollen river torrents and storm-tossed seas, as well as angry men like Achilles who storm across a battlefield. Consequently, the related noun *thumos* can mean a number of things: "breath," "soul," "heart," "life," "desire," "will," "courage," and "anger"—Hipponax even uses the word *thumos* to refer to an erect phallus![86] Therefore, in the Greek tradition at least, using magic to bind a man's *thumos* not only controls his anger; it also involves a much more diffuse attack on a man's will, courage, and sexual desire—character traits and emotions that are very closely tied to popular notions of masculinity.[87] In a similar manner, although the noun *orgē* primarily means "anger," in its original meaning it apparently indicated "natural impulse" or "propensity" and was closely related to the verb *organ,* which describes the state of a man "swelling with lust."[88] Thus at the base of the two Greek word-groups used to describe anger we see an intrinsic connection between a man swollen with anger and one swollen with sexual desire.

This equation between masculine anger and passion is most visible in the apparently continuous popular Greek discourse—glimpsed only intermittently in our sources—about the close link between "righteous anger" and proper male behavior. We find, for instance, that speakers in the law courts of classical Athens repeatedly describe, display, and boast about their own sometimes violent anger as a way of establishing their credentials as

86. Padel (1992) 30–32 and D. Allen (1999) chap. 2.

87. There may even have been a direct connection between *thumos* and sexual passion, for the words *epithumia,* "desire," and *epithumein,* "to desire," are often treated as synonyms of *erōs* and *eran.* See Dover (1978) 43–44. [Aristotle] *Problems* 953b34–36 asserts that those with excessive black bile "are easily moved to angers *(thumous)* and desires *(epithumias)."* Brandes (1981) discusses a similar connection in Andalusian popular thought between male genitalia, semen, and will.

88. See LSJ s.v. and Stern (1971) 171. The English word "orgasm" is derived from this word-group. My colleague Danielle Allen (1999), working on notions of anger and punishment in Attic oratory and drama, has arrived at similar conclusions about the overlap of sexual passion and anger in the Athenian mind.

"real men" in their community.[89] Indeed, in his *Wasps* Aristophanes uses the perpetually angry chorus of wasps (armed with phallic stingers) as an icon for the old-fashioned courage, virility, and rugged individualism of those Athenians who defeated the Persians.[90] Stoic arguments against the passions also connect anger and sexual desire *(erōs)* in a way that suggests they are addressing a similar widespread popular understanding—at least from the Hellenistic period onward—of the common source of these two passions and their importance to proper male behavior.[91] In sum, when wives or underlings take aim at a man's *thumos,* they are aiming at something more than his anger—something vitally connected with his individuality, his aggressiveness, and his autonomy, something that in a Mediterranean context such as this we might aptly call his *machismo.*

This preoccupation with mollifying angry, passionate men is quite explicit in the Greek discourse on the plants used in love potions. In fact I shall argue below that the unnamed love potions discussed in the previous section, such as the one used by the women in Antiphon's speech, were most probably a narcotic of some kind that sedates a man in progressive stages, beginning with cheerfulness and warm feelings (including sexual arousal) toward his wife or companions, and then—as the dosage increases—moving on to enervation and sleep. This argument directly challenges the assumption of some scholars that these unnamed drugs were very similar to the erection-producing materials discussed in Chapter 1. A pharmacologist has suggested, for instance, that the women in Antiphon's speech adulterated the wine with crushed blister beetles, which contain canthariden, a drug which in small doses causes irritation to the urogenital tract and erection in males, but which in larger doses causes cramping, internal bleeding, and even death.[92] The Greeks were in fact quite aware that erection-producing drugs were irritants and that they could cause pain

---

89. D. Allen (1999) chaps. 2 and 3.

90. Taillardet (1962) 159–160, Reckford (1977) 305–307 (on their sexual agressiveness) and Konstan (1985) 32–34.

91. Nussbaum (1994) 402–483, esp. 409, where she describes the interlocutor in Seneca's *De ira* as a representative of the typical Roman view that anger is a necessary and important part of a soldier's personality and indeed essential to masculine behavior generally.

92. W. Endres *apud* Heitsch (1983) 123–125. The Greeks in the Hellenistic period were apparently aware of the toxic effects of canthariden, but not its aphrodisiac effect; see Scarborough (1979) 73–80.

and harm if overused. Our sources are quite explicit, for example, that *saturion,* one of the most popular herbs of this type, if taken in too large an amount or over too long a period, produces a pathology known as satyriasis, a very painful state of continual erection that in fact prevents sleep.[93]

It would seem, then, that there were two diametrically opposed types of love potions used by or against men in the Greek world: irritants, such as blister beetles and *saturion* (usually self-administered), that were believed to produce erections of greater frequency or longer duration; and narcotics that were sometimes used by wives to soothe their husbands and make them more affectionate and intimate. When used in small doses, the effects of these two types of potion were perhaps difficult to distinguish, but when ingested in larger amounts the irritants induced cramping, pain, and insomnia, while the sedatives made the "victim" drowsy and eventually unconscious. The emotional effects on males would, moreover, presumably have been quite different, with the former producing irritable, phallic men like Aristophanes' chorus of *Wasps,* and the latter mollified emasculated men of the sort that so alarmed Plutarch. The narcotic type of love potion can best be illustrated in the case of wine, which the Greeks believed to be the simplest love potion known to humankind.[94] Indeed, the effect that alcohol has on the amorous inclinations of men is notoriously linked to the amount they drink. Shakespeare sums up the problem most memorably in the second act of *Macbeth,* where Macduff's Porter lists the three most pronounced effects of strong drink on a man: a flushed face, sleep, and "much urine." He cautiously adds sexual arousal as a fourth, noting: "Lechery, sir, it provokes and unprovokes: it provokes the desire but it takes away the performance" (*Macbeth* 2.3). There are in fact several ancient Greek anecdotes about male impotency induced by excessive drinking, but they are mostly concerned with Alexander and his Macedonian cronies.[95] A fragment of Euboulos, the fourth-century B.C.E. comic poet, suggests, how-

93. Gourevitch (1995) 153–154. Pliny *NH* 26.99, discussing *saturion,* describes the effect of increased proximity: "They tell us that sexual desire is aroused if the root is merely held in the hand, a stronger passion, however, if it is taken in dry wine, that rams and he-goats are given it to drink, when they are too sluggish, and that it is given to stallions from Sarmatia, when they are too fatigued in copulation because of prolonged labor."

94. Müller (1980) 134–138.

95. Plutarch *Moralia* 623e and 652d, discussed by Gerber (1988) 43. Micalella (1977) discusses the Hippocratic warning that unmixed wine causes impotence.

ever, that the Athenians in late classical times were also aware of this
contradictory pattern of effects: "Three cups of wine only do I mix for the
temperate—one for health, which they empty first, the second for sexual
passion (erōs) and pleasure, and the third for sleep, which men reputed to
be wise drink up and then go home."[96] An elegiac poem by Euenos is
predicated on a similar hierarchy, in which the debilitating effects of the
wine are linked to the ratio at which it is mixed with water; as one increases the proportion of wine, one again moves from enhanced sexual
capacity to sleep.[97]

This general belief that in small doses a narcotic acts as a stimulant
to lovemaking is reflected elsewhere in ancient Greek lore about herbal
aphrodisiacs.[98] Theophrastus mentions at least three plants—all of them
known narcotics—which were used as mood-enchancers or aphrodisiacs:
oleander, cyclamen, and mandrake. He tells us, for example, that oleander,
when administered with wine, makes a man's temper more gentle and
cheerful (praoteron kai hilarōteron), a description that—for an Aristotelian
like Theophrastus—probably implies a diminution of anger.[99] In the same
section he discusses how the root of the cyclamen plant, when steeped in
wine, makes one drunk and is useful for love potions, and how mandrake is
used as a pain-killer, a cure for insomnia, and also in love potions.[100]

96. Frag. 94 (Kock). It appears that the god Dionysus himself is the speaker here, and that
he condones the first three stages of inebriation, which seem to be a traditional triad; see De
Falco (1935), Hunter (1983) 183–189, and Gerber (1988) 42.

97. Frag. 2 (West); see Gerber (1988). The date of Euenos is problematic; see West (1974)
171.

98. It is in fact a popular and widespread misconception in most cultures. Taberner (1985)
discusses the traditional beliefs that alcohol (120–138), opiates (195–198), and other sedatives
(e.g., 118–120) are powerful aphrodisiacs. According to Taberner, modern clinical tests have
failed to substantiate any of these claims. He suggests two possible explanations for these
beliefs: (1) when used in small or moderate amounts, alcohol and most sedatives relax the
body and reduce social inhibitions about physical contact and sexual intimacy; and (2) in
moderate doses, these same drugs tend to increase the duration of the male erection by
delaying ejaculation. Taberner suggests that this second effect, as it increases the possibility
for the woman's orgasm, could well be perceived by both partners as an enhancement to
sexual congress.

99. HP 9.19.1; see Preus (1988) 87. Nussbaum (1994) 94–95 discusses Aristotle's use of the
word "mildness" (praotēs) for the appropriate virtuous disposition with regard to anger.

100. Cyclamen: HP 9.19.3 (eis philtra); mandrake: HP 9.9.1 (pros philtra); cf. Aristotle De
somno et vigilia 456b31 for further evidence that mandrake was used as a narcotic. Lloyd

Although Theophrastus does not explain why these narcotics have such a range of effects, the analogy with wine suggests that as the dose of the drug increased, so did the sedative and toxic effects. This direct relationship between increasing dosage and the movement from erotic playfulness to death is in fact explicitly documented in Theophrastus' description of yet another narcotic herb, which he calls *struchnos manikos:* "Of this a drachm in weight is given if the victim is to become playful *(paizein)* and think himself a fine fellow, two drachms if he is to go mad and see visions, three drachms if he is to be permanently mad . . . and four if it is to kill him."[101]

Unlike in Theophrastus' discussions of the medicinal properties of herbs, here he or the popular tradition he draws on clearly envisions someone inflicting these effects on another, unknowing person, that is, more like Callisthenes giving a narcotic to Lucullus than like the men who use *saturion* to increase the duration of their erections.[102] And as in the case of mandrake or cyclamen, the beneficial effects come only in the smallest dose, which puts the victim in a cheerful mood—a useful result for a wife with an angry or disaffected husband. Here, however, the middle stages of the sequence are madness, a feature of the love potions that inadvertently deranged and eventually killed Lucullus, Lucretius, and Caligula. In this light, it is perhaps somewhat easier to understand why Callisthenes might have given Lucullus a poison like *struchnos manikos* in hopes of rendering him more affectionate, and why a mistake in the size of the dose would have had such tragic consequences.

The climactic series of effects linked to the increasing doses of *struchnos* is of great interest, as it sets the initial aphrodisiac effect of the drug into a larger scheme in which a larger dose of a narcotic increasingly enervates and subjugates the male victim. This sequence is in fact re-

(1983) 130 discusses its use in ancient Greece for calming quartan fever, spasms, or a suicidal patient. For the use of mandrake as aphrodisiac in antiquity, see Randolph (1905) 501–504.

101. *HP* 9.11.6. There is some confusion about the identity of this plant, but the two likeliest candidates, *Datura stramonium* and *Atropa belladonna,* contain atropine, a drug that in small doses mildly stimulates the nervous system, but in larger doses can produce (in this order) mental disturbances, depression, and death. See Lloyd (1983) 128 and Preus (1988) 86–87.

102. Thus I follow Preus (1988) 86 in describing the male user as a "victim" instead of a "patient," as Hort and others would have it.

flected—in one way or another—in most of the *philia*-producing devices or drugs that have been discussed. (See Table 4.) Most of these devices or potions show or imply a sequence of effects linked to the amount of the dose or—in the case of an amulet—the proximity or duration of its contact. With the smallest dose or briefest exposure, the male victim is rendered more amorous or displays more affection, good humor, and playfulness; but as the dose or exposure is increased, the victim passes into states of weakness, madness, enervation, and eventually death. This idea of sedating "naturally" angry and passionate men is also reflected in the *philia*-producing amulets, which often involve the tying of knots and other techniques that suggest practitioners are binding the anger and lust of their male targets, rather than exacerbavating and irritating their sexual desires, as happens when men eat *saturion*.

Indeed, even though we do not know precisely what the women in Antiphon's speech put in Philoneus' wine, we can see from its place on the chart that it, too, had differing effects, dependent on the amount mixed in the wine: Philoneus, who was given the strongest dose, died on the spot, while the speaker's father was apparently paralyzed for a time and later died. Given the fact that the wives were acquitted on the grounds that they were trying to mix love potions, we must suppose that this unnamed *pharmakon*, when given in a very small dose, would, like mandrake or oleander, probably have had the desired aphrodisiac effect or at least a mildly narcotic one. Thus the range of expected and documented effects of this unknown *pharmakon* is quite similar to that of the narcotics discussed by Theophrastus. There is also a negative argument: in Antiphon's speech, there is no mention that the father, who lived for twenty days after he was struck ill (1.20), suffered the kind of pain or violent cramps that affect men who take overdoses of irritants like *saturion* or canthariden (blister beetles). Certainly we would have expected a seasoned speechwriter like Antiphon to make dramatic use of such details if the man had died a particularly painful death.

In the final analysis, Greek men apparently had mixed reactions to the idea that females and other subordinates used amulets, rings, and potions to manipulate the affections of their male superiors. On the one hand, we have seen that a philosophical author like Plutarch, concerned as he is with the division of mind and body, and generally suspicious of the carnality of the latter, roundly criticizes this use of aphrodisiacs, on the grounds that it

Table 4. Effects of increased doses of *philia* magic

Potion or device	Small dose	Larger dose	Very large dose
Wine according to Euboulos	health (1 glass)	arousal (2 glasses)	sleep (3 glasses)
Wine according to Euenos	—	arousal (mixed 1 to 4)	sleep (stronger)
Mandrake	used in love potions (*philtra*)	painkiller and insomnia cure	paralysis and death
Oleander	makes a male victim more gentle and cheerful	sleep?	paralysis and death
Cyclamen	used in love potions (*philtra*)	intoxication	death?
Unnamed *pharmakon* (Antiphon 1)	makes a male victim more affectionate	immobilizes Philoneus' friend	kills Philoneus immediately
Strychnos manikos	playfulness (1 drach.)	madness: temporary (2 drach.) permanent (3 drach.)	death (4 drach.)
Unnamed *pharmakon* used by Callisthenes	makes male victim more affectionate	drives him mad	eventually kills him
Kestos headband in the *Cyranides*	if touched by male victim, makes him impotent	if carried by male victim, makes him a temporary *kinaidos*	if eaten by male victim, makes him a permanent *kinaidos*

makes men docile and useless like the men who drank Circe's potions. In fact this reaction to love potions is very similar to the philosophers' view of narcotics, especially when they end up in the hands of subordinates. Plato's description, for example, in Socrates' famous fable of the mutiny on the ship of state reveals how underlings might profit from the narcotic effects of mandrake or alcohol (*Republic* 6.488c): "and after binding the well-born shipmaster with mandrake or strong drink or some other intoxicant, they (sc. the sailors) take command of the ship." According to the philosophic tradition, then, love potions attack the mind and therefore represent two different levels of rebellion against the "normal" order of things: by attacking the mind such spells threaten the "natural" superiority of the mind over the body; and when used by social inferiors against men, they jeopardize the superiority and autonomy of the putatively more rational male elites and the social institutions they command. At the heart of this system, of course, is a philosophical (and therefore minority) model of normatively rational and self-controlled masculinity.[103]

On the other hand, a superficially similar and apparently more popular strain of Greek thought treasures the carnality of the male body and accordingly sees male anger and sexual desire as very closely related passions that are crucial components of masculinity. This popular tradition also frets about the subversive use of *philia* magic by subordinates, but for a very different reason: by binding a husband's natural *thumos* a wife unwittingly unmans him, the threat that is so graphically depicted on the obsidian stone that lies at the center of the elaborate *kestos* described earlier: "a castrated man, with his genitals lying alongside his feet and his hands extended downward, gazing at his genitals." Here, of course, the threat does not lie in undermining the controlling power of mind over body, but rather the reverse: the spell will unman the victim by controlling his "natural" anger and passion. It is in the light of such a gruesome image that we can, I think, understand the deeply fearful ending of Sophocles' *Women of Trachis*—with its final presentation of a withered and feminized Heracles[104]—and the urgency of Plutarch's advice to the young brides for in different ways both underscore the anxiety of Greek males over the socially corrosive use of drugs and magic on the men who were supposedly the autonomous rulers of their families and cities.

This "subversive" aspect of love magic—its ability to reverse or at least soften traditional power relations—provides some interesting insight into the perceived roles of men and women in courtship and how desire itself changes them, a topic that I leave for the next chapter. I will, however, close

103. Foucault (1985) and (1986). For another ancient model that privileges a normatively rational and self-controlled female, see section 4.3.

104. Faraone (1994a).

this chapter by discussing an intriguing passage from Xenophon's *Memorabilia* in which Socrates, in the course of his inquiry into the sources and characteristics of friendship *(philia)*, turns to the subject of *philia* magic (2.6.10–11):

CRITOBOULOS: But how will they become friends [*philoi*]?

SOCRATES: They say there are some spells *(epōidas)* that those in the know chant against whomever they wish and thus make them friends *(philous)*, and they say that there are also love spells *(philtra)* that they use against whomever they wish and are thus loved *(philountai)* by them.

CRITOBOULOS: How, then, might we learn them?

SOCRATES: You yourself have heard from Homer the words the Sirens chanted against Odysseus. It begins something like this: "Hither, come hither, renowned Odysseus, great glory of the Achaeans" (*Od.* 12.184).

CRITOBOULOS: You mean that magic spell *(epōidēn)*, Socrates, that the Sirens chanted against other men as well and bound them so that they would not leave them once they had been charmed?

Here the Sirens' song is understood as a kind of *philia* spell which causes men to love *(philein)*, but which also binds them *(katechein)* and prevents them from leaving. The correlation between this song and *philia* magic would, of course, be profoundly disquieting to Greek males, since the fate of the men who went to the Sirens' island was so well known: first pleasure, next enervation, and then paralysis and death, precisely the sequence that we see repeated in the cases discussed above and that Plutarch found so troubling.

4

~

SOME FINAL THOUGHTS ON
HISTORY, GENDER, AND DESIRE

The synchronic sweep of the preceding chapters allows us to see that ancient Greek love charms—and the often nervous male discourse about them—divide easily into two distinct categories, those used primarily to inflame women with *erōs*, and those generally deployed against men to encourage feelings of *philia* toward their wives and other social underlings. But as is true with all synchronic studies, while we gain great insight into the larger patterns of social interaction and the beliefs that underlie them, we tend to ignore or minimize deviations from such patterns, and thereby lose sight of historical developments or other possibly important variations. This chapter seeks to address these concerns squarely, using the preceding discussion as foreground for three separate inquiries designed to encourage further debate. The first is a tentative sketch of the historical development of the most popular and best-documented genre of Greek love magic, the *agōgē* spells, with special focus on the demons and gods to whom practitioners most often appealed in their incantations. Then I turn to the dozen or so glaring exceptions to the otherwise highly gendered taxonomy of Greek love magic, as when Theocritus' Simaetha uses a charm against her boyfriend that is traditionally used by men against women. As I have hinted above, these apparent deviations will permit us to see that the gender of the agents (be they biological males or females) is often socially constructed according to their relationship with their victims. Finally I turn to the related question of how the victims of these spells were constructed as desiring subjects, and how this construction conflicts with the other, better-documented ancient Greek construction of the allegedly voracious, insatiable female, whose sexuality is said to be an omnipresent threat to households and the putatively wise and thoughtful men who oversee them.

4.1 From Aphrodite to the Restless Dead: A Brief History of the *Agōgē* Spell

Ancient Greek love magic does indeed have a history, stretching nearly two millennia, from Homer and the "Nestor's Cup Inscription" to Byzantine hagiography. As we would expect, its development follows a pattern similar to the history of other magical incentations, in which we see an important watershed around the first century B.C.E. At this time many local forms of magical charms—short spells transmitted primarily by oral tradition and practiced widely by amateurs—begin to yield to composite or "international" types of incantation apparently popularized by professional magicians using written collections of charms and elaborate handbooks that provide detailed descriptions of lengthy rituals and incantations.[1] Although our information is usually very sketchy about the Greek traditions antedating these new, polyglot forms of magic, we can make out the contours of some traditional genres of spells, most notably curses and related forms of *agōgē* spells. The latter seem to be intimately connected with the worship of three very different groups of supernatural entities: Aphrodite and her entourage (Eros, Peitho, and so on); Selene the Moon and Helios the Sun; and the denizens of the underworld, both full-fledged gods such as Hermes, Hecate, and Persephone, and lesser powers like demons and unquiet ghosts. Given the thinness of the data, we cannot rule out the possibility that all three forms existed throughout the historical period, but the extant evidence suggests that the first two groups enjoyed early popularity in Greece and were later overshadowed by the third, a shift that was perhaps facilitated by the later assimilation of celestial Selene and chthonian Hecate. It is this last form, with its nocturnal graveside ceremonies, that endures in later antiquity and forms the slim factual core for the popular caricature that we find in Roman poetry of ugly hags digging up corpses with their bare hands and uttering barbarous and frightening incantations.

At its earliest stages, however, love magic in the Greek world appar-

1. Petropoulos (1988), Kotansky (1991a), Furley (1993), and Faraone (1995) and (1996b) 80–97.

ently has much to do with Aphrodite, who in her Cyprian manifestations is closely connected with all aspects of sexuality and love.[2] Her very name comes to mean "sexual intercourse," as do related nouns and verbs like *aphrodisia* and *aphrodizein*. Just as Dionysus is experienced in part as the wild intoxication of wine or dancing, the divinity of Aphrodite seems to have been manifested in intense sexual desire or in the orgasm itself. In the Homeric hymn dedicated to her, she is celebrated in her Cyprian guise as a divine power that can conquer nearly all gods and mortals with lust, and in his *Hippolytus*, Euripides reveals the horrific results of her handiwork. And yet it is intriguing that in Greek myth Aphrodite often eschews direct intervention in human love affairs and provides instead a magical device, such as a *iunx* or a magic apple, for a mortal to use for similar ends. An equivalent in myth might involve Zeus regularly giving his worshippers rain charms or teaching them how to perform rainmaking rituals, instead of simply making it rain himself. To my knowledge the only other god who provides a similar array of magical devices to his protégés is the divine craftsman Hephaestus,[3] whom we would expect to be in precisely this sort of business. Moreover, the magical devices invented by Hephaestus and Aphrodite consistently bear a close resemblance to Near Eastern charms.[4] And this phenomenon, too, makes sense, since the worship of Aphrodite in her Cyprian guise and of Hephaestus in his Lemnian seems to have been borrowed from or heavily influenced by Near Eastern cultures at a very early time.[5]

Rarely do such magical devices work automatically; in most cases, a performative or persuasive ritual (such as an effigy melted on a fire or impaled with pins) is combined with a prayer to the goddess (or occasionally to her son Eros) and an appropriate sacrificial offering. The earliest example is Hera's prayerlike request to Aphrodite in the *kestos himas* episode ("Give me affection and desire . . ."), which, as we saw, is very similar in its simplicity and directness to many pleas found on later amulets or in invocations used with ointment spells, such as the one that asks Aphrodite:

2. This paragraph summarizes Burkert (1985) 152–156.

3. Delcourt (1957); Faraone (1987) and (1992c) 18–35.

4. We have seen the probable Near Eastern influence in the case of the *kestos himas* and the apple charms; see Faraone (1990) 239–243 for more detailed discussion. For similar parallels to Hephaestus' magical statues, see Faraone (1987) and (1992c) 18–35.

5. Burkert (1985) 152–153 (Aphrodite) and 167–168 (Hephaestus).

"Come hither to me, Cypris, every day of my life . . . give me victory, repute, beauty before all men and women."[6] Ovid, talking about the Roman Vinalia, a "Feast of the Prostitutes," reminds us that such prayerful requests to Aphrodite were probably accompanied by simple offerings: "When you have given incense, ask for beauty and popular favor *(favorem)*, ask for charm *(blanditias)* and for witty banter, and give the Mistress the mint she loves along with her myrtle and rushes fitted with roses."[7]

Sometimes prayers to Aphrodite are used without any offerings or magical devices on hand. Herodotus (2.181) preserves the intriguing story of a young Greek woman named Ladike born into the highest aristocratic circles of Cyrene (an important Greek city on the coast of Libya), who was married to her neighbor Amasis, the Egyptian pharaoh. He was, however, unable to consummate the marriage. Upset at his own impotence, he accused her of bewitching him and threatened to have her put to death.[8] Ladike, however, prayed silently to Aphrodite and vowed that if she and Amasis were able to have intercourse that night she would send a beautiful gift to the goddess' temple back home in Cyrene. Amasis was immediately *(autika)* able to make love and thereafter "cherished her mightily."[9] A wish of Aristophanes' Lysistrata (551–556) seems to reflect the same tradition, albeit in an irrepressibly comic fashion: "But if indeed heart-delighting Eros or Aphrodite Cyprogeneia begins to infuse desire down along our breasts and thighs and thus cause a pleasurable tension and a case of 'stiff penisitis' in our husbands, then I believe that one day we will be known among the Greeks as the Peacemakers." As commentators have astutely remarked, the language of traditional prayer here has some close similarities to Hera's prayerful request to Aphrodite in *Iliad* 14.[10] In fact the dactylic rhythm of Lysistrata's appeal and the invocation of Aphrodite in her

6. *SM* 63. See Faraone (1990) 223–224.

7. *Fasti* 4.863–886; see Bömer (1958) 283–284 for comments. Ovid goes on to say (line 874) that the Venus who receives these offerings was transferred to Rome from Eryx, a cult that was itself probably of Phoenician origin.

8. 2.181.3; the verb is *katapharmassein*. His accusation is similar to those discussed in section 3.3.

9. 2.181.4: the verb is *stergein*. For Aphrodite's instantaneous response, see in note 17 below the traditional stress on quick completion of a love spell.

10. Henderson (1987a) ad loc. And here, as with the *kestos himas* in the *Iliad,* the ultimate goal of the Athenian women is not sex, but the manipulation of their husbands' desires for some larger political goal: the end of the Peloponnesian War.

Cyprian aspect seems to recall the Greek tradition of hexametrical love spells that invoke this goddess to come and force another to fall in love.[11]

One might argue, of course, that Ladike, Lysistrata, and the women at the Roman Vinalia are simply praying to a goddess for help and that this activity can hardly be called a magical incantation, but in fact such a distinction is of very little help in understanding ancient Greek magical spells, which are replete with traditional prayers and hymns.[12] An excellent and early illustration of the close intertwining of prayer and incantation is Sappho's *Hymn to Aphrodite*, a deliciously playful rendition of a traditional incantation that begs the goddess to force someone to love the poet "even if she is unwilling."[13] In the middle of this sophisticated literary version, however, the goddess suddenly begins to speak,[14] gently chiding the poet and asking who it is that she, Aphrodite, should "lead" to Sappho this time, with the implication that Sappho's earlier (and repeated) prayers to the goddess were indeed in the realm of *agōgē* spells.[15] Many other details point in the same direction. Toward the end of the hymn, for example, Aphrodite predicts a sudden reversal in Sappho's erotic fortunes (21–24): "For if she flees, quickly *(tacheōs)* she will pursue, and if she refuses gifts, she will give them, and if she will not love, quickly she will love, even if she is unwilling." Scholars have shown that the peculiar syntax of the goddess' promises (conditional clause and predicted reversal),[16] coupled with the strategic repetition of the adverb "quickly"[17] and the empha-

11. See Faraone (1992b), (1995), and (forthcoming) sec. 4.2.

12. Faraone (1991a) 17–20 and Graf (1991) 194.

13. Cameron (1939) 8–10, C. Segal (1974) 148–149, Burnett (1983) 254–255, Petropoulos (1993), and Faraone (1992b) 323–324.

14. For the complex layering of poetic voices and shifting of temporal frames, see Winkler (1990) 167–176.

15. The syntax here at the beginning of line 9 is somewhat obscure, but most modern editors print the infinitive of the verb "to lead."

16. Cameron (1939) 8 cites the long list of such pairs in *PGM* IV.1511–20: "If she is sitting, let her not sit, if she is chatting with someone, let her not chat, if she is gazing at someone, let her not gaze, if she is going to someone, let her not go, if she is out walking, let her not walk, if she is drinking, let her not drink, if she is eating, let her not eat, if she is caressing someone, let her not caress, if she is enjoying some pleasure, let her not enjoy, if she sleeps, let her not sleep, but let her hold in her thoughts me alone, Mr. So-and-so."

17. Cameron (1939) 9 and Petropoulos (1993) 47. Segal (1974) 158 n. 16 notes that the placement of the caesura after the fifth syllable of lines 21 and 23 greatly emphasizes the repetition of the word "quickly." The doubling "now, now, quickly, quickly" is extremely common in erotic magical incantations, e.g., *PGM* I.262; III.35, 85 and 123; IV.973, 1593, and

sis on the victim's unwillingness,[18] clearly echoes the demands of traditional erotic spells.

In the final lines of the hymn, the poet ends her recollection of Aphrodite's past promises and reverts to her own voice (24–28): "Come to me even now and free me from difficult troubles, and bring to perfection *(teleson)* however many things my heart desires you to bring to perfection *(telessai)* for me, and you yourself be a comrade in arms." Sappho's vague reference to "however many things my heart desires" also shows up in later erotic charms,[19] as does her use of the verb "to bring to perfection" *(telein)*, which is a very common feature at the end of the hexametrical erotic spells, such as the one that Aristophanes parodies,[20] or the Hellenistic apple spell discussed in detail in section 2.3: "To whomsoever I give this *pharmakon* . . . may she not stop loving me. O Lady Cyprogeneia, bring to perfection this perfect incantation." Here, too, we have an excellent example of the fruitful combination of a performative incantation (the so-called wish-formula)[21] followed by a prayer to Aphrodite directing her to ensure that the wish will indeed be fulfilled.

This overlap between a performative incantation and a more traditional prayer is best illustrated by the peculiar term in Pindar's description of the *iunx* spell in *Pythian* 4, where Aphrodite "taught Jason skill in prayer charms." The Greek phrase *litas t' epaoidas*, translated here as "prayer charms," is a peculiar combination of two Greek nouns, the first indicating prayers usually in the form of an entreaty (*litai*, from the verb *litomai*, "to beg") and the second denoting incantations (*epaoidai*, literally "songs" [*aoidai*] sung "against" [*epi*] someone).[22] To modern scholars who insist

---

2037. One also finds the adverbs *tacheōs*, (*PGM* I.107; IV.72, 384, and 1265) and *tachista*, "very quickly" (*PGM* IV.2619, 2742, 2757, and 2782).

18. Cameron (1939) 9 and Petropoulos (1993) 47–48 also point out that Aphrodite's ability to lead the unwilling (line 24) appears in a hymn to Aphrodite embedded in an elaborate erotic spell (*PGM* IV.2935).

19. This expression may seem tame in comparison with some of the graphic descriptions quoted in Chapter 2, but they imply the deity's ability to know the thoughts of a mortal—not an uncommon idea in ancient Greece. See, e.g., a late fourth-century B.C.E. love spell: "until she does for Pausanias *whatever Pausanias wants*" (Jordan [1999] no. 3) and a second-century C.E. gold amulet that requests "success with all men, but especially with him, *whomever she herself wishes*" (*GMA* 44).

20. Frag. 29 K-A; see section 2.2.

21. Faraone (1991a) 4–7.

22. E.g., Segal (1986) 20 renders the term as "supplicatory enchantments."

on a firm Frazerian distinction between magic and religion, such a term would undoubtedly appear oxymoronic, but it does in fact capture the peculiar sequence in these texts, where performative charms are followed by prayerful invocations, as in the apple spell quoted above, where the performative language that culminates with a wish ("may she not stop loving me") is followed by an appeal to Cyprogeneia to bring the incantation itself to perfection. And in fact we have already seen that Pindar in his description of Jason's *iunx* spell seems to have this very same tradition in mind, for he, too, echoes the traditional language of love charms in his compressed description of the spell's effects and uses the telltale form of the goddess' name, Cyprogeneia.[23]

Aphrodite was, in short, a powerful goddess, to whom wives, courtesans, suitors, and many others prayed for help in perfecting their love charms. More importantly, she repeatedly appears in myth as the aboriginal source for most of the important rituals discussed earlier, for example, the *kestos himas,* the *iunx,* and the enchanted apple. And in her Cyprian guise she continues to be the focus of this tradition of hexametrical "prayer charms" that survives until the late-antique period. Consider, for example, an *agōgē* ritual in a later handbook that consists solely of a hexametrical hymn that a man is to sing to "the star of Aphrodite" while burning a special incense compounded of the blood of a white dove (a traditional bird of the goddess), untreated myrrh, and parched wormwood.[24] The star in question is, of course, the Morning-Star, or the planet of Venus, so we must imagine an early-morning rite. Although some parts of the hymn itself show Persian influence,[25] its Greek antecedents are clear in the meter, the poetic language, and the content of the final request:[26]

23. See Chapter 2, note 72, and note 11 above.

24. *PGM* IV.2891–2942. The recipe then adds: "And also have the brains of a vulture for the coercion, so that you can make the offering." Graf (1991) 194–195 shows that these "coercive procedures" are not part of the original spell, but rather seem to be used when the regular spell does not work at all or works too slowly.

25. The hymn alludes to an otherwise unknown myth about the Persian goddess Zouro/Rhouzo, who is here equated with Aphrodite because she "led" a male god, Barza ("Shining Light"), into her bed, apparently some syncretization of the Adonis myth, which is also mentioned in the hymn. For discussion, see Röscher s.v. "Zuro."

26. *PGM* IV.2902–39 = *PGM* Hymn 22.

Foam-born Cythereia,[27] mother of gods and men . . . You move holy desire *(himeros)* into the souls of men and you (move) women toward a man,[28] and you make a woman desirable *(erasmion)* to a man for all days. Our Queen, Goddess, come to these incantations *(epaoidais)*, Lady Cyprogeneia . . . and into her, Ms. So-and-so, whom Ms. So-and-so bore, throw the torch of desires *(purson erōtōn)*, with the result that she melt *(takēmenai)* with love for me for all her days.

The hymn ends with the traditional hexametrical coda discussed above: "And you, goddess Cyprogeneia, bring to perfection this perfect incantation." Thus despite the addition of some Persian lore, we can still recognize here, in a recipe of the fourth century C.E., a simple ceremony in which a man sings a hymn to Aphrodite in poetic Greek hexameters while burning an incense appropriate to the goddess (dove's blood and myrrh).

Aphrodite was not the only Greek divinity who oversaw love spells. For instance, there seems to have been another, albeit very poorly documented, tradition of asking Selene (the moon goddess) or Helios (the sun god) to help in similar ways. An ancient commentator on Theocritus' second *Idyll* tells us the following, when he explains why Simaetha in the course of her *agōgē* spell asks Selene to appear:

Pindar says in the poems separate from his *Partheneia* that among lovers *(erastōn)*, men pray for Helios to appear, but women pray for Selene to appear . . . It is common for women who are mastered by passion *(tais erōti katechomenais)* to invoke Selene in prayer, just as even Euripides makes Phaedra (i.e., invoke Selene) in his *Hippolytus Veiled*.[29]

27. This epithet is usually connected with the island Cythera, which like Cyprus had a very old temple to Aphrodite founded by the Phoenicians, and which also claimed to be Aphrodite's birthplace. Morgan (1978) has argued, however, that the title has nothing to do with the island and that it means "Goddess of Desire."

28. This sentence does not make complete sense; I suspect that something has dropped out in the middle that provided for two balanced antitheses, e.g., "You move desire in the souls of men <and in the souls of women, and you move men to women> and women to men."

29. Scholia to Theocritus 2.10b–c, which preserves Pindar frag. 104 (Maehler).

It would seem that this traditional appeal was known to Pindar, although the genre of poems "separate from the *Partheneia*" is still a mystery. The request for a deity to appear is, of course, common in hymns, but with deities like Selene and Helios, one must wonder whether there is in fact a reference to the actual rising of the moon and the sun, as we saw in the prayer to Aphrodite at the rising of the Morning-Star. The nature of these lovers' prayers is, moreover, unclear: did the female *erastēs*—itself a rare, even oxymoronic designation[30]—call on Selene to enact a love charm or did she merely ask her to cure her lovesickness? The scholiast then tells us that in the unsuccessful first version of Euripides' *Hippolytus* the lovesick Phaedra also made or was described as making a prayer asking Selene to appear.[31] Here, too, the same ambiguity abides, as it does, indeed, in Theocritus' poem, where Simaetha invokes two goddesses separately: first she calls on Selene, to whom she later reveals the course of her sad love affair, with presumably some therapeutic effect;[32] and then she invokes Hecate, who seems to be in charge of the magical attack on Delphis.

The scholiast's remark that male *erastai* urge Helios to appear is even more obscure, because he quotes no examples. We may, however, see some very faint traces of something like it in two later Greek spells from Egypt, but in both cases the syncretism of Helios and the Egyptian sun god, Re, make it impossible to assert whether they do indeed reflect this putative Greek tradition. The first is a very fragmentary late Hellenistic recipe for a love spell designed to lead one man into an erotic relationship with another man. It consists of a prayer to the rising sun that contains a complaint reminiscent of Sappho's *Hymn to Aphrodite*: "he does not(?) remain, I am running, but he flees from me."[33] The homosexual orientation of the spell, the appeal to Helios at dawn, and plaintive tone (much like Simaetha when

---

30. Lucian *Philopseudes* 15 describes a woman of ill repute using the odd expression *erastēs gunē*, apparently to point out the incongruity, as women were not typical *erastai*.

31. Nauck p. 491 and Barrett (1964) 19 frag. E. Because the action of the play is set during the day, Barrett thinks that some character described Phaedra's nighttime prayer. Ortega (1991) 76 quotes a Spanish love charm addressed to the moon: "Bright moon, lovely and beautiful as you appear to me, so bright and beautiful may I appear to my man."

32. Segal (1973 and 1974), Griffiths (1979), and Parry (1988).

33. *SM* 72 col. ii.9–25, with the comments of the editors. The parallel with Sappho frag. 1.21 is noted by Winkler (1991) 239 n. 55.

she talks to the moon) all fit the description given above by the scholiast, and seem to attest to a special kind of male homoerotic spell that, like Sappho's *Hymn* and Theocritus' *Idyll* 2, addresses complaints about injustice to a god and seeks redress by some kind of erotic revenge, a theme that also recurs in homoerotic epigrams of the same time period.[34] On the other hand, the spell shows strong Egyptian influence as well, when it invokes Helios "and the gods who rise with him," apparently a standard invocation to the sun god Re and the retinue that accompanies him in his solar boat. The second possible example of a love spell addressed to Helios is a later homoerotic spell that uses a myth about Helios burning Typhon with his rays as a model for the burning action of the spell: "Just as Typhon is the enemy of Helios (sc. and burns him), so too make the heart and soul of Ammoneios himself burn for Serapiakos himself, whom Threpta bore, now, now, quickly, quickly." The spell, however, invokes the Jewish magical deity Adonaios, not Helios, to do the burning, and the myth itself seems to reflect a peculiar and complicated syncresis of Egyptian traditions about the sun god's battles with Seth, and Greek traditions about Apollo (not Helios) and the serpent Typhousa.[35] Given the tattered shape of the first papyrus and the ambiguities in both spells, it seems prudent not to push too hard on this evidence.

These early and apparently independent traditions of erotic spells addressed to Aphrodite, Selene, and (perhaps) Helios give way in the Hellenistic and Roman periods to a third tradition, which seems to arise directly out of the Greek practice of invoking chthonic gods or ghosts to bind their enemies.[36] This later lack of interest in Aphrodite is quite startling. For although she or her magical names continue to appear regularly in connection with *philia*-producing spells, especially rings and amulets, she is virtually absent from later *erōs*-producing charms. Selene, on the other hand, is by the Roman period assimilated to Hecate in her chthonic form as over-

---

34. See section 2.4 on the similarities between some erotic spells and "judicial prayers." The fact that this theme shows up in pederastic poetry from the Hellenistic period onward— see Giacomelli (1980)—suggests that such a form may have had special appeal to gays who used love magic (discussed in the next section).

35. *PGM* XXXIIa. and note 61 below.

36. See, e.g., Petropoulos (1988), Faraone (1991a) 14–15, and Gager *CTBS* p. 81, who discuss the evolution of *defixiones* into erotic spells. Johnston (1999) 127–160 gives a detailed discussion of ghosts as the agents of Greek binding curses.

seer of the restless dead,[37] and is invoked in a number of erotic spells. We do not know precisely when Hecate and Selene were first conjoined in an erotic spell, but they appear side by side without any sense of contradiction in Theocritus' second *Idyll,* an early third-century B.C.E.[38] poem that describes and enacts an *agōgē* ritual set on the Greek island of Cos.[39] Scholars have shown repeatedly that the various ritual actions performed in the spell—especially the burning rites—have close parallels in the *agōgē* spells discussed above in Chapter 2,[40] and they have argued more recently that some features of its form and syntax reflect Theocritus' knowledge of traditional Greek binding charms sung in hexameters.[41] For instance, when Simaetha begins to perform a number of persuasive and performative rituals, she invokes a well-known goddess in dactylic hexameters and asks her to bring her spell to its final goal *(telos):*

> Now I shall bind him down with spells of burnt offerings. Appear in beauty, Selene! For to you, goddess, shall I sing softly, and to Hecate Chthonia, before whom even dogs tremble as she moves among the graves and the dark blood of the dead. Hail, horrible Hecate! Accompany us to our goal *(telos)* and make these *pharmaka* no less potent than those of Circe or Medea or golden-haired Perimede.
>
> You, *iunx,* drag him to my house, my man![42]

On a formal level, Simaetha's request here reflects the traditional closing line of hexametrical incantations that ask Aphrodite Cyprogeneia to

37. See Johnston (1999) 203–249.

38. Hopfner (1939). This assimilation is sometimes subtle; e.g., Lucian *Philops.* 15 describes an elaborate *agōgē* spell which must be performed at the full moon, but which invokes Hecate in her chthonic aspects.

39. See Gow (1952) vol. 1 p. xx, Dover (1971) 96–97, and Sherwin-White (1973) 291 and 321–322.

40. For the parallels in content, see Sutphin (1902), Schweizer (1937), and the commentaries of Gow (1952) and Dover (1971). Graf (1997b) 176–184 suggests that the poet is well informed about all the individual details, but that he has combined them in an unconvincing manner.

41. For the importance of the hexametrical form and the "performative future," see Faraone (1992b and 1995), comparing *inter alii* two third-century B.C.E. hexametrical *katadesmoi.*

42. *Idyll* 2.10–17. I translate Gow's (1952) text.

"perfect this perfect incantation."[43] In this poem, however, Simaetha also invokes Hecate in her most frightening and chthonic aspects, which along with the graveyard setting of her epiphany are, in fact, commonplace in both the binding spells and *agōgē* spells of the Roman era. This common tradition is most evident in lines 44–45 of Theocritus' poem: "Thrice do I make libation, Lady (i.e., Hecate), and thrice cry this: 'Whether it be a woman that lies by him now, or whether man, may he clean forget them as once, men say, Theseus forgot the fair-tressed Ariadne on the island of Dia.'" As we have seen, binding spells aimed at the victims' memory of their spouses or family are part of the oldest extant strata of Greek erotic magic,[44] and continue to appear in a number of later spells of the Roman period.[45]

Many later *agōgē* spells invoke or mention underworld deities, were discovered in a grave or necropolis, or were written on lead, all features suggesting that they developed historically out of the Greek tradition of binding spells *(katadesmoi)*. Until quite recently it was believed that this melding of Greek *katadesmoi* with *agōgē* spells was a peculiar development of Roman North Africa,[46] but Simaetha's hybrid spell performed on the island of Cos and a recently published lead tablet from a graveyard in Chalcidian Acanthus suggest that this combination had occurred in the Aegean before these types of spells were disseminated during the Hellenistic period. This new text, in fact, dates to the late fourth or early third century B.C.E., perhaps a century before Theocritus penned his *Idyll* 2:

> Pausanias puts a binding spell *(katadesmos)* on Sime, daughter of Amphitritos, until she does whatever Pausanias wants. And neither

---

43. Faraone (1992b) 324.

44. See Petropoulos (1988) 218–220 and above, Chapter 2, note 182.

45. To the examples cited by Petropoulos (1988) 220 nn. 30 and 31, add *DT* 266 (2d cent. C.E., Hadrumentum): "I bind the perception, the sagacity, the discernment, and the will of Vettia, whom Optata bore, in order that she may love me, Felix, whom Fructa bore, from this day and this hour, (and) in order that she forget her father, her mother, her own [neighbors], and all her friends, and [other] men on account of her love for me, Felix"; and Audollent (1908) nos. I and II (also 2d cent. C.E., Hadrumentum): "Persephone, bind [name missing] . . . from this day, this hour, so that she forgets her father and mother and all her own . . . of insane [love?] . . . but [burning?] with love and desire [for me?]."

46. So Faraone (1991a) 14–15.

may she be able to touch a victim sacrificed to Athena, nor let
Aphrodite be gracious to her, before Sime embraces Pausanias.[47]

In this tablet we see for the first time the pattern that will become widespread: an incantation that calls itself a "binding spell" *(katadesmos)* but at
the same time acts like an *agōgē* spell, when it ties the cessation of the
binding magic to the arrival of the female victim in the arms of the man
who uses the spell.[48] Theocritus shows a somewhat different combination
of these two traditions: a series of burning rituals that use "persuasive
analogies" to burn Delphis and "draw" him back to Simaetha's door; and a
binding ritual addressed to Hecate of the underworld that binds his memory and affection for "whoever is holding him now."[49]

We can often discern the same Greek ritual that Simaetha uses in the
syncretistic erotic spells of later antiquity. Take, for instance, an elaborate
hymn composed almost entirely in dactylic hexameters and sung in the
context of a simple offering ritual: the recipe directs the user to compound
incense from Ethiopian cumin and goat fat and then burn it on a rooftop
on the thirteenth or fourteenth of the month, presumably while singing the
hymn.[50] The text falls neatly into four sections, each of which begins by
invoking Hecate in various guises.[51] The first and third sections summon
the goddess from a variety of far-off places by her different names, for

47. Jordan (1999) no. 3; Jordan's translation. The reverse binds another person of indeter-
minable gender: "Pausanias puts a binding spell on Ainis (the victim's name can be either
male or female). May s/he neither be able to touch a victim nor may s/he be able to become
possessed of any other good, before Ainis is gracious to Pausanias. May no one other than
Pausanias undo these things" (translation by D. R. Jordan). For the peculiar stipulations in
curses against performing sacrifice, see Versnel (1985).

48. Martinez (1995) uses the term "vow of renunciation" to describe the sorts of curse that
aim to force a desired action, as opposed to conditional curses, which are designed to prevent
an undesired action; see above, section 2.1.

49. Theocritus' debt to *defixiones* was not readily appreciated until the early part of this
century, when an early papyrus text revealed that in three places where Simaetha describes
the general effect of the spell (lines 3, 10, and 159) the manuscript reading of the key verb
katathusomai ("I shall burn") was incorrect and had somehow replaced Theocritus' original
katadēsomai ("I shall bind"). See Schweizer (1937) 16–17 and 2–25.

50. *PGM* IV.2714–83. See Faraone (1997) for full translation and commentary.

51. Three of these sections begin with the invocation "Hither Hecate" *(deur' Hekate)*. The
Greek adverb *(deuro,* "hither") that opens this text is a standard marker of a cletic hymn; see
Chapter 3, note 46.

example, Persephone-Kore, Baubo from Persia, Artemis from Lydia, Ereschigal from Assyria; and a number of other divinities whose names are
unfamiliar to us.[52] The second and fourth sections, however, focus primarily on the request: to drive the female target mad with insomnia so that she
abandons her family and comes immediately to the door of the man singing the hymn.[53]

> *Section 2:* Hither Hecate, goddess of the crossroads, with your fire-
> breathing ghosts, you (i.e. the ghosts) who have got as your allot-
> ment horrible ambushes and irksome haunts, I call you, Hecate,
> with those ghosts who have died before their time and with those of
> the heroes who, hissing wildly holding anger in their hearts,[54] have
> died without wife or children. You (i.e., ghosts) stand above her
> head and take sweet sleep from her. May her eyelids never be closely
> joined with each other, but rather let her be worn out over her
> wakeful thoughts about me. And if she is lying down with another
> man in her embrace, let her push that man away and let her put
> me down into her heart, and let her immediately forsake him and
> quickly come stand near my doors, subdued in her soul for my
> wedding bed.

> *Section 4:* Hither Hecate of the fiery will, I call you to my incanta-
> tions.[55] May she come to my doors driven mad, immediately forget-
> ting the intimacy of her children and parents, and hating the entire
> race of men and women, except this (sc. race?) of mine, Mr. So-and-

52. This type of syncretism is the hallmark of Greek hymnody from the later Hellenistic
period onward, e.g., the so-called Isis Aretalogies, which assimilate that Egyptian goddess
with scores of other goddesses linked to specific cities or lands throughout the eastern
Mediterranean.

53. *PGM* Hymn 21.10–21 (sec. 2) and 27–33 (sec. 4). Note that in section 2 the spell invokes
Hecate's ghostly companions to harass the victim, but in the final section it calls on Hecate
herself to accomplish the spell.

54. The papyrus indicates that the scribe or his source knew an alternate version of the end
of this line. At this point he writes: "Others (sc. read): 'holding the form of winds'" (i.e.,
instead of "holding anger in their hearts").

55. At this point the scribe inserts an unmetrical *voces magicae,* perhaps because he did not
understand that the reference here to *epaoidai* ("incantations") refers self-reflexively to the
hexameters themselves.

so, and may she come and stand near holding me alone, subdued in
her heart by the strong necessity of love.

Here we see a full-fledged example of the later "international style" of
Greek erotic incantation. In the invocations in the first and third sections
of the poem, Hecate is openly assimilated with a wide range of foreign
goddesses, but in the actual requests quoted above we see no foreign elements at all,[56] but rather a very traditional Greek *agōgē* spell that asks
Hecate and the ghosts under her sway to force the female victim to come to
the man who is burning incense on a rooftop at night and chanting this
incantation in Greek hexameters.

4.2 Courtesans, Freedmen, and the
Social Construction of Gender

We have seen that ancient Greek love spells generally fall into two very
distinct categories, one group traditionally used by men in the hope of
instilling uncontrollable passion *(erōs)* in women, and another group usually deployed by women against men in the hope of inducing or regaining
philia and other forms of affection. There are, however, some consistent
exceptions or anomalies to this pattern, especially with regard to the genders of the users and victims of these charms. These anomalies do not,
however, invalidate the taxonomy but rather they reinforce it by revealing
how gender itself is socially constructed in the world of love magic. As we
have already seen in the discussion of *philia*-producing amulets in section
3.1, in the Near East and Greece men and women alike could use these
devices to gain the esteem, friendship, and goodwill of men in positions of
authority. A similar flexibility appears in the case of love potions, although
the variations are not as widespread. Thus, although the great preponder-
ance of evidence—from Sophocles' Deianeira to Plutarch's "Marital Advice"—suggests that wives were the traditional users of love potions and
husbands were invariably their victims, we saw how Callisthenes, Lucullus'
Greek freedman, apparently used the same kind of "wifely" magic when he

---

56. Graf (1991) discusses several other examples in *PGM* in which the invocation portions
of traditional Greek prayers or hymns are loaded with the names of foreign deities and
demons.

found himself in a similar social situation. In the case of *philia*-producing magic, then, it is fairly obvious that the female gender of the user is constructed in such a way as to include socially inferior males, a common feature of ancient Greek culture that feminist scholars and others have noted for some time.[57]

We find a similar set of anomalies when we turn to the gender of those who deploy *erōs*-producing magic, especially in the case of the extant *agōgē* spells, the great majority of which are aimed by men at women. To begin with, there are some obvious exceptions in the literary renditions. The best known, of course, is Sappho's playful *Hymn to Aphrodite*, which, as we saw, clearly reflects the content and language of traditional erotic spells used by men. Similarly, in *Idyll* 7, Theocritus seems to mimic an *agōgē* spell when a character asks Pan, the special patron of homoerotic attraction,[58] to bring a desired boy uninvited into the arms of his friend Aratus.[59] Such anomalies suggest that we might identify a special subset of gay erotic spells, but of the eighty or so extant *agōgē* spells, only four seem designed for same-sex liaisons.[60] Two are used against men: the spell discussed earlier that is designed to "make the heart and soul of Ammoneios . . . burn for Serapiakos,"[61] and another, unpublished Greek spell from Tyre

57. See Richlin (1991) for a survey of the early feminist contributions of Keuls, Hallett, Skinner, and others. Dover (1978) 100–110, Foucault (1985) and (1986), Winkler (1990) 17–44, and Halperin (1990), esp. 266, have discussed in detail how such hierarchical notions play out in classical Athenian homoerotic love as the distinctions between the masculine *erastēs* (the "lover," who penetrates) and the "feminized" *erōmenos* (the "beloved," who is penetrated). Gleason (1990) profitably extends this type of analysis to the culture of the late-antique orators, and Loizos (1994) 71–74 discusses similar modern Greek notions. The Foucauldian tradition has been extremely useful in its close examination of male homosocial interactions, but it has rightly been criticized for its dependence on philosophic texts, its "erasure" of women, and its failure to acknowledge adequately the earlier contributions of feminists and Dover. See, e.g., Katz (1989) 167, Richlin (1991) 173–174, Dean-Jones (1992), Cohen (1992) 150–151, and Foxhall (1994).

58. Borgeaud (1988) 74–75.

59. *Idyll* 7.103–114. Fantuzzi and Maltomini (1996) show how Theocritus parodies erotic spells here, especially those that promise gifts or punishment to a deity or ghost if the wish is not fulfilled, as in, e.g., *PGM* IV.2065–66 and *DT* 270.21.

60. For the total numbers, see Chapter 2, note 9. If we include two other possible, but not probable, examples (see notes 62 and 63 below), the total number is still insignificant.

61. *PGM* XXXIIa, discussed by Montserrat (1996) 196–198. The two examples of the formula "Just as Typhon is the enemy . . . " occur in this spell and *PGM* LXVIII (partially

that uses sleeplessness to a similar end: "May Juvinus lie awake on account of his affection for me, Porphyrios."[62] The two lesbian spells are again typical of the *agōgē* genre, asking that a female victim be burned and whipped until she comes to the woman who performs the spell.[63] Most intriguing is an elaborate spell that closes with the following request (*SM* 42): "Lead Gorgonia, whom Nilogenia bore, to love Sophia, whom Isara bore; burn, set on fire the soul, the heart, the liver, the spirit of burned, inflamed, tortured Gorgonia . . . until she comes to the bath house for the sake of Sophia." The small number of gay *agōgē* spells suggests that they were perhaps unneeded in a culture that allowed males regular access to other males and females to other females. When such spells are used on the same sex, as in the erotic spell that Sophia uses to force Gorgonia to come to the bath, we might presume that for some reason or other Sophia had difficulty coming into direct contact with Gorgonia and resorted to an *agōgē* spell to facilitate such a meeting. Thus we might speculate that the scant handful of extant gay and lesbian spells arise from special circumstances where regular same-sex contact in the home, the gymnasia, or the baths has for some reason been forestalled. In short, the use of erotic magic by gays is probably generated by the social situation, not by any intrinsic feature of homosexual desire, a fact that also explains why the few extant

---

quoted below as no. 3 in note 64). Both come from Hawara, Egypt, date roughly to second–third century c.e., and target a male victim, who is an atypical victim of this type of spell. In Egypt, where Typhon is assimilated to the male god Seth, this myth makes great sense, but in earlier Greek myth (e.g., Hesiod; see Faraone [1988] 281–282 n. 8) Typhon was female, begging the question: was this originally a Greek burning spell designed, as usual, for use against women, which was later adapted in Egypt for use against males, because in Egypt Seth-Typhon is male?

62. Jordan (1985b) 223 n. 16. *DT* 38 (= *SM* 54) may also be a gay spell, as it asks chthonic deities to melt the flesh of Ionikos and see to it that he remembers no one but Annianos, the man who wrote or commissioned the tablet. But elsewhere the spell seems to curse Ionikas outright; the editors' comments in *SM* ad loc. suggest that this spell combines facets of an erotic spell and a judicial binding spell; Jordan (1994b) sees only a judicial curse.

63. See also *PGM* XXXII, a spell by Heraeis aimed at leading *(agein)* Sarapias to her. See Monserrat (1996) 158–159 and Brooten (1996) 77–90 who gives a detailed commentary on both lesbian spells and adds *SM* 37 as a third example. The gender of the beneficiary (named Pantous or Paitous) of that spell has been debated, as the relative pronoun that twice follows it is feminine, but the Pa– prefix clearly indicates a male Egyptian name. I follow the editors of *SM* in assuming that the name is masculine and the pronouns are mistakenly written.

gay *agōgē* spells do not differ either in content or in form from their heterosexual counterparts.

As it turns out, the greatest number of spells that deviate from the usual pattern are those *erōs*-producing spells which women use to attract men. In the corpus of extant spells, there are seven examples[64]—again perhaps an insignificant number, but the fact that later handbook recipes for *agōgē* spells sometimes insert parenthetical variations that allow for male targets suggests that such charms could be adapted for that purpose.[65] Of course this might have been the result of a social change in Greek culture over time. Some scholars plausibly argue, for example, that the growing emancipation of women in Roman Egypt (the source for five of our seven examples) encouraged them to act upon their desires and to usurp male techniques of seduction.[66] But in fact literary evidence beginning in the classical period suggests that one special group of women regularly co-opted these traditionally male forms of magic: courtesans and prostitutes. Socrates' banter with Theodote, for example, hints quite

64. (1) *PGM* XV: "I shall bind you, Nilos . . . with great evils . . . and you will love me, Capitolina . . . You will forget your parents, your children, your friends"; (2) *PGM* XXXIX: ". . . in order that you lead Herakles, whom Taaipis bore, to Allous, (she) whom Alexandria bore, quickly, quickly, now, now"; (3) *PGM* LXVIII: "Just as Typhon is the enemy of Helios (sc. and Helios burns him), so, too, burn the *psuche* and heart of Eutuches, (he) whom Zosime bore, for her Eriea, now, quickly, quickly"; (4) *DT* 270, a second-century C.E. lead tablet from Hadrumentum (lines 5–9): "Let Sextilius, son of Dionysia, not sleep, let him burn in madness . . . let him think of me, Septimia, daughter of Amoena"; (5) *DT* 271 (same provenence as 270): "Lead Urbanus, whom Urbana bore, to Domitiana, whom Candida bore, desiring, maddened, sleepless, in his affection and desire and begging her to come to his house (and) be his lifemate"; (6) *PGM* XVI: "Make Sarapion, whom any womb bore, waste away and melt down in passion for Dioskorous, (she) whom Tikoi bore"; and (7) *PGM* XIXb.1–4, a very fragmentary handbook, includes a *logos* that asks: ". . . might carry Mr. So-and-so to Ms. So-and-so."

65. The male target and female agent are usually parenthetical insertions: *PGM* IV.2087–95: "proceed to wherever this female (or this male) lives and lead her to me, Mr. So-and-so"; XII.24: "make all people *(anthrōpoi)* and all women *(gunaikes)* turn to the desire *(erōs)* of me, Mr. So-and so (or Ms. So-and-so); XIII.238–239: "It leads a woman to a man (or a man to a woman), so that you will be amazed"; and XXXVI.69–70: "It leads men to women and women to men and makes virgins leap out of their houses"—the *logos* that follows, however, mentions only a woman as a victim (80–85): "So too may the *psuche*, the heart of Ms. So-and-so, burn . . . until she comes loving me, Mr. So-and-So."

66. Graf (1997a) 93.

openly that courtesans learned and used such spells on their clients, and the speech of "Just Argument" in Aristophanes likewise suggests that the apple spell—used traditionally by men against women—was also deployed by prostitutes in hopes of gaining new customers.[67] Commentators on the Aristophanic passage regularly note the popular Greek motif of the ballistic apple in seduction scenes, but they are baffled by the inverted genders of the participants, arguing, for instance, that the apple is a way that the girl might suggest to the man that "she would let him try and seduce her."[68] It seems far more likely, however, that prostitutes were thought to perform these apple rituals with the goal of seducing young men directly. Indeed I would stress the importance of the aggressive stance of the whore, who by using a traditionally male form of erotic magic clearly signals her intent to be the seducer herself.

In fact courtesans and prostitutes appear regularly in later literary evidence as users of *agōgē* spells. Lucian, for example, depicts two Athenian *hetairai,* Melitta and Bacchis, swapping tales and recipes. He begins with Melitta's plea for some help in retrieving a lost boyfriend (*Dialogues of the Courtesans* 4.1): "Do you know of any old women of the kind called 'Thessalians'? . . . They sing incantations and they make women desirable *(erasmious)* even if they are entirely despised." Contrast Melitta's goal here of being sexually desirable *(erasmios)* with that of the Athenian housewives (discussed in section 3.2) who give their husbands love potions so that they will be more loved or esteemed *(philēsomenas).* It turns out that Bacchis does not know any "Thessalians," but she describes how a Syrian sorceress living near the Ceramicus once performed a ritual that successfully led back Phanias, a boyfriend who had apparently gone off to live with another woman:

> She hangs these (i.e., the clothes or hairs of the man) from a peg and heats them up with burning sulfur, sprinkling salt over the fire, and says in addition the names of both people, his and yours. Then she brings out from her bosom a *rhombos* and whirls it round while speaking with a rapid tongue some incantation of barbaric and frightening names . . . And not long afterward . . . he came to me led

67. Xenophon *Memorabilia* 3.11.16 (discussed at the beginning of Chapter 1) and Aristophanes *Clouds* 996–997.

68. Dover (1968) ad loc.

(agomenos) by the incantation, despite the fact that his buddies had told him off and Phoebis, the girl with whom he was living, kept pleading with him.

Lucian clearly has in mind some kind of *agōgē* spell that uses fire and the whirling device known as a *rhombos,* similar to many of the later *agōgē* spells in which a man tortures a woman and forces her to come to him.[69] In this incident narrated by Bacchis, however, there is an inversion of the usual gender of the participants: she penetrates the "house" of her boy-friend's current "family" (his new girlfriend and his male drinking companions) and forces him to return to her.

We see a similar reversal of traditional gender roles in an anonymous Hellenistic epigram that takes the form of a dedicatory inscription, which begins:[70] "To you, Cypris (= Aphrodite), is dedicated Niko's *iunx,* which knows how to draw a man from across the sea and youngsters[71] from the women's quarters." Most commentators assume that Niko dedicates this *iunx,* like other dedicators of prized tools, because she is retiring from her successful trade as a sorceress;[72] but it seems unlikely that a professional magician at this period would dedicate a *iunx* to Aphrodite instead of to Hecate or some other, more appropriate patron of the magical arts, and

69. Note the use of the verb *agein* to describe the effect of the spell: Phanias was being "led *(agomenos)* by the incantation." Most scholars—e.g., Dedo (1904) 21 and Abt (1967) 182—understand this to be a description of a *Feuerzauber* (a subset of *agōgē* spells), but Eitrem (1934) 246 suggests (wrongly in my view) a purification ritual.

70. *AP* 5.205, which Gow and Page (1965) 207 date to the Hellenistic period.

71. Following Paton (1916) 231. The Greek word here is *paides,* a gender-neutral term meaning "children" or "youngsters." Gow/Page ad loc. and Alan Cameron (1981) suggest that it refers to young *girls* whom the *iunx* drew out of their bedrooms for the benefit of male clients. Segal (1973) 39–40 suggests that it could mean either. If, as I argue below, Niko was a courtesan, then *paides* here probably refers to young men drawn out of their natal homes (i.e., their mother's bedroom) or more likely out of the bedrooms of other courtesans. Charinus, the jealous young lover of the courtesan Melitta, is called a *pais* (Lucian *Dial. Court.* 4.3). See also *DTA* 78, a binding spell that seeks to prevent a man from "marrying" other women or young men *(paides).*

72. See, e.g., Gow and Page (1965) 207, who apparently understand the word *xeinia* in the final line of the poem—"the guest-gifts *(xeinia)* of the sorceress *(pharmakis)* of Larissa"—to refer to the act of Niko's dedication, when in fact it most probably refers to the *iunx* that a Thessalian witch once gave to Niko as a hospitality gift, the most common meaning of the word *xeinia.*

that she would on her monument boast only of her knowledge of love magic, and not, say, divination, healing rites, and cursing. If we recall, however, that Niko is a popular name for a courtesan and that other hetaerae—like Theodote and Socrates, the sham courtesan—seem to use their own *iunx* spells, it seems far more likely that Niko was a successful courtesan, who often had cause to use the arts of erotic magic, and who at the end of a long career dedicated this valuable device to Aphrodite, the patron goddess of her profession. Moreover, when Niko claims to have used her *iunx* to draw "youngsters" out of the women's quarters, she is probably referring humorously to seducing a wealthy young man who was either still living in his parents' home or, like Bacchis' boyfriend in Lucian's dialogue, had recently been seduced away by another woman and was spending all his time in her bedroom.[73]

The logistical problem faced by both Bacchis and Niko—"leading" or "drawing" a lover out of the house of a rival—is in fact precisely the one faced in Theocritus' second *Idyll*, where Simaetha performs an elaborate erotic spell designed to get her boyfriend Delphis away from *his* new lover. Here, too, the ritual has all the hallmarks of an *agōgē* spell. Simaetha and her servant use a *rhombos*, like the one employed by Lucian's Syrian sorceress, and they burn various household items such as barley, bay leaves, and wax in hopes of burning the victim until he returns. The following lines illustrate the technique:

> Delphis vexed me and I burn this laurel against him. And just as these laurel leaves shriek loudly as they catch fire and suddenly burst into flames and we cannot even see their ashes, so too may Delphis completely consume his flesh in flame!
>
> You, *iunx*, drag him to my house, my man!
>
> Just as I melt this wax with the goddess' help, so too may Delphis of Myndus immediately *(autika)* be melted by passion. And just as this brazen *rhombus* is spun with the help of Aphrodite, so too may he be spun before our gates!
>
> You, *iunx*, drag him to my house, my man![74]

73. At 4.3 Lucian describes the boyfriend as "shut up inside with the girl."

74. *Idyll* 2.23–32, in the order they appear in the manuscript tradition. I leave untranslated the word *rhombos*, which is some kind of spinning device (see the Glossary), and the word

As mentioned earlier, commentors have long noted that nearly all the magical actions performed in this poem find direct parallels in the Greek magical papyri.[75] Scholars have, however, repeatedly failed to realize that the forms of magic used by Simaetha are those traditionally used by *males* to get females out of their homes.

As it turns out, Simaetha's apparent appropriation of traditionally male forms of erotic magic fits in very well with recent analyses of the poem which stress her aggressive, masculine role, especially in the detailed description of her first encounter with Delphis, where she puts herself in the role of the male viewer and makes Delphis the object of her own erotic gaze—a startling co-optation of the traditional male role in homosexual courtship.[76] This equation of Simaetha with an *erastēs* is helpful in showing how in her behavior she inverts traditional Greek expectations of the female as the passive partner in an erotic encounter. In the past, this peculiar independence of Simaetha has also been interpreted as a sign of the increased mobility and power of all women in Hellenistic cities like Alexandria,[77] but I would argue that the character of Simaetha in the second *Idyll* is—like that of the unnamed whore in Aristophanes' *Clouds*, of Niko in the anonymous Hellenistic epigram, or of Lucian's Athenian courtesans—most

---

iunx, which can at this period refer to a bird, a wheel, or more generally to an incantation. Virgil, in his imitation and adaptation of this poem (*Eclogue* 8), replaced the word *iunx* in his refrain with *mea carmina* ("my incantations"), suggesting that he at any rate understood the word *iunx* to mean "incantation"; for discussion see Chapter 1, note 107.

75. See note 40 above.

76. See, e.g., Walker (1980) 97 and esp. Griffiths (1981) 266–67, who notes perceptively that she pursues a fickle but beautiful object of desire, that she is attracted by Delphis' well-oiled and athletic body, and that her lament in the second half of the poem is similar to those of the aging pederasts in *Idylls* 29 and 30. More recently Burton (1995) 43–44 stresses that Simaetha assumes the male initiative in courtship and that she falls in love at first sight, another topos of pederastic infatuation.

77. See, e.g., Gow (1952) 33, Burton (1995) 69–73, and Alan Cameron (1996) 497, who aptly summarizes this widespread view when he describes Simaetha as "a poor but respectable maiden, a virgin until she gave herself to the faithless Delphis." This line of argument depends in large part on two erroneous suppositions: (1) that Simaetha lives in Alexandria, where we do have evidence for the increased financial and social autonomy of women; most scholars, however, think the setting of the poem is the Greek island of Cos (see note 39 above); and (2) that Simaetha's self designation as *aparthenos* must mean that she has been deflowered by Delphis. The word *parthenos*, however, seems to mean "marriageable" without (as Sissa [1990] has shown) any reference to the hymen. This should make us rethink the

probably drawn from a traditional literary stereotype of the courtesan, who was often especially forthright in her pursuit of men and thus was liable to perform the sort of aggressive erotic magic that was otherwise typical of men. In short, Theocritus seems to present Simaetha in a situation that would have been instantly recognizable to his ancient audience as typical of a courtesan who was trying to get a former lover to return to her.

I am not, of course, the first to suggest that Simaetha is a courtesan. Scholars have long noted several peculiarities about her status and life-style.[78] Her name, for instance, is a combination of the Greek words for "monkey" and "goat"—typical of the degrading animal nicknames given to prostitutes—and Aristophanes even mentions a whore named Simaetha (*Acharnians* 525). Theocritus' Simaetha, moreover, seems to be the head of her household, having taken over after the recent death of her mother. There is absolutely no mention of male relatives from her extended family to whom an allegedly deflowered young woman might turn.[79] One could, of course, imagine a series of tragic events that might lead to such a scenario, but Simaetha's domestic situation is strikingly similar to that of fifth-century courtesans like Theodote and Neara, several courtesans in New and Roman Comedy, and many courtesans of the Renaissance, who live together in an all-female "family" headed by an aging courtesan who has "adopted" younger women, passed them off as her own daughters, and taught them the tricks of the trade.[80]

The suspicion that prostitutes and mistresses used aggressive types of *erōs* magic is, moreover, widespread in later Mediterranean and European

---

meaning of *aparthenos*, which in fact appears only one other time in classical Greek (Euripides *Hecuba* 612), where it is used to describe a girl who actually died a virgin, and in doing so lost her marriageability, not her virginity. I suspect that it is used by Simaetha euphemistically (as *gamos*, "marriage," and other words are used in the slang of courtesans' relationships) to indicate the lost opportunity of a steady boyfriend.

78. For what follows, see Gow (1952) ad loc. and Dover (1971) 95–96. Arnott (1996) 60 notes that Simaetha is associated by various details with the lifestyle of a courtesan.

79. Gow (1952) 33 gives a helpful summary: "S. is apparently living alone with a single slave . . . her gossips have been the nurse in a neighbor's house (line 70) and the mother of a girl who plays the flute (line 74)."

80. Theodote lived in her own house with her "mother" (Xenophon *Memorabilia* 3.11.4) and many beautiful servant girls, who—as Keuls (1985) 197 suspects—were probably courtesans in training (no men are mentioned). Neaeira was purchased as a child by a freedwoman named Nicarete (no husband is mentioned), who called her and six other bought girls her

history. The church father John Chrysostom warns married men to stay away from such women because they use magic to alienate men from their wives,[81] an accusation that recurs in Byzantine and medieval sources,[82] in the especially detailed records of the Florentine and Venetian Inquisitors,[83] in the trials and tribulations of the English royal house,[84] and in sixteenth-century Modena and modern Algeria.[85] Such accusations, however, are undoubtedly exaggerated and sometimes even manufactured by the under-standable desire to save face: how else might a family explain such un-seemly behavior by an errant husband or son? The prosecution of such women for erotic magic is further complicated by issues of social class; there is evidence from premodern Italy and Spain, for example, that lower-class prostitutes who allegedly captivated upper-class youths with magic spells were much more frequently and more severely punished by the authorities than were upper-class courtesans who used the same devices.[86] The detailed testimony and court records of the Italian Inquisition show, however, that these accusations were not simply invented out of whole cloth, but were based on a core of historically documented practices. In

"daughters"; [Demosthenes] 59.18–19; see Fantham (1975) 50 n. 9. Alexis frag. 98 seems to describe an older courtesan teaching her girls the tricks of the trade. Konstan (1993) 145–147, Fantham (1975) 58–62, and Rosivach (1998) 145 discuss similar situations in New and Roman comedy, e.g., in Plautus' *Cistellaria*, in which Selenion is the "foster daughter" of a whore. Ruggiero (1993) 26–29, 42–43, and 120 collects several examples of all-female "families" of courtesans working in Renaissance Florence.

81. *PG* 51.216. I thank M. Dickie for this reference.

82. Kazhdam (1995) 78 and Kieckhofer (1991) 31–35 and 44.

83. Brucker (1963) 9–10 and Freedberg (1989) 269 discuss the case of a Florentine mer-chant who in 1375 accused a prostitute of using a doll stuck with iron pins to cause his brother to desert his wife, children, and business. Ruggiero (1993) mentions other accusa-tions in Florence, e.g., a whore who marries a young nobleman and then is prosecuted by his family for using magic (28–31); see also pp. 43–45, 47–48, 93, and 99–103. For Venice, see Ruggerio (1985) 35. Brucker (1963) 11 and 18 mentions a brother and sister accused of using magic to attract customers to their brothel.

84. Kelly (1977) 215 (Alice Perrin's alleged use of magic on Edward III), 219–220, and 226–227 (Eleanor Cobham, mistress to the Duke of Gloucester, accused of using a local witch to force him to divorce his wife and marry her), 235–236 (Henry VIII privately accused Anne Boleyn of using love magic).

85. O'Neil (1987) 99–102 and 111–112 n. 41; Janson (1987) 188.

86. Ruggiero (1993) 28–31 and (1985) 35. O'Neil (1987) 99, 111–112 n. 41, and 113 n. 61.

short, most courtesans and prostitutes seem to know and use erotic magic, although not all of them are prosecuted.[87]

In fact it makes good sense that courtesans in the ancient Greek world would use these types of aggressive "male" magic, once we realize that as a group they are in many ways quite similar to Greek men, especially in their economic autonomy and their education. The successful ones, at least, live in their own houses, provide for their own income, fall in love at first sight, aggressively hunt out their lovers,[88] and employ other types of public stances and gestures that were traditionally limited to males. Even the notorious fact that they were mentioned by name in Athenian oratory and comedy—usually interpreted as contempt for their low status[89]—can be taken as a backhanded compliment, for such treatment was usually reserved for the notable men of the city. Indeed, they were apparently very popular on the comic stage. Athenaeus cites dozens of lost fifth- and fourth-century Attic comedies that reveal how well educated these women were and how they excelled in the games and wit of the symposium, another exclusively male domain.[90] This peculiar "maleness" of prostitutes and courtesans has in fact been noted by ethnographers working on circum-Mediterranean cultures. Prostitutes in Morocco and Algeria, for instance, regularly co-opt aspects of male dress and behavior, as well as certain types of body language that are culturally defined as male—such as sitting or standing with legs spread apart or leaning on doorposts.[91]

The courtesan, in fact, is a doubly interesting case, for depending on her social circumstances at any given time she seems to use both forms of

87. Ruggiero (1985) and (1993).

88. Fantham (1986) 47–48 notes that the courtesans in New Comedy seem to exhibit the violent emotions and actions of the traditional male *erastēs*.

89. Schaps (1977).

90. *Deipnosophistae* 13. Regarding these comic fragments Cooper (1995) 317 n. 39 says aptly: "courtesans are characterized as witty, sophisticated, quick at repartee, and associating with philosophers, poets and politicians." Henry (1985) and Keuls (1985) 187–203 are generally skeptical of this image, the latter (pp. 199–200) pointing out that the dirty jokes they tell are not refined. Perhaps not, but such jokes only strengthen my argument that courtesans co-opted male practices and performance modes.

91. Janson (1987) 179–183.

love magic. If she is in a settled, monogamous relationship with a lover, playing the role of a *pallakē* (mistress or concubine),[92] she is much more likely to use the forms of *philia* magic appropriate for a wife. For instance, when Philoneus' *pallakē* in Antiphon's speech hears that he is going to break off their domestic relationship and send her back to the brothel, she uses a love potion typical of a married woman, because at this point in her life her social role is very similar to that of a wife and she makes similar emotional demands on her partner. She administers the fatal potion because she wishes to be more loved *(mallon philēsomenē)* by him, not because she wants to seduce him. Indeed, even the notorious Neara left one of her live-in lovers "because she had not been loved *(ēgapato)* as she had expected to be."[93] This also seems to be the case of Hermione, the courtesan[94] described in Asclepiades' epigram, who wears an amuletic girdle like the Homeric *kestos himas* to ensure the continued affection of a lover and to control his anger. The best illustration, however, of how a courtesan uses the whole spectrum of love charms is the intriguing passage from Xenophon's *Memorabilia,* quoted at the very beginning of this book, in which Socrates ironically pretends to have used "love potions *(philtra)*, incantations *(epōidai)*, and *iugges*" like a courtesan to attract young men to his ambit and keep them there. As in his more famous allusions to himself as a midwife, Socrates again assimilates himself to a class of "working women" in Athens, although in this case the connection admittedly carries much more baggage with it.[95] In the earlier part of their dialogue, he and Theodote use imagery that identifies each explicitly as an aggressive hunter and lover of young men *(erastēs)*; this imagery is appropriate in the usual homoerotic sense for Socrates as an older male Athenian citizen, but not at first glance for the female Theodote. But here, again, the cultural identifica-

92. Konstan (1993) 138–143 and 145–147 and Rosivach (1998) 144–145, using the evidence in Menander and Roman comedy. The Greek nomenclature is quite fluid, as *hetaira, pallakē,* and *pornē* are often used interchangeably. See Dover (1978) 21, Halperin (1990a) 111–112, and Henry (1985) 2–5.

93. [Demosthenes] 59.35.

94. These terms are used very loosely, but I—following Cairns (1998) 4–6—am not convinced by Alan Cameron (1993) 500–501, who asserts that Hermione is not a *hetaira,* but "simply a flirt, a girl 'who can't say no.'"

95. Satyrus, quoted by Athenaeus 13.584a4–9, also equated philosophers and *hetairai.*

tion of an autonomous courtesan as "male" helps us make better sense of this conversation.

This regular equation of courtesan and autonomous male has obvious parallels in the popular suspicions that powerful queens like Cleopatra used love magic to attract and then control men.[96] Such accusations, of course, have great explanatory value, for how else might a Roman understand why a soldier's soldier like Mark Antony would ignominiously flee the battle of Actium? Aristophanes slyly alludes to this exchange of "natural" roles when the chorus praises Lysistrata for her skillful use of erotic magic (1108–11): "Hail, O most manly *(andreiotatē)* of all woman, since the most powerful of the Greeks have been seized by your *iunx* spell and have come to you en masse." This is figurative language, of course, but quite appropriate for a stage full of Greek men with painful erections. I am, however, most interested in the fact that Lysistrata, in her putative role as expert handler of a *iunx* spell, is called "most manly." This odd understanding of the maleness of women who use erotic magic also shows up in the stereotypical representations of witches in later Roman literature. Horace alludes to the "masculine passion" of Canidia—perhaps a "working girl" herself—who performs an erotic spell,[97] and in Apuleius' *Metamorphoses* the protagonist Lucius is warned that the wife of his host is a "witch of the first order" and "expert in every kind of graveside incantation" who, like a typical male *erastēs*, falls in love at first sight and uses erotic magic to have her way:

> No sooner does she catch sight of some young man of attractive appearance than she is consumed by his charm and immediately directs her eye and her desire at him. She . . . attacks his soul and binds him with everlasting shackles of passionate love . . . I advise you to beware of her, for she is always on fire, and you are quite young and handsome enough to suit her.[98]

96. See the beginning of section 3.3.

97. *Epistle* 5.41: "mascula libido." Scholiasts at *Epode* 3.7–8 identify her as Gratidia, a Neapolitan perfume-seller *(unguentaria)*, and Dedo (1904) 42–44 suggests that the character is based on a real woman. Such *unguentariae* apparently worked as prostitutes as well; see Alan Cameron (1981) 286–287.

98. *Metamorphoses* 2.5, in the translation of Hanson (1989).

Widows—especially in the Roman period, when they seem to have an autonomy similar to that of a courtesan—were also thought to be prone to erastic behavior, as in the scandalous case of Ismenodora, a young widow who "though previously blameless" was influenced by "the divine force of Eros" and began to pursue a younger man of lower social status, eventually kidnapping and marrying him. In doing so she, too, appropriates a traditionally male act of aggression, bridal theft,[99] which, as we have seen, is similar in important ways to the genre of *agōgē* spells. Ismenodora, it would seem, accomplished with her own hands and slaves what other independent women of means attempted with erotic spells.

It would seem, then, that gender is a crucial criterion for the taxonomy and study of ancient Greek love magic, but that the notions of gender that emerge from this material, although they are most often represented in myth and anecdote as isomorphic with biological sex, turn out upon closer inspection to be much wider social constructions based on Greek hierarchical notions of the "femininity" of subordinates or the "masculinity" of the socially autonomous. Thus in the case of *philia*-inducing magic the female gender of the user is constructed vertically according to Greek ideas of social rank and therefore includes males in subservient positions like the freedman Callisthenes. In the erotic magic charms, however, the male gender of the user is constructed according to the relative positions of a protected, ideally chaste victim on the inside and independent agent on the outside, who tries to force his or her victim from their family. As such, *agōgē* spells are equally useful to males, who desire the daughters and wives of other men, and to courtesans and prostitutes, who face similar problems when they need to force rich young men away from their parents or rival girls. By abandoning strict biological definitions of gender, we can also better understand why courtesans seem to use both forms of love magic depending on where they are in the cycle of forming new relationships or maintaining old ones. Thus if they find themselves in a settled long-term relationship, they seem to use the magic favored by wives and other social inferiors—magic designed to curtail the man's anger and to maintain his

99. Ismenodora's story provides the dramatic frame for Plutarch's *Erotikos;* for an engaging recent discussion see Goldhill (1995) 146–161. On the financial power of widows during the Roman period, see Fantham (1995). Pitt-Rivers (1977) 80–84 and Brandes (1981) 226–227 note the popular Andalusian belief that widows take on "the predatory male attitude toward sexual promiscuity" and that their image is often blurred with that of the witch.

affection and esteem. But if they should one day find themselves without a steady lover or in need of winning back a lost one, they can also resort to enchanted apples, like the prostitute in Aristophanes' *Clouds,* or to more elaborate *agōgē* spells, like Simaetha, Niko, or the courtesans in Lucian's fourth *Dialogue of the Courtesans.*

4.3 Aelian's Tortoises and the Representation of the Desiring Subject

In addition to giving us some special insights into how the ancient Greeks constructed gender, the forms of love magic surveyed in this book give us some interesting new vantage points for seeing how males and females were contructed as desiring subjects. We have already seen that the burning, madness, and bodily torture demanded in the erotic spells are also mirrored in Hippocratic and hagiographic descriptions of female adolescent hysteria and in mythographic accounts of the daughters of Proetus, indicating perhaps that these are features of a Greek understanding of female desire. We find a very similar description of this kind of desire—also incited by an erotic spell—in a most unlikely source and pertaining to a most unlikely population. Aelian, an early third-century c.e. natural historian, reports that a species of land tortoise employs a special herb to facilitate sexual intercourse, an act that—according to his source, a Roman senator named Demostratus—is normally a difficult one, for although the male is by nature a "most lustful creature," the female is coy and fearful of mating (*On the Nature of Animals* 15.19):

> This, then, is what the females dread . . . and since they are chaste (*sōphronousai*) and prefer personal safety to pleasure, the males are unable to coax them to the act. And so by some mysterious instinct the males hold out to them an erotic *iunx* spell (*iugga erōtikēn*) and a "banisher of all fear."[100] But it turns out that the *iugges* of an amorous male tortoise are not songs, by Zeus, such as those that Theocritus, the composer of playful herding songs, sings, but a strange herb of which Demostratus admits that neither he nor anyone else knows the name. Apparently the males adorn them-

100. An allusion (quoting half of *Od.* 4.221) to the *pharmakon* used by Helen that makes people forget their fear.

selves with this herb . . . [corruption in the text] . . . At any rate, if
they hold this herb in their mouths, there ensues the exact opposite
to what I have described above, for the male becomes enervated
(thruptetai), while the female, who hitherto was fleeing *(pheugousa)*
now is burning *(phlegomenē)*; she is made wild with frenzy *(exoistratai)* and desires intercourse.

I suspect that this passage tells us far more about the popular understanding of the effects of contemporary love spells than it does about the
actual habits of tortoises, but since both Aristotle and Theophrastus tell
us explicitly that people learn about the properties of herbs by watching
the behavior of wild animals[101] we should perhaps keep an open mind on
the subject. In any event, the moderate character of the female tortoise
(*sōphronousa*: "chaste" or "self-controlled"), who is then burned and made
"wild with frenzy," accords well with the anticipated effects of the *agōgē*
spells discussed earlier. Familiar, too, is the report that the magic charm
enervates the male, a pattern that I traced in my discussions of the social
context of amulets and potions used to induce *philia*. Demostratus, however, tells us that both of these changes occur together in complementary
fashion, for, according to his account, the same herb can reverse the "natural"[102] desires of both genders and thereby invert the normal courtship
roles of the species. The famous orator Polemo, writing about a century
earlier than Aelian, has a similar understanding about the changes that
erotic magic brings about in a female victim. In a thinly veiled diatribe, he
accuses his rival Favorinus of fraudulently claiming knowledge of magic:
"On top of this, he was a charlatan in the magic arts . . . He made men
believe that he could compel women to pursue men the way men pursue
women." [103] Here we have one side of the equation given by Aelian: erotic
magic forces women to pursue the male practitioner in the same manner as
men are ("naturally") predisposed to pursue women.

This idea of "turning tables" or "trading places" is, as we have seen,
implicit in other literary treatments of love magic, most famously in Sap-

---

101. Preus (1988) 83–85.

102. Throughout this section I use "natural" in quotation marks to indicate that this is a
conventional Greek belief; see Winkler (1991) 17–44.

103. Polemo *De physiognomia* in *Scriptores physiognomonici Graeci* 1.160–164. See Gleason
(1995) 7–8 for this translation and a detailed discussion.

pho's *Hymn to Aphrodite* ("for if she flees, quickly she will pursue"), and reminds us that the images of "pursuing" and "fleeing" that we find in both Aelian and Polemo are indeed more commonly applied to homosexual relationships.[104] When applied to heterosexual encounters, however, these descriptions suggest a wholesale change in the "natural" gender role of the victim as a desiring subject. In what follows, I use Aelian's tortoises as a suggestive model for understanding the wider ramifications of the use of love magic in ancient Greek society, for it seems—broadly speaking—that the technologies discussed throughout this book aim in similar ways at reversing the "natural" courtship roles of men and women. Fear of such reversal is, for example, palpable in Plutarch's anxiety about women's using magical spells to enervate and control their otherwise "naturally" passionate male superiors. The flip side of this argument is, of course, that Greek women are "by nature" moderate like Aelian's female tortoises and that erotic magic somehow manages to reverse their traditional antipathy or coolness to sexual intercourse. As we shall see, both of these assumptions— that men are "naturally" wild and sexually aggressive, while women are "naturally" self-controlled—are potentially controversial, since they fly in the face of much scholarly work that sees male fear of the "natural" wildness and promiscuity of women as a primary cause of ancient Greek misogyny.[105] In other words, the representation of the victims in ancient Greek love magic as desiring subjects seems to presuppose an inverted model, according to which it is rampant *male* sexuality that needs to be controlled by chaste and thoughtful women.

This construct of the "naturally" chaste female is by no means limited to the arcana of ancient Greek magical practices or to the later beliefs of Roman-era authors such as Polemo or Aelian. Indeed, the image of aggressive male pursuit of a reluctant young woman is a staple of Greek myth and is often depicted on vase paintings.[106] Hesiod and Alcaeus, moreover, reveal a very early understanding of "normative" female chastity when they discuss the noxious effects of the Dog-Star (Sirius):[107]

104. Giacomelli (1980) for the general pattern.

105. For a good summary, see Cantarella (1987) 24–51 and 66–69, who uses mainly literary evidence.

106. Zeitlin (1986) and Sourvinou-Inwood (1987).

107. Hesiod *Works and Days* 585–588 and Alcaeus, frag 347(a). See Carson (1990) 139–141 for discussion. For the danger of the star's rising, see esp. the simile of the Dog-Star rising at

... then ... women are most lustful *(machlotatai)* and men most weak *(aphaurotatoi)*, since Sirius dries out their head and knees and their skin is withered by the heat. (Hesiod)

Soak your lungs in wine, for the star is on the rise and the season is harsh and all things are thirsty in the heat ... and now women are most polluted *(miarōtatai)* and men are weak *(leptoi)*, since the Dog-Star dries out their head and knees. (Alcaeus)

The controversial textual relation between these two passages need not detain us, as they are both obviously drawn from the same stratum of folk belief.[108] Indeed, it can hardly be a coincidence that the Adonia—a festival of Aphrodite devoted to female sexuality and a traditional lightning rod for male suspicions about female licentiousness—was held at the rising of the Dog-Star.[109] Later authors certainly understand that both Hesiod and Alcaeus are referring explicitly to the Dog-Star's effect on the sexual desire of females and males. Thus Pliny the Elder paraphrases (*Natural History* 22.86): "They have written that when the song of the cicada is most piercing, women are most keen for lust, and men are most sluggish for sexual intercourse."

The author of the Aristotelian *Problems* explains the rationale behind this belief (879a26–28):

QUESTION: Why is it that in summer men are less able to make love but women more able, just as the poet says of the time when the thistle blooms: "Women are most wanton and men most weak"?

ANSWER: Because hot natures collapse in summer by excess of heat, while cold ones flourish. Since a man is hot and dry, but a woman cold and moist, the power of a man is diminished at that time, but a woman's power flourishes.

This discussion, with its focus on physical ability and power, obscures Hesiod's peculiar and asymmetrical emphasis on female lust—Hesiod says

---

Iliad 22.25–32 ("it brings great fever to mortals"). Scholtz (1937) 10–12 discusses dog-sacrifice and other Roman aversive rituals used to ward off agricultural blight at the rising of the Dog-Star.

108. See Nagy (1990) 462–463 and Petropoulos (1994) 17 for a summary of the debate.

109. Winkler (1991) 188–209.

that women become lascivious and the men get weak. It does, however, connect this early understanding of the seasonal effects of hot summer weather to traditional Greek beliefs about the bodily humors, whereby men are generally believed to be "naturally" dry and hot, and females cool and wet.[110] Thus, the Dog-Star, said to "dry out" and "wither" the heads and knees in a period when "all things are thirsty," would logically have the effect of changing normally moist and cool women into dry and hot men, that is, into "naturally" lascivious beings like Aelian's male tortoises. This belief, moreover, fits well with the advice of ancient Greek animal-herders that one must artificially heat up and dry out the females of the herd in order to encourage them to mate,[111] and may explain the great popularity of those *agōgē* spells that aim mainly at burning the female victim (the so-called *empura*). In Chapter 2 I argued that these spells should be understood against the shared ritual background of erotic magic and curses, but here we have indications that fire may have been an especially attractive form of torture precisely because it was connected with this traditional idea that heat has a special effect on the cool and wet female body; thus a burning spell *(empuron)*, like the blistering heat at the rising of the Dog-Star, dries and heats women and thereby alters their "naturally" cool and moist disposition.

The second and third columns of Table 5 summarize my previous conclusions about how ancient Greek love spells construct the genders of

110. There is some difference of opinion about the relative temperatures of males and females. The Hippocratics generally thought that women were moist and hot, whereas Aristotle and the Hippocratic author of *Regimen* 1 thought they were moist and cold, a theory that won out in the end. See Dean-Jones (1991) 134 n. 31. Carson (1990) 137–138 discusses the idea in early Greek philosophy that "dryness" is the soundest human condition and that therefore "a dry soul was wisest and best" (Heraclitus B118 VS) and that consumption of alcohol, on the other hand, makes the soul wet, leading to loss of wisdom and self-control.

111. Aristotle reports that "the warmer the weather" the more eagerly do cows and mares desire to mate (*HA* 572a30-b4). Virgil notes that horse-breeders deny mares water and food to increase their ardor for mating, since this makes them "thirsty for seed" (*Georgics* 2.130 ff.). Pliny (*NH* 10.181) tells us that male horses, dogs, and swine prefer mating in the morning (i.e., when it is cooler and wetter), while the females prefer the afternoon (i.e., when it is hotter and dryer). Similar beliefs may underlie Aelian's advice (*NA* 9.48) concerning the breeding of asses, goats, and horses: rub salt and sodium carbonate on the genitals of the females to produce a greater appetite for sexual intercourse (it makes the females "go mad for" [*epimainontai*] the males).

Table 5. Inversion of the "natural" genders of victims

Type of spell	Agent constructed as:	"Natural" state of victim	Effect of spell on victim
erōs spells	autonomous *erastēs*	moderate, chaste	becomes an *erastēs* temporarily
philia spells	social inferior	angry, passionate	becomes moderate, calm, subordinate

both agent and victim; the final column characterizes the victim's anticipated response. This summary provides some valuable new insights into
the theme of "table-turning" that frequently turns up in love spells and
confirms my suspicions that such spells are often thought, like Aelian's
unnamed herb, to invert the "natural" gender of their victims. Thus males
and other *erastai,* such as courtesans and widows, use erotic magic to
project the burning desire and madness typical of *erastai* onto their female
(or feminized) victims, while in the case of *philia* charms, moderate and
chaste women and other subordinates seek to calm and control their angry
and passionate superiors. We must, of course, be careful not to oversche-
matize the difference, since we have seen, for instance, that *erōs* spells can
also be used to dominate and subordinate the victim, though in a very
different way (see section 2.4).

   This startling flexibility in the victim's constructed gender seems to
presuppose a belief that men and women are essentially of the same species
and partake of the same "nature" *(phusis),* a belief associated with Aristotle
and with later medical writers such as Hierophilus, Soranus, and Galen,[112]
who with the help of human dissection in the Hellenistic and Roman
periods were able to contest the alternate Hippocratic theory that men and
women were essentially two separate species, with different flesh, organs,
and diseases.[113] Soranus, for example, noted that excessively active women,
like professional acrobats and dancers—that is, those who most closely
approximated a physically demanding male lifestyle—often stopped men-
struating, while men who adopted a sedentary lifestyle were thought to
grow soft and effeminate.[114] Likewise, we can explain why the rising Dog-
Star or an erotic magic spell can, for a time at least, turn "naturally" chaste

112. Laquer (1986) 2–5 and Gleason (1990) 380 n. 4.
113. Dean-Jones (1991) 115–117 and Gleason (1990) 390 summarize the differences.
114. Soranus *Gynaeceia* 1.4.22–23. See Gleason (1995) 96–97.

females into *erastai,* since according to this popular Aristotelian model, at least, environment played an important role in the gendering of an individual. In the light of this cultural background, it is not surprising that Greek ideas about the effects of the environment and magic on human sexuality also presuppose Aristotelian, not Hippocratic, ideas about the bodily humors.

It would seem, then, that the practice of ancient Greek love magic reflects a flexible understanding of the gender of the agents of these spells and employs an equally flexible model of the victim as desiring subject, according to which "natural" female chastity and "natural" male lasciviousness can be altered by seasonal and other environmental factors, which like love magic can change and even reverse the "natural" proclivities of both males and females. However, this model of the desiring subject runs counter to recent understandings of a popular misogynist vein of Greek thought—running from Hesiod to Aristotle—that sees women as physically, intellectually, and morally inferior to men.[115] This negative view of women, moreover, is thought to be connected in various ways with a deeply felt Greek male fear that females are "naturally" wild and promiscuous and that it is incumbent upon moderate and self-controlled males—in their roles as fathers, brothers, and husbands—to imprison their womenfolk in the house and control their sexuality so that it can be deployed only in the context of an arranged marriage.[116] My interpretation of ancient Greek love magic suggests, however, the existence of an alternative to this misogynist model—we might call it a misandrist model[117]—according to which men must torture and burn women, because like Aelian's female tortoises women are by nature self-controlled and sedate, and reluctant to have intercourse. Conversely, women use soporific potions and knotted cords to control the anger and the passion—recall the semantic slippage of *thumos* and *orgē*—of their "naturally" wild husbands, because like Aelian's male tortoises they are otherwise passionate and difficult to control.

115. See, e.g., Keuls (1985), Cantarella (1987) 24–51 and 66–69, and Carson (1990).

116. Apparently a common belief of Mediterranean males; see Brandes (1981) for discussion and earlier bibliography and Cohen (1991a) 138–145 for ancient Athens.

117. See Winkler (1991) 139–140 and 205–207 for misandrist discourse as an alternate and subordinated or "muted" ideology that women use in patriarchal cultures to resist, complement, and (at times) even accommodate the dominant ideology. Cohen (1991a) 137–141 (discussing the confused image of women in Greek literature) sees conflicting normative ideals about women, one of praise and another of contempt.

The prevailing orthodoxy of the misogynist model has in fact been eroded in recent years by studies that question the once widespread scholarly consensus that the ancient Greeks—and indeed modern Mediterranean peoples in general—rigorously seclude their women because they fear their wild sexuality. Indeed it now appears that it is wholly inappropriate to apply the word "seclusion" to what is really the "separation" of men and women into two different areas of social activity: for the men, the civic centers such as the agora and the courts; and for the women, their homes, the houses of their neighbors, and some public spaces, such as the local fountain, places for washing clothes, and (in agricultural areas) the family fields.[118] Other studies, moreover, suggest that a cultural belief or ideology about the "natural" inferiority or lasciviousness of women is usually not monolithic, but rather manifests itself in the public "coffeehouse talk" of males that needs to be contrasted with the private or "muted" discourse of women.[119] As a consequence, any apparent social rules connected with these concepts (i.e., we watch over our women because they are lascivious) need to be compared closely with actual social practices,[120] since ideology itself is subject to a wide variety of pressures, especially the wealth and social status of the women.[121]

As it turns out, in this highly segregated Greek world, men are forced to be away from the house for long stretches of time, a situation that actually prevents fathers and brothers from actively patrolling the homestead and policing the activity of women; instead it appears that concerns about female infidelity and impurity are the purview of the women of the family and the neighborhood themselves, who stress ideals of loyalty to family (both natal and marital) above all else.[122] This dependence on emotional ties and female fidelity shows up, in fact, in the *agōgē* spells themselves, for although they do imagine success in terms of physically forcing the woman out of her house, these spells never attempt to remove any physical barriers to the female victim's escape, such as one might expect in

118. Gould (1980) 46–51, Walcot (1984) 37–38, Cohen (1991a) 149–154, and Katz (1992).

119. Winkler (1991) 6–7, using Ardener's terminology.

120. Walcot (1984) 38 and Cohen (1991a) 14–24, making wonderful use of P. Bourdieu's work.

121. Cohen (1991a) 150–151.

122. Cohen (1991a) 155 notes that the neighborhood is probably "one of the major mechanisms for social control" in ancient Athens and Mediterranean cultures generally.

a culture that assumed the "natural" infidelity of its women. Thus, it is striking that with all our evidence for the use of *erōs* magic against women, we have absolutely no hint that erotic-charms were needed to unbar a locked door[123] or to cast sleep on the eyes of a vigilant father or husband— situations that we might expect in a culture that actively secluded its womenfolk. The story of the bewitched Cappadocian nun discussed earlier shows, in fact, how easily the special security and surveillance at a nunnery—with its perpetually locked door and doorkeeper—might foil a traditional *agōgē* spell.

The idea that erotic magic attacks a woman's "natural" loyalty and chastity is, moreover, manifest in classical Greek texts as well. In Euripides' *Hippolytus* Phaedra appears as a paragon of female virtues and an embodiment of the ideals of shame *(aidōs)* and modesty *(sōphrosunē)*, whose "natural" state is then perverted by the attacks of Aphrodite and Eros.[124] Likewise Jason deploys his *iunx* spell in order to strip Medea of the respect *(aidōs)* that she feels for her parents, and many of the extant *agōgē* spells aim specifically at making the woman forget her parents, children, husband, siblings, friends, and neighbors, that is, all those people who make up her moral community. Occasionally the extant erotic spells directly attack a woman's moral character, for instance: "Make her cease from her arrogance, her thoughtfulness *(logismou)*, and her sense of shame *(aischunēs)*."[125] In short, it would appear that the main obstacles to the users of

---

123. See, e.g., *PGM* XII.160–178, a spell used to escape prison, which reads in part: "let the doors be opened for him"; or *PGM* XXXVI.312–320, which is addressed to the door bolt. In his list of things that magicians claim to do, Arnobius lists opening doors and inflaming women with passion separately and far apart as if they were two separate operations *(Adversus gentes* 1.43): ". . . that they send lethal decay to whomever they want, disrupt family relations, open locked doors without a key, reduce mouths to silence, speed or slow down horses in chariot races, send the flames of love and furious desires to housewives."

124. Zeitlin (1985) 52–53. We should remember, moreover, that this play won first prize at Athens, while his earlier attempt at this story, in his lost play *Hippolytus Veiled,* had been widely condemned precisely because the poet had portrayed Phaedra as wildly enamored woman who shamelessly propositions her stepson directly. See Barrett (1964) 11–15 for discussion.

125. *PGM* XVIIa, discussed by Petropoulos (1993) 50 n. 46. See also *PGM* IV.1759–60, where the god Eros, in the midst of an elaborate hexametrical hymn used in an *agōgē* spell, is described as "you, who obscure self-controlled thoughts *(sōphronas logismous)* and instill dark frenzy *(oistron).*"

these spells is not the locked door or the males who guard it, but rather the "natural" modesty of young women and the reverence and loyalty they feel toward their parents, their husbands, or their community. This is not to say, of course, that there were not "easy" women in ancient Greek society, but rather that there was no need to use erotic magic to get at them. Indeed, this is the point of a comic tale about a foolish rich youth who pays an enormous sum to a magician to perform an erotic spell against the wife of another man; but this woman (as Lucian tells us with a grin) was a "lusty and forward lady," who would have come to him anyway, and for a fraction of the sum he paid to the magician.[126]

Finally, although I argue that this misandrist model of the chaste female and the wild, passionate male is widely reflected in the practices of ancient Greek love magic, I do not assert that this model is more pervasive or important than the misogynist, which is widely attested in literary texts, albeit primarily in those surviving from Athens. I would argue instead for the existence of two (perhaps even more) competing constructions of and discourses about gender and desire among the Greeks, some of which privilege the male and others the female. We might characterize these competing ideologies as "opposed" or "complementary" or suggest a hierarchy with the terms "dominant" and "muted,"[127] but such fixed and neat schemata usually run the risk of missing the fluidity in the conceptions of gender that we find regarding love magic. We have noticed, in particular, that courtesans can use either *erōs* magic or *philia* magic depending on their current social situation and needs. Similar indications of what I would call "situational gender"[128] surface in those Greek myths (discussed in section 2.4) in which "naturally" chaste and obedient girls are driven from their homes precisely because it is "*un*natural" for them to remain forever modest and devoted to their parents. Thus in some sense it is correct to say that the misandrist model describes and prescribes a "natural" state for prepubescent and married women, while the misogynist model does the same for adolescent girls, whose wild and lascivious behavior is sanctioned and can even be explained theologically as the result of

126. Lucian *Philopseudes* 13–15; see Winkler (1991) 88 for discussion.

127. Winkler (1991) 139–140 and 205–207.

128. See Foxhall (1994) 134–135 for a general discussion, and Cornwall (1994) for the astonishing fluidity in the gender roles adopted by Brazilian sex-workers.

divine anger or human magic, or medically as the result of excess blood in their systems.

Confusion arises, then, when scholars wrongly argue for a mysogynist model that sees *all* women as wild and lascivious *all* the time, when in fact such behavior seems to be a kind of developmental pathology limited to the period of adolescence, when they must of necessity (according to patriarchal views, at least) make the transition from their roles as daughters in their fathers' home to their new roles as wives and then mothers in the homes of their husbands.[129] Such a flexible and situational model of desire allows Greek women to be both chaste daughters and wives but also desirable and desiring brides, a split that appears elsewhere in our sources, for example, in the treatment of women in Aristophanes' *Lysistrata,* in which the older women are portrayed in positive, rational, and even patriotic roles, while the younger women appear as slaves to their desires for wine and sex who must to be locked up in the Acropolis by Lysistrata.[130] This notion of rabid female passion as a necessary transitional or developmental phase is implicit in the mythological pattern examined at the end of Chapter 2, in which female adolescent hysteria (often eroticized) is to be "cured" by marriage and childbirth. This belief is also implicit in the legal testimony of a fifth-century B.C.E. cuckold, who says that *after* his first child was born he relaxed his scrutiny of his young wife's behavior and gave her the keys to the house[131]—hoping, I would argue, that the all-male jury will see this as an appropriate male response to the end of his wife's "natural" adolescent desire and the beginning of the subsequent period of her equally "natural" moderation. Did he, in fact, keep close scrutiny over her prior to the birth of the first child? We have no way of knowing, of course, since this is precisely the "coffeehouse talk" that we would expect from a Mediterranean male. Indeed, in the narrative of his discovery of his wife's affair we learn that he often worked late in the fields outside the city, and there is no reason to think that his work schedule would have been any different before his child was born.

It is at this point, I think, that the evidence for ancient Greek magic

129. Sourvinou-Inwood (1987) 136–139 and Seaford (1988).

130. Faraone (1997b) 39. The division of female characters by generation and the generally more positive presentation of the older generation is a feature of Old Comedy; see Henderson (1987b).

131. Lysias 1.

gives us a new vantage point. If we look only at the evidence of Aristophanes' *Lysistrata* and the legal testimony of the cuckold in *Lysias* 1—that is: male pronouncements in very public arenas—then we might see evidence that Greek males actively secluded their women, at least during the period of adolescence, when they were "naturally" lascivious. The discourse over *agōgē* spells and the evidence for the extant spells themselves suggest, however, that Medea in Pindar's *Pythian* 4 and the other female victims of these spells would have remained chaste had it not been for the intervention of supernatural magical spells. What we have, in fact, is a richly ambivalent and contradictory collection of competing explanations for what the Greeks perceived as the sometimes violent sexual desire of adolescent females, which was variously explained as a "natural" sign that it was time for young woman to marry and have children, that a god was angry at them or their family and had to be appeased, or that they were the victim of a magical attack. It is extremely interesting, however, that despite this broad disagreement on the aetiology of this desire, all of these sources seem to agree on the symptoms or outward manifestations of it, a fact which suggests, to me at least, that we should consider seriously Winkler's suggestion that the imagined effects of erotic magic might indeed give us a faint and rare glimpse of ancient Greek women as desiring subjects. I would agree wholeheartedly, but I suggest that the Greeks might limit the period of such a snapshot to the brief years of optimum marriageability, to the effects of magic apples and *iunx* spells or to the few weeks each year when the Dog Star rises and brings its own brief period of female lust.

These final forays into history, gender, and desire hopefully offer a richer, fuller, and much more untidy view of ancient Greek love magic than the necessarily overschematized and synchronic studies presented in the preceding two chapters. They also illustrate how a detailed analysis of what at first glance may appear to be a marginal and sometimes unsavory social practice can yield new readings of familiar texts and new insights into important questions about the dynamics of gender and desire in ancient Greek culture. I hope, too, that my closing discussions of the construction and flexibility of Greek concepts of gender have in particular provided an improved method for interpreting the role-reversal that sometimes appears in erotic spells, a phenomenon which has generated the currently popular therapeutic and psychological explanations of Winkler and others. Indeed, by abandoning or at least drastically revising this psychological model of a pathological user of erotic magic—be she Sophocles' Deianeira or the putatively lovesick male users of *agōgē* spells—we might begin to see the techniques of both *philia* charms and erotic spells as Socrates and Theodote seem to see them in the Xenophontic dialogue quoted at the beginning of this book: as unremarkable but useful devices that were probably used widely in ancient Greece by clearheaded individuals for very practical purposes.

GLOSSARY

ABBREVIATIONS

BIBLIOGRAPHY

INDEXES

GLOSSARY

agapan To love, esteem (rarely in an erotic manner)

agapē Love, affection (rarely sexual)

agōgē (pl. *agōgai*) Derived from the verb *agein*, "to lead, to drive," this handbook rubric designates an erotic spell that burns or tortures the victim (usually female) and thereby leads or drives her away from her home and to the practitioner (usually male)

charis In love spells, the outward charm, beauty, or charisma of an attractive person

charitēsion (pl. *charitēsia*) A spell or device (usually an amulet or a facial oil) designed to enhance the *charis* of the person who uses it

defixio (pl. *defixiones*) A binding spell; the Latin term for Greek *katadesmos (see below)*

empuron (pl. *empura*) Literally, an "in-the-fire spell," usually a type of *agōgē (see above)* that burns herbs or *ousia (see below)* in a fire to force the victim (usually female) out by means of sympathetic or persuasive analogy

epaoide (pl. *epaoidai*) The uncontracted, poetic form of the word *epōide (see below)*

epikleros (pl. *epikleroi*) An heiress, who according to Athenian law can be forced to marry a relative if the family lacks a male heir to inherit

epōidē (pl. *epōidai*) An incantation; literally, "a song sung over or against someone"

erastēs (pl. *erastai*) The older, active "lover" who in a male homoerotic relationship pursues and educates his "beloved" *(erōmenos)*

erōmenos (pl. *erōmenoi*)　The younger, passive "beloved" in a male homo-erotic relationship

erōs (pl. *erōtes*)　Sexual love, bodily passion

hetaira (pl. *hetairai*)　Courtesan

iunx (pl. *iugges*)　A salacious bird and a type of *agōgē* spell that involves a sympathetic or persuasive ritual in which this bird is tied to a wheel. It can also mean "erotic spell." In the Roman period it can designate spinning tops and *rhomboi (see below)*.

katadesmos (pl. *katadesmoi*)　A binding spell, usually inscribed on a lead tablet and buried underground or deposited in an underground body of water, such as a well

kestos himas　The magical "perforated strap" that Aphrodite lends to Hera in *Iliad* 14; in later Greek it is designated simply as the *kestos*.

mēlon (pl. *mēla*)　Any fruit that grows on trees; can refer to apples and quinces, but can also designate tree-fruit with stones, such as peaches and apricots

nikētikon (pl. *nikētika*)　Victory spell

oistros　Strong or mad passion

orgē　Disposition, anger, lust

ousia　The "material" or "stuff" used in magical spells, e.g., bits of hair, fingernails, or garment threads used to target the victim

pallakē (pl. *pallakai*)　Mistress

"persuasive analogy"　Stanley Tambiah's useful reformulation of Frazer's concept of sympathetic magic

pharmakon (pl. *pharmaka*)　Drug, poison, or incantation

philein　To love, esteem, be affectionate (generally in a nonerotic manner)

philia　Affection, love (generally of the nonerotic sort), friendship

philtron (pl. *philtra*)　A magic spell that creates *philia;* later used generally to designate any kind of magic spell or potion *philtrokatadesmos* (pl. *philtrokatadesmoi*)   Literally "a binding love spell," a handbook rubric used to designate a hybrid spell (popular in later antiquity) that combines a love spell *(philtron)* with a binding spell *(katadesmos)*

psuche   Commonly designates the human "spirit" or "soul," but in slang and in erotic spells it can also mean "female genitals"

rhombos   A device whirled at the end of a string, used in the worship of Rhea and Dionysus and in love spells; in later Greek equated or confused with the *iunx* wheel and the spinning top

saturion   Derived from the word "satyr," denotes plants in the orchid family thought to produce erections and male lust

stergein   To love, esteem, be affectionate, often of love within the family (never in an erotic manner)

"sympathetic magic"   Frazer's term to explain the widespread belief that, e.g., by destroying an image of your enemy, you can destroy him

sumplegma (pl. *sumplegmata*)   An effigy of a couple entwined in an erotic embrace, used in erotic spells

thumokatochon (pl. *thumokatocha*)   A handbook rubric designating a spell that binds anger *(thumos)*

thumos   Spirit, will, anger

voces magicae   Magical names like "abracadabra" which appear to the uninitiated as gibberish, but which seem to designate the names of powerful supernatural forces

Abbreviations

Abbreviations for oft-cited books, journals, and reference works appear in the list below. Full citations of all other references to modern works can be found in the Bibliography. References to ancient authors and their works are given in full in English or in their common Latin titles as they appear in the *OCD* pp. xvii–liv. For easy access to an excellent translation, the fragments of the Greek lyric poets are cited according to the numbers used by Campbell (1982–93).

ABSA	*Annual of the British School at Athens*
ACM	M. Meyer and R. Smith, eds., *Ancient Christian Magic: Coptic Texts of Ritual Power* (San Francisco 1994)
AEMT	J. F. Borghouts, *Ancient Egyptian Magical Texts* (Leiden 1978)
AJA	*American Journal of Archaeology*
AJP	*American Journal of Philology*
ANRW	*Aufstieg und Niedergang der römischen Welt*
AP	*Palatine Anthology*
APF	*Archiv für Papyrusforschung*
ARW	*Archiv für Religionswissenschaft*
BICS	*Bulletin for the Institute for Classical Studies*
BIFAO	*Bulletin de l'Institut Français d'archéologie orientale*
CA	*Classical Antiquity*
CCC	*Civiltà classica e cristiana*

CJ	*Classical Journal*
CP	*Classical Philology*
CQ	*Classical Quarterly*
CR	*Classical Review*
CRAI	*Comptes rendus de l'Académie des Inscriptions et Belle Lettres*
CTBS	John G. Gager, ed., *Curse Tablets and Binding Spells from the Ancient World* (Oxford 1992)
DT	A. Audollent, *Defixionum tabellae* (Paris 1904)
DTA	R. Wünsch, *Defixionum tabellae atticae, Inscriptiones Graecae* 3.3 (Berlin 1897)
EPRO	Etudes préliminaires aux religions orientales dans l'empire romain
GMA	R. Kotansky, *Greek Magical Amulets: The Inscribed Gold, Silver, Copper, and Bronze Lamellae, Part I: Published Texts of Known Provenance*, Papyrologica Coloniensia 22.1 (Opladen 1994)
GMPT	H. D. Betz, ed., *The Greek Magical Papyri in Translation* (Chicago 1986)
GRBS	*Greek, Roman and Byzantine Studies*
HSCP	*Harvard Studies in Classical Philology*
HThR	*Harvard Theological Review*
ICS	*Illinois Classical Studies*
JHS	*Journal of Hellenic Studies*
JAOI	*Jahreshefte des österreichischen archäologischen Instituts*
JEA	*Journal of Egyptian Archaeology*
JRS	*Journal of Roman Studies*
JWCI	*Journal of the Warburg and Courtauld Institutes*

KAR E. Ebeling, *Keilschrifturkunden aus Assur religiösen Inhalts,* 2 vols. (Leipzig 1915–1923)

LIMC *Lexicon Iconographicum Mythologiae Classicae* (Zurich 1981–)

LSJ Liddell, Scott, Jones et al., eds., *A Greek-English Lexicon*[9] with revised Supplement (Oxford 1996)

OCD S. Hornblower and S. Spawforth, eds., *Oxford Classical Dictionary*[3] (Oxford 1996)

PCPS *Proceedings of the Cambridge Philological Society*

PDM Demotic Egyptian magical papyri as translated by J. Johnson in *GMPT*

PG J.-P. Migne, ed., *Patrologiae Cursus Completus, Series Graeca* (Paris 1857–1936)

PGM K. Preisendanz and A. Henrichs, eds., *Papyri Graecae Magicae: Die griechischen Zauberpapyri*[2] (Stuttgart 1973–74)

PL J.-P. Migne, ed., *Patrologiae Cursus Completus, Series Latina* (Paris 1844–1900)

PP *La parola del passato*

PSI *Pubblicazioni della Società Italiana per la ricerca dei papiri greci e latini in Egitto* (Florence 1912–1979)

QUCC *Quaderni Urbinati di cultura classica*

RA *Revue d' assyriologie et archéologie orientale*

RAC *Reallexikon für Antike und Christentum*

RE A. Pauly and G. Wissowa, eds., *Real-Encyclopädie der classischen Altertumswissenschaft* (Stuttgart 1894–)

REA *Revue des études anciennes*

REG *Revue des études grecques*

RGVV Religionsgeschichtliche Versuch und Vorarbeiten

RhM	*Rheinisches Museum*
SAK	*Studien zur altägyptischen Kultur*
SAOC	Studies in Ancient Oriental Civilization
SEG	*Supplementum Epigraphicum Graecum* (Leiden 1923–)
SGD	D. Jordan, "A Survey of Greek Defixiones not Included in the Special Corpora," *GRBS* 26 (1985) 151–197
SIFC	*Studi italiani di filologia classica*
SMA	C. Bonner, *Studies in Magical Amulets, Chiefly Greco-Egyptian* (Ann Arbor 1955)
SM	R. W. Daniel and F. Maltomini, eds., *Supplementum Magicum*, Papyrologica Coloniensia 16.1 and 2 (Opladen 1990–1992)
SO	*Symbolae Osloenses*
SP	*Studia Papyrologica*
TAPA	*Transactions of the American Philological Association*
Supp. Hell.	H. Lloyd-Jones and P. Parsons, eds., *Supplementum Hellenisticum* (Berlin 1983)
WS	*Wiener Studien*
ZA	*Zeitschrift für Assyriologie*
ZPE	*Zeitschrift für Papyrologie und Epigraphik*

BIBLIOGRAPHY

Abel, E. 1881. *Orphei Lithika.* Berlin.

Abrahamse, D. De F. 1982. "Magic and Sorcery in the Hagiography of the Middle Byzantine Period." *Byzantinische Forschungen* 8:3–17.

Abt, A. 1967. *Die Apologie des Apuleius von Madaura und die antike Zauberei.* Geissen. Originally published 1908.

Abusch, T., et al., eds. 1990. *Lingering over Words: Studies in Ancient Near Eastern Literature in Honor of William L. Moran.* Harvard Semitic Studies 37. Atlanta.

Alexiou, M., and P. Dronke. 1971. "The Lament of Jephta's Daughter: Themes, Traditions, Originality." *Studi Medievali* 12:919–963.

Allen, D. 1999. *The Politics of Punishing in Classical Athens.* Princeton.

Allen, T. W., W. R. Halliday, and E. E. Sikes, eds. 1936. *The Homeric Hymns.* Oxford.

Arnott, W. G. 1996. "The Preoccupations of Theocritus: Structure, Illusive Realism, and Allusive Parody." In Harder, Regtuit, and Wakker (1996) 55–70.

Audollent, A. 1908. "Rapport sur deux fragments de lamelles de plomb avec inscription découverts à Sousse (Tunisie)." *Bulletin archéologique du Comité des Travaux Historiques et Scientiques* 290–296.

Bain, D. 1991. "Six Greek Verbs of Sexual Congress." *CQ* 41: 51–77.

——— 1998. "Salpe's *Paignia:* Athenaeus 322A and Pliny *HN* 28.38." *CQ* 48:262–268.

Barb, A. A. 1950. "The Eagle Stone." *JWCI* 13:316–318.

——— 1963. "The Survival of the Magic Arts." In Momigliano (1963) 100–125.

——— 1971. "Mystery, Myth, and Magic." In Harris (1971) 138–169.

Barrett, W. S. 1964. *Euripides: Hippolytus.* Oxford.

Bates, D. G. 1974. "Normative and Alternate Systems of Marriage among the Yoruk of South-Eastern Turkey." *Anthropological Quarterly* 47:270–287.

Beckh, H. 1895. *Geoponica sive Cassiani Bassi scholastici de re rustica eclogae.* Leipzig.

Benveniste, E. 1973. *Indo-European Language and Society.* Trans. E. Palmer. London.

Bernand, A. 1991. *Sorciers grecs.* Paris.

Besnier, M. 1920. "Récents travaux sur les *defixionum tabellae* latines, 1904–1914." *Rev. Phil.* 44:5–30.

Betz, H. D. 1982. "The Formation of Authoratative Tradition in the Greek Magical Papyri." In Meyers and Sanders (1982) 161–170.

Bevilacqua, G. 1997. "Un incantesimo per odio in una *defixio* di Roma." *ZPE* 117:291–293.

Bierstack, A. 1989. "Local Knowledge, Local History: Geertz and Beyond." In Hunt (1989) 72–74.

Biggs, R. D. 1967. *SA.ZI.GA: Ancient Mesopotamian Potency Incantations.* Locust Valley, N.Y.

Blanchet, M. 1923. "Venus et Mars sur les intailles magiques et autres." *CRAI* 220–234.

Blok, J., and P. Mason, eds. 1987. *Sexual Asymmetry: Studies in Ancient Society.* Amsterdam.

Bobonich, C. 1991. "Persuasion, Compulsion, and Freedom in Plato's *Laws*." *CQ* 41:366–367.

Boll, F. 1910. *Griechischer Liebeszauber aus Aegypten.* Sitzungsberichte der Heidelberger Akademie der Wissenschaften No. 2. Heidelberg.

Bömer, F. 1958. *P. Ovidius Naso: Die Fasten.* Heidelberg.

Bonner, C. 1932a. "Demons in the Bath." In *Studies Presented to F. L. Griffith.* London. Pp. 203–208.

———— 1932b. "Witchcraft in the Lecture Room of Libanius." *TAPA* 66:34–44.

———— 1939. "Hades and the Pomegranate Seed (*Hymn to Demeter* 372–374)." *CR* 53:3–4.

———— 1942. "Two Studies in Syncretistic Amulets." *Proceedings of the American Philosophical Society* 85.5:466–471.

———— 1943. "Techniques of Exorcism." *HTR* 36:41–47.

———— 1949. "KESTOS HIMAS and the Saltire of Aphrodite." *AJP* 70:1–6.

———— 1950. *Studies in Magical Amulets Chiefly Graeco-Egyptian.* University of Michigan Studies, Humanistic Series 49. Ann Arbor.

Borgeaud, P. 1988. *The Cult of Pan in Ancient Greece.* Trans. K. Atlass and J. Redfield. Chicago.

Bowersock, G. W., W. Burkert, and M. C. J. Putnam, eds. 1979. *Arktouros: Hellenic Studies Presented to Bernard M. W. Knox on the Occasion of His 65th Birthday.* Berlin.

Bowra, C. M. 1944. *Sophoclean Tragedy.* Oxford.

Brandes, S. 1981. "Like Wounded Stags: Male Sexual Ideology in an Andalusian Town." In Ortner and Whitehead (1981) 216–239.

Brashear, W. M. 1979. "Ein Berliner Zauberpapyrus." *ZPE* 33:261–278.

———— 1992. "Ein neues Zauberensemble in München." *Studien zur Altägyptischen Kultur* 19:79–109.

———— 1995. "The Greek Magical Papyri: An Introduction and Survey with an Annotated Bibliography." *ANRW* II 18.5:3380–3684.

Braswell, B. K. 1988. *A Commentary on the Fourth Pythian Ode of Pindar*. Berlin.

Brazda, M. K. 1977. *Zur Bedeutung des Apfels in der antiken Kultur*. Diss. Bonn.

Bremmer, J. N. 1984. "Greek Maenidism Reconsidered." *ZPE* 55:267–86.

————, ed. 1987. *Interpretations of Greek Mythology*. London.

Brenk, F. E. 1977. "Aphrodite's Girdle: No Way to Treat a Lady." *Classical Bulletin* 54:17–20.

Broadhead, H. D. 1960. *The Persae of Aeschylus*. Cambridge.

Brooten, B. J. 1996. *Love between Women: Early Christian Responses to Female Homoeroticism*. Chicago.

Brown, C. G. 1991. "The Power of Aphrodite: Bacchylides 17.10." *Mnemosyne* 44:327–335.

Brucker, G. A. 1963. "Sorcery in Early Rennaisance Florence." *Studies in the Renaissance* 10:7–24.

Burian, P., ed. 1985. *Directions in Euripidean Criticism: A Collection of Essays*. Durham, N.C.

Burkert, W. 1983a. *"Homo Necans": The Anthropology of Ancient Greek Sacrificial Ritual and Myth*. Trans. P. Bing. Berkeley.

———— 1983b. "Itinerant Diviners and Magicians: A Neglected Area of Cultural Contact." In Hägg (1983) 111–119.

———— 1985. *Greek Religion*. Trans. J. Raffan. Cambridge, Mass.

———— 1987. "Oriental and Greek Mythology: The Meeting of Parallels." In Bremmer (1987) 10–40.

———— 1992. *The Orientalizing Revolution: Near Eastern Influence on Greek Culture in the Early Archaic Age*. Trans. M. E. Pinder and W. Burkert. Cambridge, Mass.

Burnett, A. P. 1971. *Catastrophe Survived: Euripides' Plays of Mixed Reversal*. Oxford.

———— 1983. *Three Archaic Poets: Archilochus, Alcaeus, Sappho*. London.

Burton, J. B. 1995. *Theocritus' Urban Mimes: Mobility, Gender, and Patronage*. Berkeley.

Bury, J. B. 1886. "*Iunx* in Greek Magic." *JHS* 7:157–159.

Buxton, R. G. A. 1982. *Persuasion in Greek Tragedy*. Cambridge.

Cairns, F. 1998. "Asclepiades and the *Hetairai*." *Eikasmos* 9:1–21.

Cameron, Alan 1981. "Asclepiades' Girlfriends." In Foley (1981) 275–302.

———— 1982. "Strato and Rufinus." *CQ* 32: 163–173.

———— 1993. *The Greek Anthology from Meleager to Planudes*. Oxford.

———— 1996. *Callimachus and His Critics*. Princeton.

Cameron, Archibald. 1939. "Sappho's Prayer to Aphrodite." *HThR* 32: 1–17.

———— 1964. "Sappho and Aphrodite Again." *HThR* 57: 237–239.

Cameron, A., and A. Kuhrt, eds. 1983. *Images of Women in Antiquity*. Detroit.

Campbell, D. 1983. *The Golden Lyre: The Themes of the Greek Lyric Poets*. London.

———— 1982–1993. *Greek Lyric*. 5 vols. Cambridge, Mass.

Campbell, J. K. 1964. *Honour, Family, and Patronage.* Oxford.

Cantarella, E. 1987. *Pandora's Daughters: The Role and Status of Women in Greek and Roman Antiquity.* Trans. M. Fant. Baltimore.

Capponi, F. 1981. "Avifauna e magia." *Latomus* 40:292–301.

Carlini, A., et al., eds. 1978. *Papiri letterari greci.* Biblioteca degli studi classici e orientali 13. Pisa.

Carson, A. 1986. *Eros the Bittersweet.* Princeton.

——— 1990. "Putting Her in Her Place: Woman, Dirt, and Desire." In Halperin, Winkler, and Zeitlin (1990) 135–169.

Cartledge, P., P. Millett, and S. von Reden, eds. 1998. *Kosmos: Essays in Order, Conflict, and Community in Classical Athens.* Cambridge.

Caven, B. 1990. *Dionysius I.* New Haven.

Clogan, P. M., ed. 1976. *Studies in Medieval and Renaissance Culture.* Cambridge.

Cohen, D. 1989. "Seclusion, Separation, and the Status of Women in Classical Athens." *Greece and Rome* 36:3–15.

——— 1991a. *Law, Sexuality, and Society: The Enforcement of Morals in Classical Athens.* Cambridge.

——— 1991b. "New Legal History." *Rechtshistorisches Journal* 10:7–39.

——— 1992. "Review Article: Sex, Gender, and Sexuality in Ancient Greece." *CP* 87:145–160.

Cohen, D., and R. Saller. 1994. "Foucault on Sexuality in Greco-Roman Antiquity." In Goldstein (1994) 35–59.

Connor, W. R. 1984. *Thucydides.* Princeton.

Cook, A. B. 1914. *Zeus: A Study in Ancient Religion.* Vol 1. Cambridge.

——— 1925. *Zeus: A Study in Ancient Religion.* Vol 2. Cambridge.

Cooper, C. 1995. "Hyperides and the Trial of Phryne." *Phoenix* 49:303–318.

Cornwall, A. 1994. "Gendered Identities and Gender Ambiguity among *Travestis* in Salvador, Brazil." In Cornwall and Lindisfarne (1994) 111–132.

Cornwall, A., and N. Lindisfarne, eds. 1994. *Dislocating Masculinity.* London.

Craik, E. M., ed. 1990. *Owls to Athens: Essays on Classical Subjects Presented to Sir Kenneth Dover.* Oxford.

Cunliffe, B. W., ed. 1988. *The Temple of Sulis Minerva at Bath.* Vol. 2: *Finds from the Sacred Spring.* Oxford.

Cunningham, I. C. 1971. *Herodas Mimiambi.* Oxford.

Cyrino, M. S. 1995. *In Pandora's Jar: Lovesickness in Early Greek Poetry.* Lanham, Md.

Daniel, R. 1975. "Two Love Charms." *ZPE* 19:249–264.

——— 1991. *Two Greek Magical Papyri in the National Museum of Antiquities in Leiden.* Papyrologica Coloniensia 19. Opladen.

Davies, M. 1989. "Deianeira and Medea: A Footnote to the Pre-History of Two Myths." *Mnemosyne* 42:469–472.

———— 1991. *Sophocles: Trachiniae.* Oxford.

Dean-Jones, L. 1989. "Menstrual Bleeding according to the Hippocratics and Aristotle." *TAPA* 119:177–191.

———— 1991. "The Cultural Construct of the Female Body in Classical Greek Science." In Pomeroy (1991) 111–137.

———— 1992. "The Politics of Pleasure: Female Sexual Appetite in the Hippocratic Corpus." *Helios* 19:72–91.

———— 1994. *Women's Bodies in Classical Greek Science.* Oxford.

Dedo, R. 1904. *De antiquorum superstitione amatoria.* Gryphia.

de Falco, V. 1935. "Un frammento di Eubulo." *Dionisio* 5:73–77.

Degani, E. 1962. "Hipponactea" *Helikon* 2:627–629.

De la Genière, J. 1958. "Une roue à oiseau du Cabinet des Medailles." *REA* 60:27–55.

Delatte, A., and P. Derchain. 1964. *Les intailles magiques gréco-égyptiennes.* Paris.

Delcourt, M. 1957. *Héphaistos ou la légende du magicien.* Bibliothèque de la Faculté de Philosophie et Lettres de l'Université de Liège 146. Paris.

Denich, B. S. 1974. "Sex and Power in the Balkans." In Rosaldo and Lamphere (1974) 243–262.

Derenne, E. 1930. *Les procès d'impiété intentés aux philosophes a Athènes.* Liège.

Detienne, M. 1979. *Dionysos Slain.* Trans. M. Muellner and L. Muellner. Baltimore.

Dickie, M. W. Forthcoming. "Bolus of Mendes: The Learned Magician and the Collection and Transmission of Magical Lore in Hellenistic Egypt."

Dodds, E. R. 1951. *The Greeks and the Irrational.* Berkeley.

Dover, K. J. 1968. *Aristophanes: Clouds.* Oxford.

———— 1971. *Theocritus: Select Poems.* Glasgow.

———— 1974. *Greek Popular Morality in the Time of Plato and Aristotle.* Berkeley.

———— 1978. *Greek Homosexuality.* London.

———— 1984. "Classical Greek Attitudes to Sexual Behavior." *Arethusa* 6:59–73.

Dubisch, J., ed. 1986. *Gender and Power in Rural Greece.* Princeton.

du Boulay, J. 1986. "Women: Images of their Nature and Destiny in Rural Greece." In Dubisch (1986) 139–168.

du Bourguet, P. 1975. "Ensemble magique de la période romaine en Egypt." *Revue du Louvre:* 255–257.

Dunbabin, K. M. D. 1989. "*Baiarum Grata Voluptas:* Pleasures and Dangers of the Baths." *BSR* 57:6–46.

Easterling, P. E. 1968. "Sophocles, *Trachiniae.*" *BICS* 15:58–69.

———— 1982. *Sophocles: Trachiniae.* Cambridge.

Ebeling, E. 1925. *Liebeszauber im Alten Orient,* Mitteilungen der Altorientalischen Gesellschaft 1.1. Leipzig.

Edmunds, L., ed. 1990. *Approaches to Greek Myth.* Baltimore.

Egger, R. 1948. "Liebeszauber." *JOAI* 37:112–120.

Eitrem, S. 1925. *Papyri Osloenses.* Fasc. 1: *Magical Papyri.* Oslo.

———— 1928. "Necromancy in the *Persae* of Aeschylus." *SO* 6:1–16.

———— 1933. "Das Ende Didos in Vergils Aeneis." In *Festskrift til Halvdan Koht.* Oslo. Pp. 29–41.

———— 1934. "Aus 'Papyrologie und Religionsgeschichte': Die Magische Papyri." In Otto and Wenger (1934) 243–263.

———— 1939. "Die magischen Gemmen und ihre Weihe." *SO* 19:57–85.

———— 1940. "Eleusinia—Les mystères et l'agriculture." *SO* 20:133–151.

———— 1941. "La magie comme motif littéraire chez les Grecs et les Romains." *SO* 21:39–83.

———— 1942. "Excursus: Les roues magiques." *SO* 22:78–79.

Erler, M., and M. Kowaleski, eds. 1988. *Women and Power in the Middle Ages.* Athens, Ga.

Errondonea, I. 1927. "Deianeira vere DEI-ANEIRA." *Mnemosyne* 55:145–164.

Evans Grubbs, J. 1989. "Abduction Marriage in Antiquity: A Law of Constantine (*CTh* IX.24.1) and Its Social Context." *JRS* 79:59–83.

Fantham, E. 1975. "Sex, Status, and Survival in Hellenistic Athens: A Study of Women in New Comedy." *Phoenix* 29:44–74.

———— 1986. "ZHLOTUPIA: A Brief Excursion into Sex, Violence, and Literary History." *Phoenix* 40:45–57.

———— 1995. "Aemilia Pudentilla or a Wealthy Widow's Choice." In Hawley and Levick (1995) 220–232.

Fantuzzi, M., and F. Maltomini. 1996. "Ancora magia in Teocrito (VII 103–114)." *ZPE* 114:27–29.

Faraone, C. A. 1985. "Aeschylus' *Hymnos Desmios* (*Eum.* 306) and Attic Judicial Curse Tablets." *JHS* 105:150–154.

———— 1987. "Hephaestus the Magician and the Near Eastern Parallels for the Gold and Silver Dogs of Alcinous (*Od.* 7.91–4)." *GRBS* 28:257–280.

———— 1988. "Hermes without the Marrow: Another Look at a Puzzling Magical Spell." *ZPE* 72:279–286.

———— 1989a. "An Accusation of Magic in Classical Athens (Ar. *Wasps* 946–48)." *TAPA* 119:149–161.

———— 1989b. "Clay Hardens and Wax Melts: Magical Role-Reversal in Vergil's Eighth *Eclogue.*" *CP* 84:294–300.

———— 1990. "Aphrodites' KESTOS and Apples for Atalanta: Aphrodisiacs in Early Greek Myth and Ritual." *Phoenix* 44:224–243.

———— 1991a. "The Agonistic Context of Early Greek Binding Spells." In Faraone and Obbink (1991) 3–32.

———— 1991b. "Binding and Burying the Forces of Evil: The Defensive Use of 'Voodoo Dolls' in Ancient Greece." *CA* 10:165–205.

———— 1992a. "Sex and Power: Male-Targeting Aphrodisiacs in the Greek Magical Tradition." *Helios* 19:92–103.

———— 1992b. "Aristophanes *Amphiaraus* Frag. 29 (Kassel-Austin): Oracular Response or Erotic Incantation?" *CQ* 42:320–327.

———— 1992c. *Talismans and Trojan Horses: Guardian Statues in Ancient Greek Myth and Ritual.* Oxford.

———— 1993a. "The Wheel, the Whip, and Other Implements of Torture: Erotic Magic in Pindar *Pythian* 4:213–19." *CJ* 89:1–19.

———— 1993b. "Molten Wax, Spilt Wine, and Mutilated Animals: Sympathetic Magic in Early Greek and Near Eastern Oath Ceremonies." *JHS* 113:60–80.

———— 1994a. "Deianeira's Mistake and the Demise of Heracles: Erotic Magic in Sophocles' *Trachiniae.*" *Helios* 21:115–135.

———— 1994b. "Three Notes on Greek Magical Texts." *ZPE* 100:81–85.

———— 1995. "The 'Performative Future' in Three Hellenistic Incantations and Theocritus' Second *Idyll.*" *CP* 90:1–15.

———— 1996a. "The *Mystodokos* and the Dark-Eyed Maidens: Multicultural Influences on a Late Hellenistic Charm." In Meyer and Mirecki (1996) 297–334.

———— 1996b. "Taking the Nestor's Cup Inscription Seriously: Conditional Curses and Erotic Magic in the Earliest Greek Hexameters." *CA* 15:77–112.

———— 1997a. "Hymn to Selene-Hecate-Artemis from a Greek Magical Handbook (*PGM* IV 2714–83)." In Kiley (1997) 195–199.

———— 1997b. "Salvation and Female Heroics in the Parodos of Aristophanes' *Lysistrata.*" *JHS* 117:38–59.

———— Forthcoming a. *Incantation as Poetic Genre in Ancient Greece.*

———— Forthcoming b. "The Ethnic Origins of a Roman Era *Philtrokatadesmos* (*PGM* IV 296–434)."

Faraone, C. A., and D. Obbink, eds. 1991. *Magika Hiera: Ancient Greek Magic and Religion.* New York.

Ferrante, J. 1988. "Public Postures and Private Maneuvers: Roles Medieval Women Play." In Erler and Kowaleski (1988) 213–229.

Fick, N., and J.-C. Carriere, eds. 1991. *Mélanges Étienne Bernard.* Paris.

Finley, M. L. 1971. *The Use and Abuse of History.* Harmondsworth.

Finnegan, R., and R. Horton, eds. 1973. *Modes of Thought.* London.

Flint, V. I. J. 1991. *The Rise of Magic in Early Medieval Europe.* Princeton.

Foley, H., ed. 1981. *Reflections of Women in Antiquity.* New York.

Fortenbaugh, W. W., and W. Sharples, eds. 1988. *Theophrastean Studies on Natural Sciences, Physics, Metaphysics, Ethics, Religion, and Rhetoric.* Rutgers University Studies in Classical Humanities 3. New Brunswick, N.J.

Foster, B. O. 1899. "Notes on the Symbolism of the Apple in Classical Antiquity." *HSCP* 10:39–55.

Foucault, M. 1985. *The History of Sexuality.* Vol. 2: *The Uses of Pleasure.* Trans. R. Hurley. New York.

———— 1986. *The History of Sexuality.* Vol. 3: *The Care of Self.* Trans. R. Hurley. New York.

Fowden, G. 1986. *The Egyptian Hermes: A Historical Approach to the Late Pagan Mind.* Oxford.

Fox, R. L. 1986. *Pagans and Christians.* New York.

Fox, W. S. 1912. *The Johns Hopkins Tabellae Defixionum,* Supplement to *AJP* 129. Baltimore.

Foxhall, L. 1989. "Household, Gender, and Property in Classical Athens." *CQ* 39:22–44.

———— 1994. "Pandora Unbound: A Feminist Critique of Foucault's *History of Sexuality.*" In Cornwall and Lindisfarne (1994) 133–146.

Freedberg, D. 1989. *The Power of Images.* Chicago.

Freudenburg, K. 1995. "Canidia at the Feast of Nasidienus (Horace *S.* 2.8.95)." *TAPA* 125:207–219.

Furley, W. D. 1993. "Besprechung und Behandlung: Zur Form und Funktion von *Epôidai* in der griechischen Zaubermedizin." In Most, Petersmann, and Ritter (1993) 80–104.

Gantz, T. 1993. *Early Greek Myth: A Guide to Literary and Artistic Sources.* Baltimore.

Garcia-Ruiz, E. 1967. "Estudio linguistico de las defixiones latinas no includas en el corpus de Audollent." *Emerita* 35:55–59.

Gardiner, E. A. 1888. *Naukratis.* Vol. 2. London.

Gellie, G. H. 1972. *Sophocles: A Reading.* Melbourne.

Gerber, D. E. 1988. "The Measure of Bacchus." *Mnemosyne* 41:39–45.

Giacomelli, A. 1980. "The Justice of Aphrodite in Sappho Fr. 1." *TAPA* 110:135–142.

Giedke, A 1983. *Die Liebeskrankheit in der Geschichte der Medizin.* Diss. Düsseldorf.

Gigante, G. E. V. 1991. "La kourotrophos Samia e un epigramma omerico." *PP* 256:33–36.

Gleason, M. W. 1990. "The Semiotics of Gender: Physiognomy and Self-Fashioning in the Second Century C.E." In Halperin, Winkler, and Zeitlin (1990) 389–415.

———— 1995. *Making Men: Sophists and Self-Presentation in Ancient Rome.* Princeton.

Goff, B. 1991. *The Noose of Words: Readings of Desire, Violence, and Language in Euripides' Hippolytos.* Cambridge.

Golden, L. 1989. "*Dios Apate* and the Unity of *Iliad* 14." *Mnemosyne* 42:1–11.

Goldhill, S. 1995. *Foucault's Virginity: Ancient Erotic Fiction and the History of Sexuality.* Cambridge.

———— 1998. "The Seductions of the Gaze: Socrates and His Girlfriends." In Cartledge, Millett, and von Reden (1998) 105–124.

Goldstein, J., ed. 1994. *Foucault and the Writing of History*. Oxford.

Gould, J. 1980. "Law, Custom, and Myth: Aspects of the Social Position of Women in Classical Athens." *JHS* 100:38–59.

Gourevitch, D. 1995. "Women Who Suffer from a Man's Disease: The Example of *Satyriasis* and the Debate on Affections Specific to the Sexes." In Hawley and Levick (1995) 148–166.

Gow, A. S. F. 1934. "IUNX, ROMBOS, RHOMBUS, TURBO." *JHS* 54:1–13.

———— 1952. *Theocritus*. 2 vols. Cambridge.

Gow, A. S. F., and D. Page. 1965. *The Greek Anthology: Hellenistic Epigrams*. Cambridge.

Graf, F. 1991. "Prayer in Magical and Religious Ritual." In Faraone and Obbink (1991) 188–213.

———— 1992. "An Oracle against Pestilence from a Western Anatolian Town." *ZPE* 92:267–278.

———— 1995. "Excluding the Charming: The Development of the Greek Concept of Magic." In Meyer and Mirecki (1995) 29–42.

———— 1997a. "How to Cope with a Difficult Life: A View of Ancient Magic." In Schäfer and Kippenberg (1997) 93–114.

———— 1997b. *Magic in the Ancient World*. Cambridge, Mass.

————, ed. 1998. *Ansichten griechischer Rituale: Geburtstags-Symposium für Walter Burkert*. Stuttgart.

Greenfield, R. P. H. 1995. "A Contribution to the Study of Palaeologan Magic." In Maguire (1995) 138–146.

Griffiths, F. T. 1979. "Poetry as Pharmakon in Theocritus' *Idyll* 2." In Bowersock, Burkert, and Putnam (1979) 81–88.

———— 1981. "Home before Lunch: The Emancipated Woman in Theocritus." In Foley (1981) 247–273.

Griffiths, J. G. 1991. *Atlantis and Egypt and Other Selected Essays*. Cardiff.

Gurney, O. R., and J. J. Finkelstein. 1957. *The Sultantepe Tablets*. London.

Hägg, R., ed. 1983. *The Greek Renaissance of the Eighth Century B.C.: Tradition and Innovation*. Stockholm.

————, ed. 1994. *Ancient Greek Cult Practices from the Epigraphic Evidence: Proceedings of the Second International Seminar on Ancient Greek Cult*. Stockholm.

Halizer, S., ed. 1987. *Inquisition and Society in Early Modern Europe*. London.

Hall, E. 1989. *Inventing the Barbarian*. Oxford.

Halleux, R., and J. Schamp. 1985. *Les lapidaires grecs*. Paris.

Halperin, D. M. 1990. "Why Is Diotima a Woman? Platonic *Eros* and the Figuration of Gender." In Halperin, Winkler, and Zeitlin (1990) 257–308.

Halperin, D. M., J. J. Winkler, and F. I. Zeitlin, eds. 1990. *Before Sexuality: The Construction of Erotic Experience in the Ancient Greek World*. Princeton.

Hanson, A. E. 1990. "The Medical Writers' Woman." In Halperin, Winkler, and Zeitlin (1990) 309–337.

Hanson, J. A. 1989. *Apuleius: Metamorphoses.* Cambridge, Mass.

Harder, M. A., R. F. Regtuit, and G. C. Wakker, eds. 1996. *Theocritus.* Hellenistica Groningana 2. Groningen.

Harris, J. R., ed. 1971. *The Legacy of Egypt.* 2d ed. Oxford.

Hawley, R., and B. Levick, eds. 1995. *Women in Antiquity: New Assessments.* London.

Headlam, W. 1902. "Ghost-raising, Magic, and the Underworld." *CR* 16:52–61.

Heitsch, E. 1983. *Antiphon aus Rhamus.* Mainz.

Henderson, J. 1987a. *Aristophanes: Lysistrata.* Oxford.

———— 1987b. "Older Women in Attic Old Comedy." *TAPA* 107:105–129.

Henrichs, A. 1972. *Die Phoinikika des Lollianos.* Bonn.

———— 1974. "Die Proitiden in hesiodischen Katalog." *ZPE* 15:297–301.

Henry, M. M. 1985. *Menander's Courtesans and the Greek Comic Tradition.* Studien zur Klassichen Philologie 20. Frankfurt am Main.

———— 1995. *Prisoner of History: Aspasia of Miletus and Her Biographical Tradition.* Oxford.

Herzfeld, M. 1985. *The Poetics of Manhood: Contest and Identity in a Cretan Mountain Village.* Princeton.

———— 1986. "Within and Without: The Category of 'Female' in the Ethnography of Modern Greece." In Dubisch (1986) 215–233.

Herzig, O. 1940. *Lukian als Quelle für die antike Zauberei.* Diss. Tübingen.

Hester, D. A. 1980. "Deianeira's 'Deception Speech.'" *Antichthon* 14:1–8.

Hexter, R., and D. Selden, eds. 1992. *Innovations of Antiquity.* New York.

Holt, P. 1981. "Disease, Desire, and Deianeira: A Note on the Symbolism of the *Trachiniai.*" *Helios* 8:63–73.

Hooker, J. 1987. "Homeric *Philos.*" *Glotta* 65:44–65.

Hopfner, T. 1938. "Ein neues *Thumokatochon:* Uber die sonstigen *Thumokatocha, Katochoi, Hypotaktika,* und *Phimotika* der griechischen Zauberpapyri in ihrem Verhältnis zu den Fluchtafeln." *Archiv Orientální* 10:128–148.

———— 1939. "Hekate-Selene-Artemis und Verwandte in der griechischen Zauberpapyri und auf den Fluchtafeln." In *Pisciculi: Festschriften F. J. Dölger.* Münster. Pp. 125–145.

Hornum, M. B. 1993. *Nemesis, the Roman State, and the Games.* Leiden.

Horton, R., and R. Finnegan, eds. 1973. *Modes of Thought.* London.

Humphry, J. H. 1988. *The Circus and a Byzantine Cemetery at Carthage.* Vol. 1. Ann Arbor.

Hunt, L., ed. 1989. *The New Cultural History.* Berkeley.

Hunter, R. C. 1983. *Eubolus: The Fragments.* Cambridge.

Hunter, V. 1989. "Women's Authority in Classical Athens." *Echos du monde classique* 33:39–48.

———— 1994. *Policing Athens*. Princeton.

Ieranò, G. 1989. "Il ditirambo XVII di Bacchilide e le feste apollonee di Delo." *QS* 30:157–183.

Ingallina, S. S. 1974. *Orazio e la magia*. Palermo.

Jameson, M. H., D. R. Jordan, and R. D. Kotansky. 1993. *A Lex Sacra from Selinous*. *GRBS* Monograph 11. Durham.

Janko, R. 1988. "Berlin Magical Papyri 21243: A Conjecture." *ZPE* 72:293.

———— 1992. *The Iliad: A Commentary on Books 13–16*. Cambridge.

Janson, W. 1987. *Women without Men: Gender and Marginality in an Algerian Town*. Leiden.

Jebb, R. C. 1892. *Sophocles: The Plays and Fragments*. Vol. 5: *The Trachiniae*. Cambridge.

Jenkins, I. 1983. "Is There Life after Marriage? A Study of the Abduction Motif in Vase Paintings of the Athenian Wedding Ceremony." *BICS* 30:137–145.

Jocelyn, H. D. 1980. "A Greek Indecency: *Laikazein*." *PCPS* 206:12–66.

Johansen, H. F. 1962. "Sophocles 1939–59." *Lustrum* 7:94–288.

Johnston, S. I. 1990. *Hekate Soteira: A Study in Hekate's Roles in the Chaldean Oracles and Related Literature*. Atlanta.

———— 1991. "Crossroads." *ZPE* 88:213–220.

———— 1994. "Penelope and the Erinyes: *Od.* 20.61–82." *Helios* 21:137–159.

———— 1995. "The Song of the Iunx: Magic and Rhetoric in *Pythian* 4." *TAPA* 125:177–206.

———— 1999. *Restless Dead: Encounters between the Living and the Dead in Ancient Greece*. Berkeley.

Joly, R. 1968. *Le vocabulaire chrétien de l'amour est-il original? Philein et agapan dans le grec antique*. Brussels.

Jordan, D. R. 1976. "*CIL* VIII 19525 (B).2: QPVVLVA = Q(VEM) P(EPERIT) VVLVA." *Philologus* 120:127–132.

———— 1977. "A Ghost-Name *ENEMEPESEPTA*." *ZPE* 24:147–149.

———— 1985a. "The Inscribed Gold Tablet from the Vigna Codini." *AJA* 89:162–166.

———— 1985b. "*Defixiones* from a Well Near the Southwest Corner of the Athenian Agora." *Hesperia* 54:205–255.

———— 1988a. "A Love Charm with Verses." *ZPE* 72:245–259.

———— 1988b. "New Archaeological Evidence for the Practice of Magic in Classical Athens." In *Praktika of the 12th International Congress of Classical Archaeology*. Athens. Pp. 273–277.

———— 1988c. "A New Reading of a Papyrus Love Charm in the Louvre." *ZPE* 74:231–246.

———— 1988d. "New Defixiones from Carthage." In Humphry (1988) 117–134.

———— 1992. "The Inscribed Lead Tablet from Phalasarna." *ZPE* 94:191–194.

———— 1994a. "Inscribed Lead Tablets from the Games in the Sanctuary of Poseidon." *Hesperia* 63:111–126.

———— 1994b. "Magica Graeca Parvula." *ZPE* 100:321–335.

———— 1994c. "Late Feasts for Ghosts." In Hägg (1994) 131–143.

———— 1996. "Notes from Carthage." *ZPE* 111:115–123.

———— 1999. "Three Greek Curse Tablets." In Jordan, Montgomery, and Thomasson (1999).

Jordan, D. R., H. J. C. Montgomery, and E. Thomasson, eds. 1999. *Magic in the Ancient World: Proceedings of the First International Samson Eitrem Seminar, Norwegian Institute Athens, 4–7 May 1997*. Bergen.

Kagarow, E. G. 1929. *Griechische Fluchtafeln, Eos* Suppl. 4. Leopoli.

Kaimakis, D. 1976. *Die Kyraniden*, Beiträge zur klassichen Philologie 76. Meisenheim am Glan.

Kambitsis, S. 1976. "Une nouvelle tablette magique d'Egypte, Musée du Louvre Inv. E27145, 3e/4e siècle." *BIFAO* 76:213–223.

Kamerbeek, J. C. 1959. *The Plays of Sophocles*. Vol. 2: *Trachiniae*. Leiden.

Käppel, L. 1992. *Paian: Studien zur Geschichte einer Gattung*, Untersuchungen zur antiken Literatur und Geschichte 37. Berlin.

Katz, M. B. (Arthur) 1989. "Sexuality and the Body in Ancient Greece." *Métis* 4:155–179.

———— 1992a. "Ideology and 'The Status of Women' in Ancient Greece." *History and Theory* 31:70–97.

———— 1992b. "Patriarchy, Ideology, and the Epikleros." *SIFC* 10:692–708.

Kazhdam, A. 1995. "Holy and Unholy Miracle Workers." In Maguire (1995) 73–82.

Kelly, H. A. 1977. "English Kings and the Fear of Sorcery." *Mediaeval Studies* 39:206–238.

Keuls, E. 1985. *The Reign of the Phallus*. New York.

Keyser, P. 1989. "Horace *Odes* 1.13.3–16:Humoural and Aetherial Love." *Philologus* 133:75–81.

Kieckhefer, R. 1991. "Erotic Magic in Medieval Europe." In Salisbury (1991) 30–55.

Kiley, M., ed. 1997. *Prayer from Alexander to Constantine*. London.

King, H. 1983. "Bound to Bleed: Artemis and Greek Women." In Cameron and Kuhrt (1983) 109–127.

Kirk, G. S., J. E. Raven, and M. Schofield. 1983. *The Presocratic Philosophers: A Critical History with a Selection of Texts*. Cambridge.

Kitto, H. D. F. 1966. *Poesis: Structure and Thought*. Sather Classical Lectures 36. Berkeley.

Kofler, D. 1949. *Aberglaube und Zauberei in Lukians Schriften*. Diss. Innsbruck.

Konstan, D. 1985. "The Politics of Aristophanes' *Wasps*." *TAPA* 115:27–46.

———— 1993. "The Young Concubine in Menandrian Comedy." In Scodel (1993) 139–160.

———— 1996. "Greek Friendship." *AJP* 117:71–94.

———— 1997. *Friendship in the Classical World.* Cambridge.

Kotansky, R. 1991a. "Incantations and Prayers for Salvation on Inscribed Greek Amulets." in Faraone and Obbink (1991) 107–137.

———— 1991b. "Magic in the Court of the Governor of Arabia." *ZPE* 88:41–60.

———— 1995. "Greek Exorcistic Amulets." In Meyer and Mirecki (1995) 243–278.

Kovacs, P. D. 1980. *The Andromache of Euripides: An Interpretation.* Chico, Calif.

Kovacsovics, W. K., ed. 1990. *Die Eckterrasse and der Gräberstrasse des Kerameikos.* Kerameikos 14. Berlin.

Kuhnert, E. 1894. "Feuerzauber." *RhM* 49:37–54.

Kuster, B. 1911. *De tribus carminibus papyri parisinae magicae.* Königsberg.

Lacey, W. K. 1968. *The Family in Ancient Greece.* Ithaca.

Lain Entralgo, P. 1970. *The Therapy of the Word in Classical Antiquity.* Trans. L. J. Rather and J. M. Sharp. New Haven.

Laquer, T. W. 1996. *Making Sex: Body and Gender from the Greeks to Freud.* Cambridge, MA.

LaRue, J. A. 1965. *Sophocles' Deianeira: A Study in Dramatic Ambiguity.* Diss. Berkeley.

Lawson, J. C. 1934. "The Evocation of Darius." *CQ* 28:79–89.

Leick, G. 1994. *Sex and Eroticism in Mesopotamian Literature.* London.

Levi, P. 1975. "The Prose Style of the Magical Papyri." In *Proceedings of the XIV International Congress of Papyrologists.* London. Pp. 211–216.

Littlewood, A. R. 1967. "The Symbolism of the Apple in Greek and Roman Language." *HSCP* 72:147–179.

———— 1974. "The Symbolism of the Apple in Byzantine Literature." *Jahrbuch der Osterreichischen Byzantinistik* 23:33–59.

Lloyd, G. E. R. 1979. *Magic, Reason, and Experience.* Cambridge.

———— 1983. *Science, Folklore, and Ideology.* Cambridge.

Lockwood, W. C. 1974. "Bride-Theft and Social Maneuverability in Western Bosnia." *Anthropological Quarterly* 47:253–269.

Loizos, P. 1994. "A Broken Mirror: Masculine Sexuality in Greek Ethnography." In Cornwall and Lindisfarne (1994) 66–81.

LoMonaco, F. 1989. "*Plumbo o rhombo?* A proposito di Ovidio *Fast.* 2.575." *Aevum Antiquum* 2:251–271.

Loraux, N. 1995. *The Experiences of Tiresias: The Feminine and the Greek Man.* Trans. P. Wissing. Princeton.

Lugauer, M. 1967. *Untersuchungen zur Symbolik des Apfels in der Antike.* Diss. Erlangen.

Maas, P. 1942. "The Philinna Papyrus." *JHS* 62:33–38.

———— 1944. "EPENIKTOS" *Hesperia* 13:36–37.

MacDowell, D. M. 1978. *The Law in Classical Athens.* Ithaca.

Maehler, H. 1990. "Symptome der Liebe in der Roman und in der griechischen Anthologie." *Groningen Colloquia on the Novel* 3:1–12.

Maguire, H., ed. 1995. *Byzantine Magic.* Washington, D.C.

Malinowski, B. 1948. *Magic, Science, and Religion.* New York.

Maltomini, F. 1978. "*P. Mon. Gr.* Inv. 216: Formulario magico." In Carlini et al. (1978) 237–266.

———— 1979. Review of Moke (1975). *Aegyptus* 59:273–284.

———— 1980. "Osservationi al testo di alcuni papiri magici greci, II." *CCC* 1:371–377.

Mandilaras, B. G., ed. 1988. *Proceedings of the XVIII International Congress of Papyrology, Athens, 25–31 May 1986.* Athens.

Manning, C. E. 1970. "Canidia in the *Epodes* of Horace." *Mnemosyne* 23:393–401.

March, J. R. 1987. *The Creative Poet: Studies in the Treatment of Myths in Greek Poetry. BICS* Suppl. 49. London.

Markwald, G. 1986. *Die Homerischen Epigramme.* Beiträge zur klassichen Philologie 165. Königstein.

Martinez, D. G. 1991a. *P. Michigan XVI: A Greek Love Charm from Egypt (P. Mich. 757).* American Studies in Papyrology 30. Atlanta.

———— 1991b. "T. Köln inv. 2.25 and Erotic *Damazein.*" *ZPE* 83:235–236.

———— 1995. "May She Neither Eat nor Drink . . .: Love Magic and Vows of Abstinence." In Meyer and Mirecki (1995) 335–360.

Mattes, J. 1970. *Der Wahnsinn im griechischen Mythos und in der Dichtung bis zum Drama des 5. Jahrhunderts.* Bibliothek der Altertumswissenschaften 36. Heidelberg.

McCall, M. 1972. "The *Trachiniae:* Structure, Focus, and Heracles." *AJP* 93:142–163.

McCartney, E. S. 1925. "How the Apple Became a Token of Love." *TAPA* 56:70–81.

Meyer, M., and Mirecki, P., eds. 1996. *Ritual Power in the Ancient World.* Leiden.

Meyers, B. F., and E. P Sanders, eds. 1982. *Self Definition in the Greco-Roman World.* Jewish and Christian Self-Definition 3. Philadelphia.

Micalella, D. 1977. "Vino e amore: Ippocrate, *Antica Medicina* 20." *QUCC* 24:151–155.

Moke, D. F. 1975. *Eroticism in the Greek Magical Papyri: Selected Studies.* Diss. Univ. of Minnesota.

Momigliano, A., ed. 1963. *The Conflict between Paganism and Christianity in the Fourth Century.* Oxford.

Mondi, R. 1990. "Greek and Near Eastern Mythology." In Edmunds (1990) 141–198.

Montserrat, D. 1996. *Sex and Society in Graeco-Roman Egypt.* London

Morgan, G. 1978. "Aphrodite Cythereia." *TAPA* 108:115–120.

Most, G. W., H. Petersmann, and A. M. Ritter, eds. 1993. *Philanthropia kai Eusebeia: Festschrift für A. Dihle zum 70. Geburtstag.* Göttingen.

Mouterde, R. 1930. *Le glaive de Dardanus: Objects et inscriptions magiques de Syrie.* Mélanges de l'Université Saint-Joseph 15.3. Beirut.

Muir, E., and G. Ruggiero, eds. 1990. *Sex and Gender in Historical Perspective.* Baltimore.

Müller, H. M. 1980. *Erotische Motive in der griechischen Dichtung bis auf Euripides.* Hamburg.

Myres, J. L. 1938. "Persephone and the Pomegranate (*H. Dem.* 372–374)." *CR* 52:51–52.

Nagy, G. 1990. *Pindar's Homer: The Lyric Possession of the Past.* Baltimore.

Neitzel, H. 1975. *Homer-Rezeption bei Hesiod: Interpretation ausgewahlter Passagen.* Bonn.

Nelson, G. W. 1946. "A Greek Votive Iynx-Wheel in Boston." *AJA* 64:443–448.

Nock, A. D. 1925. "Magical Notes 1: The Sword of Dardanus." *JEA* 11:154–158.

Nussbaum, M. C. 1994. *The Therapy of Desire: Theory and Practice in Hellenistic Ethics.* Princeton.

O'Neil, M. 1987. "Magical Healing, Love Magic, and the Inquisition in Late-Sixteenth Century Modena." In Halizer (1987) 88–114.

Onians, R. B. 1951. *The Origins of Western Thought.* Cambridge.

Ortega, M. H. S. 1991. "Sorcery and Eroticism in Love Magic." In Perry and Cruz (1991) 58–92.

Ortner, S. B., and H. Whitehead, eds. 1981. *Sexual Meanings: The Cultural Construction of Gender and Sexuality.* Cambridge.

Otto, W., and L. Wenger, eds. 1934. *Papyri und Altertumswissionshaft.* Munich.

Padel, R. 1983. "Women: Model for Possession by Greek Daemons." In Cameron and Kuhrt (1983) 3–19.

———— 1992. *In and Out of the Mind: Greek Images of the Tragic Self.* Princeton.

Page, D. L. 1972. "The Mystery of the Minstrel in the Court of Agamemnon." In *Studi classici in onore di Quintino Cataudella.* Vol. 1. Catania. Pp. 127–131.

———— 1973. *Folktales in Homer's Odyssey.* Cambridge, Mass.

———— 1981. *Further Greek Epigrams.* Cambridge.

Pálsson, G. 1991. "The Name of the Witch: Sagas, Sorcery, and Social Context." In Samson (1991) 169–178.

Parker, H. H. 1993. "Sappho Schoolmistress." *TAPA* 123:308–352.

Parker, R. 1983. *Miasma: Pollution and Purification in Early Greek Religion.* Oxford.

———— 1996. *Athenian Religion.* Oxford.

Parry, H. 1988. "Magic and the Songstress: Theocritus *Idyll* 2." *ICS* 13:42–55.

———— 1992. *Thelxis: Magic and Imagination in Greek Myth and Poetry.* Lanham, Md.

Paton, W. R. 1919. *The Greek Anthology.* Vol. 1. Cambridge, Mass.

Patterson, C. B. 1991a. "Marriage and the Married Woman in Athenian Law." In Pomeroy (1991) 48–72.

———— 1991b. "Plutarch's 'Advice on Marriage': Traditional Wisdom through a Philosophical Lens." *ANRW* 2.33.6:4709–23.

Pelling, C. B. R. 1988. *Plutarch: Life of Antony.* Cambridge.

Perry, M. E., and A. J. Cruz, eds. 1991. *Cultural Encounters: The Impact of the Inquisition in Spain and the New World.* Berkeley.

Petropoulos, J. C. B. 1988. "The Erotic Magical Papyri." In Mandilaras (1988) 215–222.

———— 1993. "Sappho Sorceress: Another Look at Frag. 1 (L-P)." *ZPE* 97:43–56.

———— 1994. *Heat and Lust: Hesiod's Midsummer Festival Scene Revisited.* London.

Pfister, F. 1940. "Daimonismus." *RE* Suppl. 7:100–114.

Pharr, C. 1932. "The Interdiction of Magic in Roman Law." *TAPA* 63:269–295.

Phillips, C. R. 1986. "The Sociology of Religious Knowledge in the Roman Empire to A.D. 284." *ANRW* 2.16.3:2677–2773.

———— 1991. "*Nullum Crimen sine Lege:* Socioreligious Sanctions on Magic." In Faraone and Obbink (1991) 260–276.

Photiades, P. P. 1958. "Pan's Prologue to the *Dyscolos* of Menander." *Greece & Rome* 5:108–122.

Picard, C. 1942–43. "Une peinture de vase lemnienne archaïque d'après l'hymn de Démodocus." *RA* 20:97–124.

Pirenne-Delforge, V. 1993. "L'iynge dans le discours mythique et les procédures magiques." *Kernos* 6:277–289.

Pitt-Rivers, J. 1977. *The Fate of Shechem.* Cambridge.

Pleket, H. W. 1981. "Religious History as a History of Mentality: The 'Believer' as Servant of the Deity in the Greek World." In Versnel (1981) 152–192.

Pomeroy, S. B. 1981. "Women in Roman Egypt (A Preliminary Study Based on Papyri)." In Foley (1981) 303–322.

———— 1984. *Women in Hellenistic Egypt from Alexander to Cleopatra.* New York.

————, ed. 1991. *Women's History and Ancient History.* Chapel Hill.

Preisendanz, K. 1918. "Ousia." *WS* 40:5–8.

———— 1928. "Die griechischen und lateinischen Zaubertafeln." *APF* 9:119–154.

———— 1923. "Ein Strassburger Liebeszauber." *ARW* 16:548–549.

———— 1933. "Die griechischen und lateinischen Zaubertafeln." *APF* 11:153–164.

———— 1972. "Fluchtafel (Defixion)." *RAC* 8:1–29.

Preus, A. 1988. "Theophrastus' Psychopharmacology (*HP* IX)." In Fortenbaugh and Sharples (1988) 76–99.

Randolph, C. B. 1905. *The Mandragora of the Ancients in Folklore and Medicine.* Proceedings of the American Academy of Arts and Sciences 40.12. New York.

Reckford, K. 1977. "Catharsis and Dream Interpretation in Aristophanes' *Wasps.*" *TAPA* 107:283–312.

Redfield, J. 1982. "Notes on the Greek Wedding." *Arethusa* 15:181–201.

———— 1995. "Homo Domesticus." In Vernant (1995) 153–183.

Reiner, E. 1966. "La magie babylonienne." In *Le monde du sorcier.* Sources Orientales 7. Paris. Pp. 69–98.

———— 1990. "Nocturnal Talk." In Abusch et al. (1990) 421–424.

———— 1995. *Astral Magic in Babylonia*. Transactions of the American Philosophical Society 85.4. Philadelphia.

Reinhardt, K. 1979. *Sophocles*. Trans. H. Harvey and D. Harvey. Oxford.

Renehan, R. 1992. "The Staunching of Odysseus' Blood: The Healing Power of Magic." *AJP* 113:1–4.

Richardson, N. J. 1974. *The Homeric Hymn to Demeter*. Oxford.

Richlin, A. 1991. "Zeus and Metis: Foucault, Feminism, Classics." *Helios* 18:160–180.

Riess, E. 1893. "Zu den Canidiagedichten des Horatius." *RhM* 48:307–311.

———— 1895. "On Ancient Superstition." *TAPA* 26:40–55.

———— 1896a. "Pliny and Magic." *AJP* 17:77–83.

———— 1896b. "Superstitions and Popular Beliefs in Greek Tragedy." *TAPA* 27:5–34.

———— 1897. "Superstitions and Popular Beliefs in Greek Comedy." *AJP* 18:189–205.

———— 1903. "Studies in Superstition: Pindar and Bacchylides." *AJP* 24:423–440.

———— 1938. "Etude sur le folklore et les superstitions: Les poètes élégiaques romains." *Latomus* 2:164–189.

Ritner, R. 1993. *The Mechanics of Ancient Egyptian Magical Practice*. SAOC 54. Chicago.

———— 1995. "Egyptian Magical Practice under the Roman Empire: The Demotic Spells and their Religious Context." *ANRW* 2.18.5:3333–79.

Rives, J. B. 1995. *Religion and Authority in Roman Carthage from Augustus to Constantine*. Oxford.

Robert, L. 1967. "Une autre épigramme de Rufin ou l'utilité du grec moderne." *Rev. Phil.* 41:77–81.

———— 1981. "Amulettes grecques." *Journal des Savants* 3–44.

Robinson, D. 1990. "Homeric *Philos*: Love of Life and Limbs, and Friendship with One's *Thumos*." In Craik (1990) 97–108.

Rosaldo, M. Z., and L. Lamphere, eds. 1974. *Woman, Culture, and Society*. Stanford.

Roscher, W. H. 1898. "Die 'Hundkrankheit' *(kuōn)* der Pandareostöchter und andere mythische Krankheiten." *RhM* 53:169–204.

Rosenmeyer, T. G. 1951. "EROS-EROTES." *Phoenix* 5:11–22.

Rosenqvist, J. O., ed. 1986. *The Life of St. Irene, Abbess of Chrysobalanton*. Uppsala.

Rosivach, V. J. 1998. *When a Young Man Falls in Love: The Sexual Exploitation of Women in New Comedy*. London.

Ruggiero, G. 1985. *The Boundaries of Eros: Sex Crime and Sexuality in Renaissance Venice*. New York.

———— 1993. *Binding Passions: Tales of Magic, Marriage, and Power at the End of the Renaissance*. New York.

Ruschenbusch, E. 1966. *Solonos Nomoi: Die Fragmente des Solonischen Gesetzwerkes*. Historia Einzelschriften 9. Wiesbaden.

Salisbury, J. E., ed. 1991. *Sex in the Middle Ages*. New York.

Saller, R. P. 1994. *Patriarchy, Property, and Death in the Roman Family.* Cambridge.

Samson, R., ed. 1991. *Social Approaches to Viking Studies.* Glasgow.

Scarborough, J. 1978. "Theophrastus on Herbals and Herbal Remedies." *Journal of the History of Biology* 11:353–385.

———— 1979. "Nicander's Toxicology II: Spiders, Scorpions, Insects, and Myriapods." *Pharmacy in History* 21:3–34 and 73–92.

———— 1991. "The Pharmacology of Sacred Plants, Herbs, and Roots." In Faraone and Obbink (1991) 175–187.

Scarpi, P. 1976. *Letture sulla religione classica: L'inno omerico a Demeter.* Florence.

Schabert, T., and R. Brague, eds. 1996. *Die Macht des Wortes.* Munich.

Schäfer, P., and H. G. Kippenberg, eds. 1997. *Envisioning Magic: A Princeton Seminar and Symposium.* Leiden.

Schaps, D. 1977. "The Woman Least Mentioned: Etiquette and Women's Names." *CQ* 27:323–330.

Scheil, V. 1921. "Catalogue de la Collection Eugene Tisserant." *Revue d'Assyriologie et d'Archéologie Orientale* 18:21–27.

Schlam, C. C. 1976. *Cupid and Psyche: Apuleius and the Monuments.* University Park, Pa.

Schmidt, K. W. 1934. Review of *PGM*, vol. 2. *Göttingische Gelehrte Anzeigen* 196:169–186.

Scholtz, H. 1937. *Der Hund in der griechisch-römischen Magie und Religion.* Diss. Berlin.

Schwartz, J. 1981. "Papyri Graecae Magicae und magische Gemmen." In Vermasseren (1981) 485–509.

Schweizer, H. 1937. *Aberglaube und Zauberei bei Theokrit.* Basel.

Scobie, A. 1983. *Apuleius and Folklore.* London.

Scodel, R. 1984. "The Irony of Fate in Bacchylides 17." *Hermes* 112:137–143.

————, ed. 1993. *Theater and Society in the Classical World.* Ann Arbor.

Scurlock, J. 1989–90. "Was There a 'Love-Hungry' *Entu*-Priestess Named Etirtum?" *Archiv für Orientforschung* 36:107–112.

Seaford, R. 1987. "The Tragic Wedding." *JHS* 107:106–130.

———— 1988. "The Eleventh Ode of Bacchylides: Hera, Artemis, and the Absence of Dionysus." *JHS* 108:118–136.

———— 1994. *Ritual and Reciprocity: Homer and Tragedy in the Developing City-State.* Oxford.

Sealey, R. 1990. *Women and Law in Classical Greece.* Chapel Hill.

Segal, A. 1981. "Hellenistic Magic: Some Questions of Definition." In van den Broek and Vermasseren (1981) 349–375.

Segal, C. 1973. "Simaetha and the *Iunx* (Theocritus *Idyll* II)." *QUCC* 17:32–43.

———— 1974. "Eros and Incantation: Sappho and Oral Poetry." *Arethusa* 7:139–160.

———— 1986. *Pindar's Mythmaking: The Fourth Pythian Ode.* Princeton.

Seltman, C. 1923–1925. "Eros in Early Attic Legend and Art" *ABSA* 26:88–105.

Shapiro, H. A. 1993. *Personifications in Greek Art: The Representation of Abstract Concepts, 600–400 B.C.* Zurich.

Sherwin-White, S. M. 1973. *Ancient Cos.* Göttingen.

Shipp, G. P. 1979. *Modern Greek Evidence for Ancient Greek Vocabulary.* Sydney.

Sijpesteijn, P. J. 1978–79. "A Syrian Phylactery on a Silver Plate." *Oudheidkundife Mededelingen uit het Rijksmuseum van Oudheden te Leiden* 59–60:189–192.

——— 1980. "Einige Bemerkungen zu einigen magischen Gemmen." *Aegyptus* 60:153–160.

Sissa, G. 1990. "Maidenhood without Maidenhead: The Female Body in Ancient Greece." In Halperin, Winkler, and Zeitlin (1990) 339–364.

Smith, J. Z. 1995. "Trading Places" in Meyer and Mirecki (1995) 13–28.

Smith, M. 1979. "Relations between Magical Papyri and Magical Gems." *Papyrologica Bruxellensia* 18:129–136.

——— 1984. "The Eighth Book of Moses and How it Grew (*P.Leid.* J 395)." In *Atti del XVIII congresso internazionale di papirologia.* Naples. Pp. 683–693.

Smith, W. 1966. "So-Called Possession in Pre-Christian Greece." *TAPA* 96:403–426.

Smither, P. 1941. "A Rameside Love Charm." *JEA* 27:131–132.

Solin, H. 1968. *Eine neue Fluchtafel aus Ostia.* Commentationes Humanorum Litterarum 42.3. Helsinki.

Sourvinou-Inwood, C. 1973. "The Young Abductor of the Lokrian Pinakes." *BICS* 20:12–21.

——— 1987. "A Series of Erotic Pursuits: Images and Meanings." *JHS* 107:131–153.

Stern, J. 1971. "The Structure of Pindar's *Nemean* 5." *CP* 66:169–173.

Strömberg, R. 1950. "The Aeolus Episode and Greek Wind Magic." *Acta Univ. Gotoburg.* 56:82–84.

Strubbe, J. H. M. 1991. "Cursed be he that moves my bones." In Faraone and Obbink (1991) 33–59.

Sullivan, S. D. 1983. "Love Influences *Phrenes* in Greek Lyric Poetry." *SO* 58:15–22.

Sutphen, M. 1902. "Magic in Theocritus and Vergil." In *Studies in Honor of Basil L. Gildersleeve.* Baltimore. Pp. 315–327.

Taberner, P. V. 1985. *Aphrodisiacs: The Science and the Myth.* Philadelphia.

Taillardat, J. 1962. *Les images d'Aristophane: Etudes de langue et style.* Paris.

Tambiah, S. J. 1968. "The Magical Power of Words." *Man* 3:175–208.

——— 1973. "Form and Meaning of Magical Acts: A Point of View." In Horton and Finnegan (1973) 199–229.

Tambornino, J. 1909. *De antiquorum daemonismo.* RGVV 7.3. Giessen.

Taplin, O. 1977. *The Stagecraft of Aeschylus.* Oxford.

Tavenner, E. 1916. *Studies in Magic from Latin Literature.* New York.

——— 1933. "Iynx and Rhombus" *TAPA* 64:109–127.

———— 1942. "The Use of Fire in Greek and Roman Love Magic." In *Studies in Honor of F. W. Shipley*. St. Louis. Pp. 17–37.

Tempkin, O. 1945. *The Falling Sickness: A History of Epilepsy from the Greeks to the Beginnings of Modern Neurology*. Baltimore.

Thee, F. C. R. 1984. *Julius Africanus and the Early Christian View of Magic*. Tübingen.

Thompson, D. W. 1936. *A Glossary of Greek Birds*. Oxford.

Thür, G. 1977. *Beweisführung vor den Schwurgerichtshöfen Athens: Die Proklesis zur Basanos*. Vienna.

Tomaselli, S., and R. Porter, eds. 1986. *Rape*. Oxford.

Tomlin, R. S. O. 1988. "*Tabellae Sulis:* Roman Inscribed Tablets of Tin and Lead from the Sacred Spring at Bath." In Cunliffe (1988) 59–277.

Trumpf, J. 1960. "Kydonische Äpfel." *Hermes* 88:14–22.

Tupet, A.-M. 1976. *La magie dans la poésie latine*. Paris.

van den Broek, R., and M. J. Vermasseren, eds. 1981. *Studies in Gnosticism and Hellenistic Religion Presented to Gilles Quispel*. EPRO 91. Leiden.

Vergote, J. 1972. "Folterwerkzeuge." *RAC* 8:113–115.

Vermasseren, M. J., ed. 1981. *Die orientalischen Religionen im Römerreich*. EPRO 93. Leiden.

Vernant, J.-P., ed. 1995. *The Greeks*. Trans. C. Lambert and T. L. Fagan. Chicago.

Versnel, H. S., ed. 1981. *Faith, Hope and Worship*. Leiden.

Versnel, H. S. 1985. "May he not be able to sacrifice. . .: Concerning a Curious Formula in Greek and Latin Curses." *ZPE* 58:247–269.

———— 1990. *Ter Unus: Isis, Dionysus, Hermes: Three Studies in Henotheism*. Leiden.

———— 1991a. "Beyond Cursing: The Appeal to Justice in Judicial Prayer." In Faraone and Obbink (1991) 65–69.

———— 1991b. "Some Reflections on the Relationship Magic-Religion." *Numen* 38:177–197.

———— 1994. "*Pepusmenos:* The Cnidian Curse Tablets and Ordeals of Fire." In Hägg (1994) 145–154.

———— 1996. "Die Poetik der Zauberspruche." In Schabert and Brague (1996) 233–297.

———— 1998. "And any other part of the entire body there may be . . .: An Essay on Anatomical Curses." In Graf (1998) 217–267.

———— 1999. "Punish those who rejoice in our misery . . .:On Curse Tablets and Schadenfreude." In Jordan, Montgomery, and Thomasson (1999) 1–40.

Veyne, P. 1987. *History of Private Life*. Vol. 1: *From Pagan Rome to Byzantium*. Trans. A. Goldhammer. Cambridge, Mass. Pp. 33–49.

Voutiras, E. 1998. *DIONUSOPHÔNTOS GAMOI: Marital Life and Magic in Fourth-Century Pella*. Amsterdam.

Waegeman, M. 1987. *Amulet and Alphabet: Magical Amulets in the First Book of Cyranides*. Amsterdam.

Ward, J. O. 1980. "Witchcraft and Sorcery in the Later Roman Empire and Early Middle Ages: An Anthropological Comment." *Prudentia* 12:93–108.

——— 1981. "Women, Witchcraft, and Social Patterning in the Later Roman Law Codes." *Prudentia* 13:99–118.

Watson, L. C. 1991. *Arae: The Curse Poetry of Antiquity*. Leeds.

Wellmann, M. 1928. *Die Physika des Bolos' Demokritos und der Magier Anaxilaos aus Larissa*. Abhand. der preuss. Akad. der Wiss. Phil.-hist. Klasse no. 7. Berlin.

West, M. L. 1965. "Alcmanica." *CQ* 15:199–200.

——— 1970. "Burning Sappho." *Maia* 22:307–330.

——— 1971. *Early Greek Philosophy and the Orient*. Oxford.

——— 1974. *Studies in Greek Elegy and Iambus*. Berlin.

West, S. 1994. "Nestor's Bewitching Cup." *ZPE* 101:9–15.

Whitman, C. 1951. *Sophocles: A Study in Heroic Humanism*. Cambridge, Mass.

Willemsen, F. 1990. "Die Fluchtafeln." In Kovacsovics (1990) 142–151.

Wills, G. 1995. *Witches & Jesuits: Shakespeare's Macbeth*. New York.

Winkler, J. J. 1990. *The Constraints of Desire: The Anthropology of Sex and Gender in Ancient Greece*. New York.

——— 1991. "The Constraints of Eros." In Faraone and Obbink (1991) 214–243.

Winnington-Ingram, R. P. 1980. *Sophocles: An Interpretation*. Cambridge.

Wittgenstein, L. 1965. "Bemerkungen über Frazers 'The Golden Bough.'" *Synthese* 18:236–258.

Wolters, P. 1911. "Faden und Knoten als Amulett." *ARW* 8:1–22.

Wortmann, D. 1968. "Neue Magische Texte" *Bonner Jahrbücher* 168:56–111.

Zeitlin, F. I. 1985. "The Power of Aphrodite: Eros and the Boundaries of Self in the *Hippolytus*." In Burian (1985) 52–111.

——— 1986. "Configurations of Rape in Greek Myth." In Tomaselli and Porter (1986) 122–151.

——— 1992. "The Politics of Eros in the Danaid Trilogy of Aeschylus." In Hexter and Selden (1992) 203–252.

Subject Index

abduction marriage. *See* bridal theft
abstractions in Greek poetry, 98–99
Acanthus, 14, 54, 143
accusations of love magic, 2, 7, 9–10, 85, 114,
    135, 155–156
Achaeans, 131
Achilles, 54, 123
Achilles Tatius, 64
Acropolis, 170
Adeimantos, 49
Adonaios, 141
Adonia, 163
Adonis, 34–35, 138
Aegisthus, 6
Aelian, 10, 20, 160–165
Aelius Dionysus, 47
Aeneas, 9
Aenesimbrota, 6
Aeolus, 39
Aeschines, 10
Aeschylus, 7, 25, 26, 60
Afghanistan, 33
Aias, 41
Ajax, 47
Alcaeus, 162–163
Alcibiades, 2
Alcinoe, 22
Alcman, 6
Alexander, 125
Alexandria, 153
Alexis, 155
Algeria, 55–56
Allous, 3, 86
Amasis, 135
Amazon, 112
Ammoneios, 141, 147

Ammonion, 3
Amorgos, 87
Amphitrite, 5, 100
Amphitritos, 143
amulets, 30, 37, 105–110, 121–122, 141
Anacreon, 44, 45, 63
Anatolia, 51
Andromache, 7, 13, 37, 100
anger (male), 97–103, 107–110, 122–128
animal breeding, 20–21
animal nicknames, 154
animals as effigies, 64–69
antaphrodisiacs, 8, 18
Antinoos, 42
Antiphon, 19, 63, 114–116, 124, 128–129, 157
Antisthenes, 1–2
Anubis, 34–35, 60–61
Apalos, 59, 61, 86
aphrodisiacs, 18–21, 126–130, 160–161
Aphrodite, 6, 12, 15, 22, 29, 36, 44, 52–54, 56–
    58, 60, 62, 64, 69, 73, 74, 75, 80, 83, 90, 93,
    97–101, 104, 109–110, 122, 133–142, 144, 151–
    152, 163, 168
Apollo, 48, 51, 141
Apollodorus, 1–2, 70
Apollonius, 3, 86
Apollonous, 56
"apples," 69–80
Apsu, 110
Apuleius, 8, 38, 62, 85, 87, 158
Arabia, 108–109
Aramaic, 16
Aratus, 22, 147
Archilochus, 44
Areopagus, 9, 115, 119
Ares, 6, 51–53

Aretaphila, 116–117, 119
Ariadne, 70, 143
Aristomache, 7
Aristophanes, 8–9, 20, 39, 46, 63, 64–65, 72–
    74, 124–125, 135, 137, 150, 154, 158, 170–171
Aristotle/Aristotelian, 10, 115, 118, 126, 161,
    163, 164, 165–166
Artemis, 47, 90, 92, 145
arugula, 19–21
Asclepiades, 9, 100–101, 151, 157
Ashur, 101–102
Aspasia, 2
Assyria/Assyrian, 31, 36–37, 75, 102–105, 145
Atalanta, 6, 28, 45, 69, 72–73, 78, 80
Athena, 22, 54, 58, 144
Athenaeus, 8, 20, 64, 156, 157
Athens/Athenian, 1, 9, 13, 32, 33, 34, 37, 49,
    65, 71–73, 77, 78, 80, 88, 110, 114–118, 123,
    126, 150–151, 153, 156–157
Attica/Attic, 12, 156
Augustus, 73
Autolycus, 39

bacchic dances, 62
Bacchis, 150–152
Bacchylides, 62, 100, 112, 119
barley, 152
Barza, 138
baths, 148
bats, 65–66
Baubo, 145
bay leaves, 152–153
Beirut, 33
Berlin, 59, 75, 77
betrothal marriages, 23, 78–80
binding, 12–14, 41–42, 51–53, 57, 62, 63, 67,
    81–82, 142–144, 158–159
birds, 64–65, 67–68, 138–139
"black magic," 30
blood, 111, 138–139
Bolus of Mendes, 11
Bostra, 109
bridal procession, 26, 56
bridal theft, 78–80, 84–88, 94–95, 159
brides, 70–72, 75, 78, 100

bulbs, 8, 20
burning, 45, 50–51, 55–56, 58–60, 141, 142,
    144, 148, 150–153, 160–161, 164
Burkert, Walter, 31, 36
Byzantine texts or ideas, 11, 56, 74, 92, 133,
    155

Cadmus' daughters, 91
Caligula, 117, 127
Callisthenes, 117, 119, 127, 129, 146, 159
Calypso, 86
Candida, 63
Canidia, 9, 50–51, 158
canthariden, 124
Cappadocia, 89, 91–92, 168
carrot, deadly, 19
Carthage, 5, 9, 14, 33, 55, 57, 67
Cassianus, 107
castration, 122, 130
cathartic model for understanding magic
    ritual, 82–84
Catullus, 9
Cebes, 1–3
Ceramicus, 37, 150
Chalcidia, 143
chameleons, 66
charisma, 103–107
Charites (Graces), 99–100
Christian texts or ideas, 5, 11, 18, 34, 74, 88–
    93
chthonic gods, 34–35, 141–142, 144–146
Circe, 6, 113, 129, 142
Claros, 51–52
clay, 41, 52, 66
Cleopatra, 121, 158
Clytemnestra, 6
Cnidus, 83, 113–114
"coffeehouse talk," 167, 170
Coptic, 74
Corybantes, 47
Cos, 37, 142
courtesans, 1–3, 13, 23, 88, 149–152, 154–155
courtship, 24
crane, 20
Creoboule, 72

Crete, 47
Creusa, 70
Critoboulos, 131
cumin, 144
cup spells, 26
curses, 30, 43–55, 81–84
cyclamen, 126, 129
Cydonian apple (quince), 70
Cypris, 109, 135, 151
Cyprogeneia, 36, 56, 64, 74–75, 134–140, 142
Cyprus/Cyprian, 33, 75, 134–136
Cyranides, 11, 121–122
Cyrene, 49–50, 116–117, 119, 135
Cythereia, 139

Dardanos, 53
Deianeira, 7, 16, 28, 110–112, 116–119, 146
Delphis of Myndus, 50, 83, 140, 144, 152–153
Demeter, 58, 76, 83, 113
Democritus, 11
Demodocus, 6
demons, 29, 34–35, 45–48, 141–143, 144–146
Demosthenes, 10, 12, 85
Demostratus, 160–162
Demotic Egyptian, 16, 19
desiring subjects, 160–171
Detienne, M., 31
Dia, 143
Dido, 9
Dike, 51, 53
Diktynna, 47
Diodorus Siculus, 118
Diogenianus, 109
Dion, 13
Dionysius I of Syracuse, 7
Dionysophon, 13
Dionysus, 58, 62, 134
Dioscorides, 18, 20, 25
Dioskorous, 94
dogs, 66–67, 90–91
Dog Star, 162–165, 171
Domitiana, 23, 63
Don Juan, 83, 85
doors, 168–169
Doris, 7

Douris, 45, 57
doves, 138–139

Earth, 70
effeminacy, 113, 121–122, 130
Egypt/Egyptian, 11, 14, 15, 16, 23, 31–36, 37, 41, 47, 52, 57, 60, 62, 92, 114, 135, 140–141, 149
"Eighth Book of Moses," 103
emancipation of women in Hellenistic world, 149, 153–154
Enuma Elish, 110
Enyalios, 47
Epaphus, 92
Epaphroditus, 87
epilepsy, 47–49
Eracura, 51
erections, 18–21, 122–124, 135
Ereschigal, 34–35, 145
Eros/Erotes, 15, 21, 49, 52, 53, 58, 60, 61, 64, 101, 133–134, 157, 168; as a demon, 44–46
eros as a disease, 48–49
erotic images, 21
Ethiopia, 144
Etruria, 36
Euboulos, 125–126, 129
Euenos, 126, 129
Euphemia, 62, 87, 89
Euripides, 7–8, 13, 25, 37, 45, 46, 47, 49, 61, 112, 154
Eus, 3
eyes, 66

facial ointments, 37, 105–106
Favorinus, 160
female adolescent hysteria, 91–92, 160
female consent to marriage, 77–80
female desire, 19, 20, 160–171
female *erastai*, 139–140, 150, 153, 157–158, 164–165
female salaciousness, 65, 67, 90–91, 162–171
feminist scholarship, 147
fertility, 7, 70, 76
fire spells, 26, 50–51, 58–60, 150–153
"first discoverer," 57–58

fish, 66, 121–122

flexibility of gender constructions, 165–166

Florence, 155

forgetting 86–89, 142–143, 168–169

Foucault, Michel, 71–72

Frazer, J. G., 81, 138

freedmen, 117

Gadara, 37

Galen, 15, 24, 26, 45, 48, 165

Ganymede, 60

gay. See homoerotic

Gaza, 88

gaze, 153, 158–159

gemstones, 15, 33, 52–53, 58, 104–105, 109, 122–123

ghosts, 34–35, 141–142, 145–146

Glaukothea, 10

Glycera, 13

goads, 59–61

goats, 144

good luck charms, 107

Gorgonia, 61, 148

Graeco-Egyptian magic, 16

Graeco-Roman magic, 16

graveyards, 133, 142–146, 158

Greek alphabet, 14

"Greek miracle," 39

Gyges' ring, 104

Hades, 28, 34, 75–78, 94

Hadrian, 42

Hadrumentum, 14

hair, 8, 51, 150

Harpies, 46

hate spells, 18

Hebrew, 16

Hecate, 22, 46–47, 88, 133, 140–146, 151

Hector, 48, 100

Helen, 37, 44, 70, 72

Heliodorus, 23

Heliopolis, 35

Helios, 105, 133, 139–141

Hellenistic texts, 6, 9, 11, 12, 23, 32, 33, 35, 36, 38, 54, 73, 77, 78, 86, 105, 113, 137, 140–141, 143, 153, 165

Hephaestus, 39, 98, 134

Hera, 5, 16, 28, 70, 90–93, 97–102, 109–110, 121–122, 134–135

Heracles, 7, 28, 110–112, 118–119

Hermes, 34, 35, 133

Hermione, 7, 13, 37, 101, 157

Hermitaris, 3

Hermoupolis, 61

Herod, 113

Herodotus, 63, 79, 135

Heronous, 3

Hesiod, 69, 73, 98, 106, 162–163, 166

hexametrical incantations, 8–9, 32, 36, 38, 39, 60, 64, 73–74, 142–146

Hieronyma, 109

Hierophilus, 165

Hippocratic texts or ideas, 48, 91–92, 125, 160, 164, 165–166

Hippolytus, 8

Hippomenes, 6, 28, 69, 73, 78, 80, 90, 93

Hipponax, 19, 123

homeopathic magic, 42

Homer/Homeric, 5, 9, 22, 37, 39, 43, 44, 45, 48, 54, 72, 75, 86, 97, 98, 99, 100–103, 109, 122, 131, 133, 157, 160, 163

homicide, involuntary, 112, 114–116

homoerotic/homosexual desire, 140, 147–149, 157

Horace, 44, 50, 51–52, 67, 68, 158

Horigenes, 41

humors, bodily, 163–164

Hyllus, 111, 119

hymns, 136–139, 144–146

Hypsipyle, 5, 100

Ibycus, 44–45

ideologies, 169–170

Inachus, 92

Inanna, 75, 102

incense, 36–40, 138–139, 144–146

initiation rites, 26

insomnia, 26–27, 65–66, 126, 145

Io, 90–92

Iole, 110, 118
Isara, 148
Ishtar, 75, 102
Isis, 105, 145
Ismenodora, 159
Italy, 155

Jason, 6, 28, 46, 56, 60, 63–69, 73, 85, 90, 92–
    94, 106, 137–138, 168
jealousy, 118
Jerome, 88, 89
Jesus, 89
Jewish texts or ideas, 16, 34–35, 103, 113,
    141
John Chrysostom, 155
judicial prayer, 12, 81–83, 85–86, 141
Julius Africanus, 21
Julius Caesar, 121
"Just Argument," 72, 150
Juvenal, 113
Juvinus, 148

Karosa, 59, 61, 86
kings, 102–104, 108
knots, 101–103
kohl, 120
Kore, 34, 145
Kourotrophos, 22
Kybele, 47

Ladike, 10, 135–136
Larissa, 151
leaping, 86, 89, 91
Lemnos/Lemnian, 134
lesbian. See homoerotic
"letters to the dead," 35
lettuce, 18
Levant, 37
Lévi-Strauss, Claude, 30
Libanius, 66
Libya, 50, 135
Lichas, 118
lizards, 66
Longus, 87
love, definitions and taxonomy of, 27–30

lovesick performer of erotic magic, 82–84,
    112–113, 118, 136–137, 139–141
Lucian, 8, 9, 18, 23, 37, 77–78, 80, 88, 140, 142,
    150–153, 160, 169
Lucius, 158
Lucretius, 117, 127
Lucullus, 117, 127
Luke, 32, 54, 89
Lycophron, 25
Lydia, 145
Lysistrata, 135–136, 158, 170–171

Macedonia/Macedonian, 13, 125
madness, 48–49, 57, 61–63, 67, 73, 88–94,
    127, 145–146, 160–161
magic, problems of definition, 16–18
magical handbooks, 4–5, 14–15, 19, 31–34, 43,
    133, 149
magnitite, 18
Malinowski, B., 81
mandrake, 126, 129–130
marriage, 70–73, 100, 101, 109–110, 113–119,
    168–171
Mark Antony, 121, 158
Martial, 21
masculinity, construction of, 122–124, 129–
    130, 153–160
Medea, 7, 25, 28, 46, 56–57, 62–69, 73, 85, 86,
    90, 92, 106, 142, 168, 171
Mediterranean cultures, 12, 14, 15, 16, 18, 19,
    29, 31, 32, 35, 52, 67, 79, 124, 154, 156, 167
Melanesian sorcerer, 81
Melampus, 90, 92
Melitta, 150–151
Menander, 8, 9, 46, 72, 114
Menelaus, 70
menstrual blood, 120
Mesopotamia/Mesopotamian, 11, 18, 23, 26,
    36–37, 89, 102–105
mint, 135
Minyas' daughters, 91
misandrist, 166–169
misogynist, 162, 166–169
Modena, 155
Moero, 22

moon, 139–141
Morning Star, 138–140
Morocco, 156
Mt. Ida, 109
Musaeus, 106
muted discourses, 166–167
mutilation, 65–66
myrrh, 26, 105–106, 138–139
myrtle, 135
mystery religions, 10

names of courtesans, 13, 154
narcotics, 125–130
"natural," 161–167
Naucratis, 12
Neara, 154, 157
Near Eastern influence on Greek ritual, 36–
    38, 134
Necessity (Anangke), 60
needles or pins, 41–42, 66–67, 134
neighbors, 167–169
Nemesis, 64
Nepos, 117
Nestor, 6
"Nestor's Cup Inscription," 12, 19, 26, 133
New Comedy, 9, 154
Nike, 56
Niko, 151–153, 160
Nilogenia, 148
Ninos, 10
North Africa, 31, 143
nudity, 52–53, 68
nuns, 88–89

oaths, 53–55, 65–66, 81
Oceanus, 97, 100, 110
Octavian, 121
Odysseus, 39, 86, 90, 131
ointments, 8, 19, 30, 112
Old Comedy, 170
oleander, 126, 129
Olympus/Olympic, 56, 65
oral tradition, 120, 133
orgasm, 123, 134
Orphic texts or ideas, 11

Osiris, 4, 65
Ovid, 20, 21, 66, 73, 135
Oxyrhynchus, 86, 107

Paitous, 56
Palestine, 37
Pamphile, 62
Pan, 22, 46, 47, 61, 147
Pandareus' daughters, 90–92
Pandora, 5, 98–100
Paris, 44
Parthenius, 22
Patrocles, 48, 54
Paul, 54
Pausanias, 14, 143–144
Peitho (Persuasion), 56, 60, 99, 133
Pelagius, 109
penis creams or ointments, 19
performative utterences or actions, 134–135,
    137–138. See also persuasive analogy
Perimede, 142
Persephone, 28, 34, 75–80, 133, 143, 145
Persia/Persian, 71, 74, 124, 138–139, 145
persuasive analogy, 42, 53, 65–66, 134–135,
    144
Petronius, 19
Phaedra, 8, 22, 44, 48–49, 139–140, 168
Phanias, 150
Pheidippides, 72
Pherecydes, 70
Philetas, 73
Philinos, 22
Philoneus, 114–115, 128–129, 157
philosophers, 157, 164
piercing, 41–42, 66–67
Pindar, 7, 17, 25, 56–67, 73, 74, 106, 137–140
Plato, 2, 49, 60, 63, 104, 129
Pliny the Elder, 18, 20, 21, 24, 25, 26, 27, 37,
    104, 106, 163, 164
Plutarch, 7, 10, 12, 48, 63, 71, 113, 116–117, 121–
    122, 125, 128, 130–131, 162
Pluto, 34, 51
Polemo, 161–162
pomegranates, 75–76
Pontus, 70

Porphyrios, 148
Poseidonios, 3
potency spells, 18–20
potions, 8, 110–119, 157
prayers, 57, 134–142
Proclus, 109
Proetus' daughters, 90–93, 160
professional magicians or sorcerers, 14–16, 21, 49, 133, 151
prostitutes, 73, 134, 149–152
Pseudo-Nachepso, 15
Psyche, 21, 53, 58, 64
psychoanalysis of the practitioner of love magic, 3, 43, 80–81
Ptolemais, 41–42
Pudentilla, 85
Pythagorean texts or ideas, 11, 36–37

quince 70–71, 78

Re, 140–141
religion, distinguished from magic, 17–18, 135–140
religious technology, 36
Renaissance, 38, 120, 154
revenge, 22, 81, 87, 141
Rhamnous, 64
rings, 37, 40, 103–104, 141
rocket. See arugula
Roman comedy, 154
Roman-era texts, 9, 10, 14, 15, 16, 20, 25, 32, 33, 35, 38, 42, 44, 52, 61, 62, 64, 73, 101, 109, 113, 141, 143, 149, 159, 165
Rome/Roman, 33, 51, 66, 87, 109, 117, 133, 135, 160
roosters, 67
root-cutters, 106
roses, 100, 135
Rhouzo, 138
Ruzzante, 38

"sacred marriage," 109–110
sadism, 3, 80–81
salt, 150, 164
Samos/Samian, 22

Sappho, 6, 44, 45, 55, 82–83, 136–137, 140–141, 147
Sarapammon, 41–43
satyr, 21
satyriasis, 21
Selene, 133, 139–141
self-control, 129–130, 160–163
Selinous, 49
Seneca, 124
separation spells, 18
Serapiakos, 141, 147
Serapion, 94
Seth Skleros, 74, 80
Sextus Julius Africanus, 11
sexual performance, 12, 18–20
shackles, 62
shame, 168–169
Sicily, 12, 33, 34
silencing, 66
Simaetha, 4, 50, 83, 132, 139–144, 152–154, 160
Sime, 14, 143–144
Simichidas, 22
Simmias, 1–3
Sirens, 6, 131
Sirius, 162–164
situational gender, 169–170
skink, 20
slang, 13
slaves, 51, 68, 85, 87
Sleep, 99
social construction of gender, 146–160
Socrates, 1–3, 10, 11, 17, 129, 131, 149, 152, 157, 172
Solon, 71–72, 80, 95
Sophia, 148
Sophocles, 7, 25, 47, 110–113, 114, 118, 121, 130
Soranus, 165
Spain, 155
Spartan, 46
spousal abuse, 100
"stealing to make friends," 84–85
Stesichorus, 70
Stoic philosophy, 124
Strabo, 70, 71
subservience, 52–53, 94

Successa, 55
Successus, 56
Suetonius, 10, 32, 117
sulphur, 150
Sumeria/Sumerian, 75, 102
summer, 162–164
sun, 139–141
"Sword of Dardanos," 53
Syedra, 51, 53
sympathetic magic, 42
symposia, 153
synchronic approach, 30–37, 132–133
Syria/Syrian, 16, 33, 37, 107, 150, 152

Taso, 108
Tethys, 97, 99–100, 110
Thebes, 1–3
Theocritus, 9, 22, 37, 38, 46, 73, 82, 83, 140, 142–144, 147, 152–154, 160
Theodote, 1–2, 10, 11, 17, 149, 152, 154, 157, 172
Theodotis, 3
Theon, 62, 87
Theonilla, 59
Theophrastus, 10, 19, 20, 105–106, 126–129, 160
Thelo, 59
Thera, 50
therapeutic model for understanding curses and erotic magic, 82–84, 140
Theseus, 47, 70, 143
Thessalians, 9, 150–151
Thessalonika, 108
Thetima, 13
Thoth, 34–35
Threpta, 141
threshold, 88
Tiamat, 110
tongues, 67
torches, 45–46, 58–59, 139
tortoises, 160–161
torture, 45–46, 51–53, 55–69, 86, 94, 159, 160
Troy/Trojan, 99, 121
Tunisia, 62
"turning tables," 161–162, 165

Twelve Tables at Rome, 87
Tyche, 64
Typhon, 141, 147–148
Typhousa, 141
Tyre, 147

unrequited love, 3
untimely dead, 34
upside-down position, 51
Urbana, 62
Urbanus, 62

Venice, 54, 66, 67, 155
Venus, 25, 138
Vernant, J.-P., 31
Victoricus, 67
victory charms, 107–109
Vinalia, 135, 136
violence, 3, 45–46, 80–81, 86
Virgil, 9, 153, 164
"voodoo dolls," 41–42
vow of abstinence, 53–55

wax, 51, 52, 62
wheel, 9, 63–64, 151–152
whip, 45, 57, 60–61, 68, 148
"white magic," 30
widow, 72, 85, 159
wine, 114–115, 125–126
Winkler, J. J., 82–85, 166, 171
witches, 151, 158–59. See also professional magicians
Wittgenstein, Ludwig, 81–84
wool, 52, 101–102
wormwood, 138

Xenophon, 1–3, 6, 24, 118, 131, 150, 154, 172

yoke, 62–63

Zachalias of Babylon, 104
Zeus, 6, 16, 44, 60, 70, 90–93, 97–101, 109–110, 121–122, 134

Index of Foreign Words

aerizousa, 104
aerizōn, 104
agapan, 29, 104, 117–119, 157
agapasthai mallon, 117–119
agapē, 27–30, 96
agein, 25, 136, 148, 151
agnus castus, 18
agōgē, 25–26, 28, 56–65, 77, 78, 80, 82, 84–89,
    92–94, 111, 133, 136–139, 142–143, 146–152,
    159–161, 164, 167–168, 172
agōgimon, 25–26
agrupnētikos, 26–28
ahoroi, 34
aidōs, 168
aischunē, 168
alutos, 62
amphiechein, 99
anakalupsis, 78
anakoptein, 47
anaseirazein, 47
andreiotatē, 158
anthrōpos, 149
aoiodai, 137
aparthenos, 153–154
aphaurotatos, 163
aphrodisiaca, 24
aphrodisiatikos, 24
aphrodisios, 73, 134
aphrodizein, 134
atelēs gamou, 13
autika, 135

ballein, 76
Barbaritha, 34
basanizein, 60–61
blanditia, 135

bromēs, 76
brya, 18
buprestis, 20

carmen, 25, 153
charis, 98–99, 103, 105–109
charitēsion, 25, 28, 107
cholos, 97
chrēsthai tini, 113

damnomenē, 59
defixio, 12
dendrites, 104
desmois alutois, 62
deuro, 109, 144
diakopē, 18
donax, 20
donein, 56, 63

edesma, 24
edodē, 76
egalkura, 102–105
eidolon, 49
eisagein, 110
ekpeplēgmenē kentrois, 49
elaunomenē oistrōi, 60–61
emballein, 76
empuron, 26, 28, 50, 58, 164
en alutōi . . . kuklōi, 62
en phrasi kaiomenē, 59–60
en phresi damnomenē, 59–60
entatikon, 25
epagōgē, 49
epaoidē, 64, 139, 145. *See also* contracted At-
    tic form *epōidē*
epaphrodisia, 105, 106, 107

epeisagein, 110
epicharis, 108
epikleros, 69, 71–72, 77–78, 80, 95
epimainein, 164
epithumia, 123
epōidē, 1–2, 6, 24, 131, 137, 157. *See also*
   epaoidē
eran, 23, 123
erasmios, 139, 150
erastēs, 139–140, 153, 157–158, 165
erōs, 7, 27–30, 44, 48, 49, 51, 78, 83, 91, 119,
   124, 126, 132, 139, 141, 146–147, 149, 165, 169
erōs manikos, 61
erōs theios, 48
erōtikos, 112, 160
eruca sativa, 19–20
eudoxia, 106
eukleia, 106
eunoia, 116, 119
excantare, 87
exhelkein, 67
exoistratai, 161

favor, 135
furens, 61

gamein, 27, 29
gamos, 13, 154
goēteia, 113, 121
gunē, 149

hamartia, 111
hebretonum, 20
helkein, 67
hilarōteros, 126
himas, 98, 122
himeros, 28, 97–98, 110, 139
hippomanes, 10, 21
homonoia, 118
hupo tēs epoidēs agomenos, 151
hupobinētiōnta brōmata, 8
hupotetachthēnai, 23, 68

iaeō, 53
ianibu, 102

incantamentum, 24
iunx, 1–2, 6, 8, 9, 17, 24, 25, 28, 56–58, 64–69,
   73, 92, 94, 137–138, 151–153, 157–158, 160–
   161, 168
iunx erotikē, 160

kaiomenē, 59–61
kakopoiea pharmaka, 114
kappa, 121
kardia, 83
katadein, 144
katadesmos, 12, 14, 34–35, 49, 143–144
katakratein, 114
katapharmakeuein, 7, 113
katapharmassein, 135
katathuein, 144
katechein, 51, 107, 131, 139
kentein, 60
kentron, 49
kēres, 46
kestos, 11, 98, 122, 129
kestos himas, 9, 11, 44, 97–102, 122, 130, 134,
   138, 157
kigklos, 65
kinaidios, 121–22
kinaidos, 121
koitēs, 86
kudonian melon, 69, 71
kuklos, 62
kurios, 72

leptos, 63
lex talionis, 83
litē, 137
lithos, 24
litomai, 137
logismos, 168
logos, 8, 57, 119
lupēthēis, 107

machlosunē, 90
machlotatai, 163
mainas, 61, 66
mainē, 66
mainomenē, 61, 66

mallon agapasthai, 117–119
mallon philēsomenē, 115, 150, 157
manes, 51
manikos, 61, 127
mastix, 45, 60
mastizomenē, 61, 63
mēlon, 69–75, 77
miarōtatos, 163
misēthron, 18, 33
misgein, 97

neikos, 97
nikētikon, 107–108
nosos, 44
nous, 44
nymphaea, 18

odi et amo, 94
oistros, 28, 60, 90, 92, 168
orchis, 20
orgē, 103, 104, 166
ousia, 8

paignia, 16
pais, 151
pallakē, 118, 157
paneion, 46
panikon, 46
parakatatithemai, 34
parakoptein, 47
parthenos, 153
peithein, 60
peplos, 76, 100
persikon melon, 69, 74
pharmakeia, 116
pharmakis, 23, 151
pharmakon, 7–9, 19, 23, 24, 37, 74, 112–119,
    121, 137, 142, 160
pharmakopolai, 19
pheugein, 161
philai, 1–2
philein, 25, 27–29, 101, 115, 117, 119, 131, 150,
    157
philia, 25, 27–30, 96, 97, 104–107, 110, 115–
    116, 119–122, 128–132, 141, 146–147, 157, 159,

    161, 165, 169, 172
philoi, 131
philon . . . poiein, 114
philostorgia, 118
philotēs, 97, 110
philtrokadadesmos, 14, 27, 28, 52, 62
philtron, 1–2, 7, 10, 12, 17, 24, 25, 28, 113–119,
    126, 129, 131, 157
phlegomenē, 161
Phōkesepseu erektathou misonktaik, 34
phrēn, 44–45, 59
phthinein, 51
phulacterion, 107
phusikleidion, 27
phusis, 3, 165
phyteuma, 20
plegai, 48
pleon . . . agapesthai, 118
pleon . . . phileisthai, 116
plokos, 8
poena, 51
pornē, 157
potērion, 26, 119
pothos, 28–29, 98, 119
pragma, 19
praoteron, 126
praotēs, 126
praxis, 16, 63
prosbolai, 48
Psēriphtha, 34
psuche, 50, 53, 58, 59, 86, 149
purson erōtōn, 139

rhombos, 8, 63, 150–152

salpē, 20
saturikon, 25
saturion, 20–21, 25, 125, 127–128
seira, 47
seirazein, 47
sophronousa, 160–161
sophrosunē, 168
staphylinus, 20
stergein, 25, 29, 111, 119, 135
stergēma, 25, 111, 119

stergēthron, 25
storgē, 28–29
streblousthai, 63
struchnos, 127, 129
sumplegma, 8, 21, 89
sunepithelgein, 87

tacheōs, 136
takēmenai, 139
telein, 137
telos, 13, 142
terebinth, 20
theios, 48
thelgein, 24, 86–87
thelktēria, 7, 24, 97

thruptetai, 161
thuein, 123
thumokatochon, 107–108, 123
thumos, 44, 107, 108, 123–124, 130, 166
tithymallus, 20

unguentaria, 158

venenum, 25
voces magicae, 52

xeinion, 151
xiphium, 20

zonion, 9

Index of Passages from Ancient Authors

Achilles Tatius 6.21: 64

Aelian, *On the Nature of Animals:* 1.44: 20; 3.17: 10; 9.48: 164; 14.18: 10; 15.19: 160

Aelius Dionysus, frag. 430: 47

Aeschylus: *Agamemnon* 385: 60; *Libation Bearers* 726: 7, 26; *Persians* 989: 25

Alcaeus, frag. 347(a): 162

Alcman, frag. 1.73–77: 6

Alexis, frag. 98: 155

Anacreon: frag. 413: 44, 45; frag., 388: 63

Antiphon: 1.9.2: 19, 115; 1.14: 114; 1.19: 114; 1.20: 128; 5.32: 63

Apollodorus 2.5.11: 70

Apuleius
  Apologia 30–32: 38
  Metamorphoses: 2.5: 62, 158; 2.32: 8, 38, 87; 3.15–18: 8, 38, 87

Archilochus: frag. 191: 44; frag. 193: 44

Aristophanes
  Acharnians: 525: 154; 1048–68: 19
  Amphiareus, frag. 29 (K-A): 8–9, 64–65, 137
  Clouds 996–997: 8, 72–73, 150
  Eccl. 1092: 20
  Frogs 620: 63
  Heros, frag. 315 (K-A): 8
  Lysistrata: 551–556: 135; 845–846: 63; 997–998: 46; 1108–11: 8
  Peace 452: 63
  Wealth: 883–885: 39; 875: 63

Aristotle
  HA: 572a30–b4: 10, 164; 577a10–15: 10
  NE: 1161a: 118; 1162a15: 118
  de Som. 456b31: 126

[Aristotle]: *Magna Moralia* 16 (= 1188b.30–38): 10, 115; *Problems* 954a3: 24

Arnobius, *Adversus Gentes* 1.43: 168

Asclepiades, *AP:* 5.158: 9, 100–101; 5.205: 9, 151

Athenaeus: 62e–64b: 8, 20; 356e–f: 8, 20; 384e–f: 20; 533f: 64; 584a: 157

Bacchylides: 11.45–46: 62; 16. 25–29: 119; 17.115–16: 100

Chariton 3.4.7: 64

Clement of Alexandria, *Protrepticus* 4.57–61: 21

Cornelius Nepos, frag. 52 (Marshall): 10, 117

Cyranides: 1.4.45–51: 104; 1.5.10–18: 21; 1.10.39–42: 104; 1.10.49–69: 121–123, 130; 1.14.10–13: 21; 1.18.50: 20; 2.29: 21

Demosthenes: 19. 281: 12; 29.40: 85

[Demosthenes]: 59.18–19: 155; 59.22: 110

Diodorus Siculus 4.38.1: 118

Diogenes Laertius 6.76: 25

Dioscorides, *Materia Medica:* 2.140: 20; 2.169: 20; 3.132: 18; 3.134: 20; 4.48: 25

Euboulos, frag. 94 (Kock): 125–126

Euenos, frag. 2 (West): 126

Eupolis, *Baptai* frag. 83 (K-A): 8

Euripides
  Andromache 155–160: 7, 13, 37
  Hecuba 612: 154
  Hippolytus: 38: 49; 141–147: 47; 236–238: 47; 256: 25; 319: 49; 509–516: 7–8, 112; 1303: 49
  Medea: 431–432: 61; 1167–77: 46
  Rhesus 36–37: 45, 46

Galen (Kühn): 12.207: 15; 12.251: 26; 14.241: 24; 18.2.18–19: 48
Geoponica: 17.5.3: 20, 21; 19.5.4: 20, 21

Heliodorus, *Aethiopica*: 2.33: 23; 3.9: 23
Herodotus: 2.89: 63; 2.181: 135; 6.65.2: 79; 7.36: 63
[Herodotus], Life of Homer 30: 22
Hesiod
    Catalogue of Women: frag. 25 (MW): 118; frag. 76 (MW): 61, 69
    Theogony 122: 44
    Works and Days: 65–66: 98; 73–74: 99
Hesychius: s.v. *anaseirazein*, 46; s.v. *harpun*, 47
[Hippocrates] *On the Sacred Disease* 1.38 (Grensemann): 48
Hipponax, frag. 78 (W): 19
Homer
    Iliad: 5.740: 98; 9.209–210: 54; 9.340–341: 72; 13.812: 45; 14.158: 100; 14.197–210: 97; 14.214–217: 44, 97; 14.294: 44; 14.313–328: 100; 16.787–796: 48; 18.535: 98; 22.25–32: 163; 22.469–472: 100
    Odyssey: 1.56–57: 86; 4.220–230: 37, 160; 5.333–335: 98; 6.235: 99; 10.19–27: 39; 12.184: 131; 23.156: 99
[Homer]
    Hymn to Demeter: 227–230: 39; 371–374: 76; 393–400: 76; 411–413: 76
    Epigram 11: 22
Horace
    Epistles 5.41: 158
    Odes 1.13: 44
    Satires: 1.8: 50, 52, 68; 2.8: 67

Ibycus: frag. 283.3–6: 44; frag. 286.8–13: 45

Jerome, *Life of St. Hilarion the Hermit* 21: 89
John Chrysostom, *PG* 51.216: 155
Josephus, *Jewish Antiquities*: 25.223–224: 113; 27.61–64: 113
Julius Africanus, *Kestoi* 3.5: 21
Juvenal 6.610–611: 113

Libanius, *Oration* 1.245–249: 66
Longus, *Daphne and Chloe* 1.27.3: 87
Lucian
    Dialogues of the Courtesans: 1.2: 23; 4: 8; 4.1: 37, 88, 150; 4.3: 151, 152; 4.4: 9; 4.5: 18; 12.1: 77
    Philopseudes 13–15: 9, 140, 142, 169
Luke
    Gospel 14:26: 89
    Acts of the Apostles: 19:19: 32; 23:12: 54
Lycophron 310: 25

Martial 3.75.3: 21
Menander: *Dyscolus* 44–46: 46; frag. 334.2–4: 72; frag. 397: 8; frag. 646: 114
Moero, *Arae*, 22

Ovid
    Ars Amatoria 421–424: 20
    Fasti: 2.577–581: 66; 4.863–886: 135
    Metamorphoses 10.666: 73
    Tristia 2.523–524: 21

Palatine Anthology: 5.79: 77; 5.158: 9, 100–101; 5.205: 9
Parthenius, *Tales of Unhappy Love* 27: 22
Petronius, *Satyricon*: 127.9: 19; 131.8: 19
Pherecydes, *FGrHist* 3 F17: 70
Philetas, frag. 18 (Powell): 73
Pindar
    Pythian: 3.47–54: 17; 4.213–219: 7, 25, 56; 4.221–223: 106
    frag. 104 (Maehler): 139
Plato
    Symposium 215b–c: 2
    Phaedrus 240d: 60
    Republic: 359d–360a: 104; 364c: 49; 488c: 129; 531b: 63
Pliny, *Natural History*: 8.165: 21; 10.181: 164; 10.182: 20; 19.154: 20; 20.28: 20; 20.32: 20; 20.47–49: 20; 20.56–57: 20; 20.68: 18; 20.105: 20; 20.110: 20; 20.143: 18; 20.214: 18; 21.162: 20; 22.20: 20, 21; 22.71: 20; 22.78: 20; 22.80: 20; 22.91: 18; 22.99: 20; 24.28: 20; 24.58–59: 18; 24.61–64: 18; 24.72:

18; 24.87: 20; 24.140: 20; 25.75: 18; 26.18:
21; 26.94–99: 18, 21, 24, 25, 26, 27; 27.65:
20, 21; 28.261–262: 20; 30.119–200: 20;
37.118: 104; 37.148: 24; 37.169: 37, 104;
38.91: 20
Plutarch
  Parallel Lives
    Antony: 25.4: 121; 37: 10, 121; 60.1: 121
    Dion 3.3: 7
    Demosthenes 14: 12
    Lucullus 43.1–2: 10, 117
    Nicias, 30: 63
    Solon 20.3: 71
  Moralia: 126: 49, 113; 138d: 71; 139a: 6;
    170a: 48; 256c: 116; 279f: 71; 623e: 125;
    652d: 125; 654: 109; 1093d: 26
Polemo, *Scriptores physiognomici Graeci*
  1.160–164: 161

Sappho: frag. 1 (*Hymn to Aphrodite*): 6, 82–
  83, 136–137, 140–141; frag. 47: 45; frag. 48:
  44, 55
Scholia: to Horace *Epodes,* 3.7–8: 158; to Pindar *Pythian* 4.381a: 67; to Theocritus *Idyll*
  2.120: 73
Seneca, *De ira,* 124
Sophocles
  Ajax 172–181: 47

Root-Cutters, frag. 536 (Radt): 7
Women of Trachis: 83–85: 118; 575–576: 111;
  576–577: 111; 717–718: 118; 727–728: 111,
  114; 1136–39: 25, 111
Soranus, *Gynaeceia* 1.4.22–23: 165
Stesichorus, frag. 187: 70
Strabo 15.3.17: 71
Suda, s.v. *iunx,* 121
Suetonius: *Augustus* 31.1: 32; *Caligula* 50:
  10, 117; *de Poetis* 16: 10, 117

Theocritus, *Idylls:* 2: 9, 38, 82; 2. 3: 144; 2.10–
  17: 142–144; 2.23–32: 83, 152–153; 2. 44–45:
  143; 2.159: 144; 2.162: 37; 3.40–43: 73; 7.103–
  117: 22, 46, 147
Theophrastus, *History of Plants:* 1.6.6: 20;
  9.9.1: 126; 9.9.3: 20; 9.11.6: 127; 9.18.9: 19;
  9.19.1–3: 106, 126; frag. 175: 10

Virgil: *Aeneid* 4: 9; *Eclogue* 8: 9, 153; *Georgics*
  2.130–135: 164

Xenophon
  Memorabilia: 2.6.10–11: 6, 131; 3.11.4: 154;
    3.11.16–17: 1–2, 150
  Hiero 3.3: 118

Index of Magical Texts

See Abbreviations for full titles.

ACM 76 74

AEMT 1 34

CTBS 34 14
 75 87
 89 114
 163 89

DT 2 83
 4 114
 38 148
 51 59
 68 86
 111 66
 112 66
 134 33
 135 33
 188 33
 190 33
 198 84
 222 67
 227 14, 56, 59
 230 57, 85
 231 14
 241 14
 252 62
 253 62
 265 61
 266 88, 143
 270 4, 59, 61, 147, 149
 271 8, 13, 23, 29, 60, 61, 63, 68, 149
 304 14

DTA 78 13, 151
 98 83

GMA 32 33
 40 108
 44 137
 48 33
 58 109
 60 107

KAR 61.8–21 75
 69.4–19 75
 69 rev. 2–12 75
 71.1–11 102
 71.21–25 102
 71 rev. 9–10 103
 237.13–17 105
 237.18–23 105

PDM xiv. 1046–55 19
 1155–62 19
 1190–95 19

 lxi. 58–62 19

PGM I.107 137
 262 136

 III.35 136
 85 136
 123 136

 IV.72 137
 191–192 27
 296–303 16, 27, 41–42, 52, 137

PGM IV. 376–381 53
973 136
1265 137
1410–14 60, 84
1496–1595 26, 50
1511–20 54
1593 136
1718–1870 53, 168
1806 85
2037 137
2065–66 147
2087–95 149
2440–41 107
2489 59
2714–83 58, 61, 88, 137, 144
2891–2942 60, 138–39, 137
2943–66 26, 43, 66
3274 66

V.304–369 13

VII.167–185 16, 20
185–186 19
191–192 19
300a–310 26, 60
340–341 50
374–376 26, 66
385–389 26. 120
390–393 107
405–406 25
459–466 25
471–472 60
593–619 26, 60
619–627 26
661–663 25
862–918 29, 94
969–971 26
973–980 26

VIII.4–26 107
923–925 107

XII.24 149
160–178 168
201–202 104
270–273 103

XII.277–280 103
374–396 26, 66

XIII.238–239 149
250–252 103, 108
319–320 26

XV 88, 149

XVI 29, 58, 94, 149

XVIIa 60, 61, 168

XIXa 59, 61, 86

XIXb 149

XX.270–273 108

XXXII 148

XXXIIa 141, 147, 148

XXXV 108

XXXVI.1–24 112
35–68 108
69–101 26, 86, 149
102–133 26, 60
161–177 108
200–201 60
211–230 105, 108
275 107
283–294 19, 27
295–311 26
312–320 168
333–360 26, 58, 86

XXXIX 149

LII.20–26 26

LXI.1–38 29, 58, 88
39–71 4, 26, 51, 66

LXVI 51

LXVIII 4, 33, 93, 147–149

CI 94

O[strakon] 2 3, 59, 86

PGM Hymn 21 145
   22 60, 138–139
   24 60

SGD 60 87
 161 14

SMA 149 108

SM 37 56, 94, 148
 38 3,14, 27
 39 85
 40 3, 59, 86
 41 61

SM 42 29, 61, 86
 45 4, 59, 61, 62, 86, 88
 46 34, 67
 47 34, 42, 67
 48 60, 88
 50 67
 54 148
 63 109, 135
 64 107
 71 57, 86
 72 35, 74, 105, 140
 73 54
 76 16, 19, 20
 83 16, 19, 20